The Ethics Toolkit

The Ethics Toolkit

A Compendium of Ethical Concepts and Methods

Julian Baggini and Peter S. Fosl

Blackwell
Publishing

BLACKWELL PUBLISHING
350 Main Street, Malden, MA 02148–5020, USA
9600 Garsington Road, Oxford OX4 2DQ, UK
550 Swanston Street, Carlton, Victoria 3053, Australia

First published 2007 by Blackwell Publishing Ltd

4   2011

Library of Congress Cataloging-in-Publication Data
Baggini, Julian.
The ethics toolkit : a compendium of ethical concepts and
methods / Julian Baggini and Peter S. Fosl.
p.   cm.
Includes bibliographical references and index.
ISBN 978-1-4051-3230-5 (hardcover : alk. paper) —
ISBN 978-1-4051-3231-2 (pbk. : alk. paper)
1. Ethics. I. Fosl, Peter S. II. Title.

BJ1012.B33 2007
170--dc22   2007005633

A catalogue record for this title is available from the British Library.

Set in 10/12.5 pt Plantin
by The Running Head Limited, Cambridge, www.therunninghead.com
Printed and bound in Singapore
by Markono Print Media Pte Ltd

For further information on
Blackwell Publishing, visit our website:
www.blackwellpublishing.com

To Joseph P. Fell and Lucy O'Brien

Contents

Alphabetical List of Entries

Acknowledgments

We would like to thank Peter's spouse, Catherine Fosl, and his children, Elijah Fosl and Isaac Fosl van-Wyke, for their patience and support; Avery Kolers for advice on the contents; Jack Furlong and Ellen Cox for their insight; Maggie Barr for proofreading the text; and Transylvania University's Jones Grant program for underwriting Peter's intercontinental travel.

We would also like to thank Jeff Dean and Danielle Descoteaux at Blackwell for their support and patience, as well as the anonymous referees for their thoughtful, thorough, helpful comments, and for their encouragement. Thanks also to Charlotte Davies, Annie Jackson, and David Williams at The Running Head for their remarkably thorough tidying up of the manuscript. We are also deeply grateful to all those who have built and who maintain the Internet. Without it, our work together and our friendship would have never come to exist.

Julian Baggini
Peter S. Fosl

Introduction

How should you think about ethics? It's a deceptively simple question. Certainly, you should think well, think clearly, think accurately, and – if it's possible in ethics – think rightly. But how exactly can you set about doing all this?

One way to approach the topic is to try to establish a general theory that attempts to do things like determine the true nature of ethics, define the meaning of ethical terms, formulate fundamental moral principles, and place those principles in a hierarchy. This way of thinking about ethics, in short, tries to produce a theory that pretty much answers all the theoretical questions anyone might ask.

Having accomplished this, of course, you also have to explain why your general theory is better than all the rest, and you have to repel the various challenges that critics are certain to advance. After producing such a theory and defending it, you next set about applying your theory to real-life moral problems, demonstrating how it resolves disputes and answers questions about what to do in various actual circumstances.

One problem with this kind of approach, however, is that more than two millennia of moral philosophy have led to little consensus about the fundamental nature of ethics, the hierarchy of moral principles, or the way to apply them in the real world. Worse, some respectable thinkers have rejected the idea that reaching consensus about such things is even possible.

Meanwhile, of course, the world goes on, tangled in the most profound sorts of moral struggle. If anything, the demand for meaningful and effective moral thinking has become greater than ever. Moral thinking and reasoning, then, despite the limitations of moral philosophy, can neither be put on hold until agreement is reached nor abandoned altogether. Even amoralists need to get clear on what they're rejecting.

The fact that theoretical consensus about moral issues hasn't been reached doesn't mean it can't be reached. But perhaps there's another method, another way to think about ethical matters, a way that can bring real intellectual force to bear upon the moral controversies that populate the world but doesn't require a univocal, general moral theory.

Rather than trying to determine a single, complete ethical theory that answers all the relevant moral questions that may arise, and defeats all its competitors, perhaps one might instead (or also) try to gain a kind of mastery or at least facility with some of the many different theories, concepts, principles, and critiques concerned with ethics that moral philosophers have produced over the ages. *The Ethics Toolkit* aspires to help those engaged in moral inquiry and reflection to do just that. By placing a selection of insights from different moral theorists and theories side by side, we hope to show readers something about ethics that may go missing in the contests among ethical theories.

We hope to show how many of the concepts and ideas collected under the umbrella of ethical theory have a wider and more complex range of application than can sometimes appear. There are many voices composing the moral discourses of our age, and these different voices address many different problems in different ways. Many tools are necessary to hear them and to respond properly to them, not a single voice or a single tool.

Indeed, anyone who wants to deliberate and converse with others about the major moral concerns that occupy people today must be able to draw upon not just a single well-crafted theory but more broadly upon the rich and diverse work of the past 2,500 years of moral philosophy. Competent thinkers simply must have in their possession a well-stocked "toolkit" containing a host of intellectual instruments for careful, precise, and sophisticated moral thinking.

By producing a compendium like this we also hope to provide readers with a deeper and subtler sense of how different ideas and methods may be enlisted so that people might not only think but also act with regard to moral matters in more effective and satisfying ways. Many of the problems that human beings have to deal with are in part conceptual and philosophical. Coming to terms with these problems will require better thinking. Medicines and machines will be needed to help make the world a better place. But, contrary to the charges that are often brought against philosophy, so will the capacity for clear thinking and sound moral deliberation. In this way, we believe that there is a connection between what the ancient Greeks called "knowing that" (theoretical knowledge) and "knowing how" (practical knowledge).

The vision of ethics underwriting *The Ethics Toolkit* is pluralistic, and unabashedly so, in the sense that it holds that the insights of, say, utilitarianism are of interest and value not only to utilitarians but also to anyone who wishes to engage in moral reflection. This vision of ethics does not, however, imply that the tools described here can simply be picked up and applied blindly to suit whatever need arises. Various tools are more appropriate to certain needs than others. That is not to say that the tools we collect here can or should only be used in a single way. Some may effectively use a screwdriver to take on the same job others would tackle with a hammer. More advanced thinkers may be able to use some of the tools in ways that beginners cannot. Moral thinkers of all abilities will use some tools more than others, using some only rarely.

There are, similarly, different ways to use this text. *The Ethics Toolkit* can be read cover-to-cover as a course in ethical reasoning. We begin in Part I with the question of the grounds on which ethics stands. We then consider in Part II the most important frameworks that have been constructed to enable us to reason about ethics. Part III describes a number of central concepts in ethical discourse. In Part IV, we look at the ways in which ethical theories and judgments may be critiqued. Finally, we look at the limits of moral reasoning in Part V.

But this sort of linear approach isn't the only way to use *The Ethics Toolkit*. It can also be used as a reference text upon which people can draw, using either the table of contents or the extensive index, to help understand a specific issue. Or alternatively, readers can simply wander about through the book, following their own muses in a nearly countless variety of ways. The cross-referencing we've appended to each entry directs readers to other entries that will complement or elaborate upon the material at hand, helping readers to make connections and articulate contrasts, sometimes in surprising ways.

Each entry is also followed by two or three suggestions for further reading. Usually these recommendations will tell you more about the subject of the entry, but sometimes we have also included details of works referred to in the entries that concern the specific examples used. Readings particularly suitable for beginners are marked with asterisks. In addition, we have tried to include concrete examples that illustrate many of the more abstract ideas of the text and also show readers how the material of the text applies to actual ethical controversies. The index includes the topic areas these examples cover. A list of societies, institutions, websites, and other resources related to the study and practice of ethics has been appended to the end of the text.

No matter how it's used, though, we hope *The Ethics Toolkit* will be a book that readers will return to again and again, whether they are students, teachers, scholars, professionals, or just people concerned with how to think better about morality.

Part I

The Grounds of Ethics

1.1 Aesthetics

"Beauty is truth, truth beauty" wrote the poet John Keats (1795–1821) in "Ode on a Grecian Urn." Was he the victim of a romantic delusion or is there really a relationship between the true, the beautiful, and even the good? Ludwig Wittgenstein (1889–1951) seemed to think there was a connection between at least the last two when he claimed that, "Ethics and aesthetics are one" (*Tractatus* 6.421). Taking at face-value a statement from any thinker as cryptic as Wittgenstein is a potentially misleading affair. But nevertheless, many have argued for links between aesthetics and ethics. Beauty can be seen as capable of representing goodness, revealing the nature of goodness, or instructing us in goodness.

Representations of good

Various ethical notions have been personified in statues and images. At the Library of Celsus in Ephesus, Turkey, you'll bump into statues of beautiful women said to be wisdom (*sophia*) and virtue (*aretē*), while justice is commonly depicted as a blindfolded woman holding a pair of scales.

Besides personifying ethical concepts, the aesthetic can have ethical import in much more abstract ways. When one looks at, for example, the Parthenon in Athens, one sees a structure that exhibits exquisite balance and harmony. The pediment and supports are carefully proportioned according to what mathematicians call the "golden section," conveying intelligence, control, and moderation. The pillars are shaped with a slight swelling (*entasis*) to give them a feeling of strength as well as rectitude. The site of the structure in an elevated, central, and historic location communicates a connection with the divine and with the past; it is the centering pole of the *polis*.

What is it, though, that such "moral" art is representing? In his *Critique of Judgment* (1790), Immanuel Kant (1724–1804) argued that art cannot directly depict moral principles, but it can offer *symbols* of morality. By this Kant meant that the way we reflect on objects of our aesthetic experience is somehow analogous to the way we reflect on the purely abstract concepts of morality. "The morally good," Kant writes, "is the intelligible that taste has in view" (*Critique*, 353–4). That's why beauty seems bound up with so many notions connected to morality. For example, says Kant, our experience of beauty is *disinterested*; we find beauty in things from which we have absolutely nothing to gain (e.g. someone else's art). Beauty can also seem *universal* in the sense that we think everyone ought to be able to see it that way – *ought to* in a way analogous to the way people ought to be moral. In short, aesthetic thought makes universal claims independent of self-interest analogous to the claims of ethical thought.

Revealing the good

The connection between aesthetics and ethics isn't restricted to art representing goodness. Nature's aesthetic qualities have also been thought to have moral significance. Ancient Pythagoreans believed that there are harmonic or at least harmonious relationships (*harmonia*) among the various structures of the natural world and that achieving a good life means replicating them in one's own soul (*psychē*), making as it were the microcosm correspond to the macrocosm. In his own ways, Plato followed them in this. Later, Romantic thinkers such as William Blake (1757–1827) and William Wordsworth (1770–1850) would find in natural beauty a source of moral restoration for those suffering from the depravity of urban, industrial society, as well as an expression of a deeper spiritual or divine goodness and beauty.

Art as instruction

Perhaps the most widespread view of art's moral dimension is that it can help develop our moral sense. For example, Aristotle's *Poetics* remarks upon the powerful and important effects of tragedy. When one walks around the remains of ancient Greece one is struck by the important location of its theaters. Directly above the great temple of Delphi is a theater. The theater of Dionysus sits snuggly at the base of the Athenian acropolis. That's because, for the ancient Greeks and many others after them, art offers not simply the exhibition of morality but instruction in it and a site for deliberation about the features of moral life.

Part of that instruction involves the cultivation of our feelings, sentiments, sympathies, and affections. Aesthetic experience can help people sympathize with the victims of war, crime, abuse, and vice. It can cultivate compassion, moral outrage, pity, pride, devotion, admiration, and respect. It can edify and elevate. Consider, for example, Picasso's painting *Guernica* (1937), the Vietnam Veterans Memorial in Washington, Arnold Schoenberg's *A Survivor from Warsaw* (Opus 46), and the Arc de Triomphe in Paris.

But not everyone agrees that art makes us better people. In his dialogue *Ion*, Plato argued that art is more likely to corrupt. Even if aesthetic experience can make a positive contribution to moral understanding, we might still question whether it offers us moral insight, cognition, deliberation, or instruction in a way nothing else can. Which raises the question: when faced with an ethical problem, is it better to turn to a theory or a poem?

See also

1.11 Harmony, 2.11 Perfectionism, 3.6 Cognitivism/non-cognitivism

Reading

Jerrold Levinson, ed., *Aesthetics and Ethics: Essays at the Intersection*, new edition (Cambridge: Cambridge University Press, 2001)
*José Louis Bermúdez and Sebastian Gardner, eds., *Art and Morality* (New York: Routledge, 2003)
Noell Caroll, "Art and the Moral Realm," in *The Blackwell Guide to Aesthetics*, edited by Peter Kivy (Malden, MA: Blackwell, 2004), 126–51

1.2 Agency

If, as the result of an earthquake, a boulder were to break off from the face of a cliff and kill an unfortunate mountaineer below, it wouldn't make sense to hold either the boulder or the Earth morally accountable for her death. If, on the other hand, an angry acquaintance dislodged the rock, aiming to kill the mountaineer for the sake of some personal grudge, things would be different. Why?

One of the key differences between the two deaths is that the second, unlike the first, involves "agency." This difference is a crucial one, as agency is often taken to be a necessary condition or requirement of moral responsibility. Simply put, something can only be held morally responsible for an event if that something is an agent. Angry colleagues are agents but the Earth is not (assuming, of course, that the Earth isn't some animate, conscious being). This seems obvious enough, but what precisely is agency, and why does it matter?

Agency for many involves the exercise of freedom. Freedom is usually taken to require the ability to act otherwise or in ways contrary to the way one is currently acting or has acted in the past. For many holding this point of view, being responsible (and thence an agent) means possessing a "free will" through which one can act independently of desires and chains of natural causes. Of course, there are also many philosophers who don't think much of this conception of freedom. Most of the critics, however, nevertheless do accept using the term for actions that proceed in a causal way from one's self or one's own character in the absence of external compulsion, coercion, or mental defect. (These philosophers are called "compatibilists.")

Conditions of agency

For thinkers following Aristotle (384–322 BCE), agency requires that one understands what one's doing, what the relevant facts of the matter are, and how the causal order of the world works to the extent that one is able to foresee the likely consequences of chosen courses of action.

It's also important that an agent possess some sort of self-understanding – that is, some sense of self-identity, knowledge of who and what one is, what one's character and emotional architecture are like, what one is capable and not capable of doing. Self-knowledge is important because it doesn't normally make sense to think of someone as a free agent who is unaware of what he or she does – for example, while asleep or during an unforeseen seizure. It can still make sense to talk of some of this kind of action as the result of agency, however, if the impairments that lead to the unconscious conduct are the result of one's own free choices. For example, consider someone who voluntarily gets drunk while piloting an airliner, knowing full well what's likely to happen; or consider someone else whose ignorance about the small child standing behind the car he has just put into gear results from negligence, from his not bothering to look out the rear window.

For Immanuel Kant (1724–1804), the ability to reason is crucial to agency. In Kant's *Critique of Practical Reason* (1788), what's important is that one act unselfishly, purely on the basis of reason or a certain kind of rational principle (a *categorical imperative*), instead of on the basis of desire or fear. Only this sort of rational action qualifies for Kant as truly moral action, because even acting well on the basis of desire ultimately boils down to the same thing as acting in other ways for the sake of desire. Desires and fears simply come over us, the result of natural and social causes beyond our control. To act strictly from desire is to be a slave to desire. Only by acting on the basis of reason alone are we, for Kant, *autonomous* – that is, self-governing beings who legislate moral laws of action to ourselves.

Other conditions of agency

But perhaps it's wrong to regard feelings and desires as irrelevant. Indeed, shouldn't moral agency also be understood to require the capacity to sympathize with others, to be distressed by their suffering, and to feel regret or remorse after harming others or acting immorally? Would it make sense to regard as a moral or free agent a robot that behaved rationally and that possessed all the relevant information but didn't have any inner, affective life? It's not obvious what the answer to this question is. *Star Trek*'s Mr Spock, for example, seemed to be a moral agent, even though the only reason he had for condemning immoral acts was that they were "illogical."

Similarly, it might be thought that the right social conditions must be in place for moral agency to be possible. Could people truly be moral agents capable of effective action without public order and security, sufficient means of sustenance, access to information and communication, education, a free press, and an open government? But again, this is far from obvious. Although it seems true that when civilization breaks down immorality or amorality rises, it also seems excessively pessimistic to conclude that moral agency is utterly impossible without many of the supports and constraints of society.

Types of agent

It may seem strange to consider things like corporations or nations or mobs or social classes as agents, but the issue often arises in reflections about whether one should make judgments that attribute collective responsibility. People did speak of the guilt of the German nation and demand that all Germans contribute to war reparations after World War I. When the government of a truly democratic nation goes to war, because its policy in some sense expresses "the will of the people," the country arguably acts as though it were a kind of single agent. People also, of course, speak collectively of the responsibilities of the ruling class, corporations, families, tribes, and ethnic groups. Because human life is populated by collectives, institutions, organizations, and other social groupings, agency can sometimes be dispersed or at least seem irremediably unclear. These "gray zones," as thinkers like Primo Levi (*The Periodic Table*, 1975) and Claudia Card (*The Atrocity Paradigm*, 2002) have called them, make determining agency in areas like sexual conduct and political action exceedingly difficult.

There are three ways of understanding how we talk about collectives as agents. One is that it's just mistaken and that collectives cannot be agents. The second is that collectives are agents in some alternative, perhaps metaphorical sense – that they are like real agents but not quite the same as them. The third is that collectives are as much agents as individual people, who are themselves perhaps not as singular, cohesive, and unified as many would like to believe.

See also

1.4 Autonomy, 2.13 Rationalism, 3.21 Moral subjects/moral agents, 5.1 *Akrasia*, 5.7 Free will and determinism

Reading

Aristotle, *Nicomachean Ethics*, edited by Sarah Broadie (Oxford: Oxford University Press, 2002), Book III
Alfred R. Mele, *Autonomous Agents: From Self-Control to Autonomy* (Oxford: Oxford University Press, 1995)
*Sandra Bartky, "Agency: What's the Trouble?" in her *Sympathy, Solidarity, and Other Essays* (Lanham, MD: Rowman & Littlefield, 2002)

1.3 Authority

> I will punish the Amalekites for what they did to Israel when they waylaid them as they came up from Egypt. Now go, attack the Amalekites and totally destroy everything that belongs to them. Do not spare them; put to death men and women, children and infants, cattle and sheep, camels and donkeys. (1 Samuel 15:2–3)

This is a pretty terrifying command. But Saul and the Israelites had one very good reason to obey it: the order came from God. Surely, God has the authority to command anything at all, even mass killing and total war. No?

It certainly seems plausible that recognizing authority figures is important to moral development. As Sigmund Freud (1856–1939) argued, we all begin our lives under the authority of some caregiver who commands us to do or not to do various things. In growing older we encounter the authority of governments, teachers, traditions, customs, religions, social groups, and even perhaps conscience – each demanding obedience to its commands. What all this seems to suggest is that actions are morally right or wrong when they are, accordingly, either commanded or prohibited by the proper authority.

Grounding ethics simply in authority is, however, deeply problematic. How can one decide among competing authorities without appealing to something independent of authority? And if authority determines right and wrong, then how can anyone possibly criticize or oppose authority? In order to ground ethics in authority, therefore, it's necessary to demonstrate that there are, in fact, legitimate authorities and then figure out what it is that they command. Logicians have a name for the mistake of justifying a claim through inappropriate or unwarranted authorities – *argumentum ad verecundiam*. Avoiding this form of error is harder than it looks.

The divine

One of the most common moral authorities to which people appeal is the divine. Some versions of this appeal may be collected under the title, "voluntarism," as they ground morality in God's "will" (*voluntas*). This strategy, however, faces two problems. The first is how one is to know what these divine commands are! Some maintain that they are apprehended through revelation, as they were for Moses and Muhammad. Others argue that they're evident in the order of nature, a position advanced by natural law theorists such as Thomas Aquinas (1224–74), Hugo Grotius (1583–1645), and the deists.

The problem here is that people appear to arrive at very different interpretations by these methods of what God or other divine beings will. The Book of Samuel, for example, admits of various interpretations; and even among those who accept the legitimacy of revelation, let alone the atheists, not everyone accepts or can even be expected to accept the authority of Abrahamic Scripture. If there's no way to achieve agreement among reasonable people about a given topic, even when the same methods for determining truth are employed, is it meaningful to say that anything can be known about it? In any case, it's certainly very hard to defend the claim to know God's will.

The second problem concerns why God should be recognized as an authority anyway. This may seem a strange question, but consider the line of inquiry developed in Plato's (427–347 BCE) well-known dialogue, *Euthyphro*. Socrates poses a dilemma that may be recast in the terms of Abrahamic monotheism this way: does God command some actions because they are morally right, or are those actions morally right because God commands them? If the answer is the former, then something besides God grounds the authority of God's commands. But if it's the latter, then God's authority and moral goodness seem to result from nothing more than a whimsical or arbitrary exercise of power.

Society, tradition, state

God, of course, isn't the only authority to which people appeal in moral matters. Many different philosophers ground morality in social authority. Social relativists hold that the authority of social conventions and agreements determines what in any given society is moral and immoral. As social agreements and conventions are variable, different, and changing, societies can and do authorize different, changing moralities. Moreover, as conventions and agreements are limited to the social order that has produced them and social orders differ widely, there may be no common moral ground across societies.

Considering the importance of traditional authorities animates critical theories as well as explanations of moral norms. Conservative thinkers like Michael Oakeshott (1901–90) and Edmund Burke (1729–97), for example, have emphasized the authority of tradition in determining moral norms, and they criticize thinkers who would ground morality in some purportedly universal rationality that speciously claims to operate independently of tradition. And, indeed, the procedures of reasoning in the sciences and elsewhere have, especially in modern times, made claim to independence, universality, and preeminence in determining what people should and shouldn't believe. (Would it be proper to call the claims of reason the commands of authority?)

The authority of the state has been justified in various ways, by appeals to divine right, nature, tradition, and conquest. During the modern era philosophers have characteristically centered their attempts to justify state authority upon the *consent* of the governed, in addition to appealing to strictly practical or utilitarian issues. For modern liberal theorists, the "will of the people" is the ultimate authority, at least in matters political.

These lines of thought, however, can lead to the undermining of critical resistance or to supine acquiescence to immorality. If society defines what's right and wrong, then taking a moral stance against the current norms of society seems to be ruled out. On what basis, for example, would Martin Luther King, Jr, or others in the US civil rights movement, have launched moral criticisms of racial segregation and discrimination? If one accepts that the state derives its authority from the consent of the people, how can anyone criticize a democratic majority that authorizes slavery, the oppression of women, or something like the Holocaust? It seems that a proper democratic theory needs, at the very least, to distinguish between government by general consent and crude majoritarianism. In *On Liberty* (1859), John Stuart Mill (1806–73) undertook to do just that.

The ancient sophist Thrasymachus (at least as he's depicted by Plato in *Republic*), the nineteenth-century German thinker Friedrich Nietzsche (1844–1900), and the French post-structuralist Michel Foucault (1926–84) all in one way or the other hold that those who are able to establish their power authorize moral norms. That is, the authority of any specific set of moral norms is the expression of power exercised by some over others. On the one hand, this position seems an amoral and cynical rejection of morality. On the other hand, perhaps it offers a critical tool for extricating people from the abuse, exploitation, and oppression of others. Perhaps some forms of power are to be preferred to others.

Wherever one falls on this issue, it's important to remember that people will do all sorts of terrible things if they feel someone with authority commands them to do it. Psychologist Stanley Milgram conducted disturbing experiments in 1961–2, in which ordinary people were found to be willing to administer dangerous electric shocks to virtual strangers – just because authoritative people wearing white lab coats commanded them to do so. If we are to obey authorities, we need to be very sure they deserve to be obeyed.

See also

1.15 Natural law, 2.6 Divine command, 5.11 Power

Reading

John Austin, *Lectures on Jurisprudence, or The Philosophy of Positive Law* [1873, 4th revised edition 1879] (Bristol: Thoemmes Press, 2002)
Michel Foucault, *Discipline and Punish: The Birth of the Prison* [1975] (New York: Pantheon Books, 1977)
*Joseph Raz, ed., *Authority* (New York: New York University Press, 1991)

1.4 Autonomy

The legitimacy of "living wills" or "advance directives" is at present a hotly contested social and moral issue. Expressing people's preferences should they become unable to do so because of illness or injury, these curious documents aim to make sure that physicians treat individuals as they wish, not as others think best. The 2005 case of Terri Schiavo, the brain-damaged American woman whose husband and parents fell into a sensational and painful legal wrangle concerning her wishes, illustrates all too well the reasons people write living wills.

Proponents of the practice argue that one of the most important bases for the human capacity to act in moral ways is the ability not only to choose and to act on those choices but also to choose for oneself, to be the author of one's own life. This capacity is known as "autonomy." But what does it mean to be autonomous?

Autonomy requires, at the very least, an absence of compulsion. If someone is compelled to act rightly by some internal or external force – for instance, to return a lost wallet packed with cash – that act isn't autonomous. So, even though the act was morally proper, because it was compelled it merits little praise.

For philosophers like Immanuel Kant (1724–1804), this is why autonomy is required for truly moral action. Kant argues in his *Critique of Practical Reason* (1788) and elsewhere that autonomously acting without regard for one's desires or interests is possible because people are able to act purely on the basis of rational principles given to themselves by themselves. Indeed, the word "autonomous" derives from the Greek for self (*auto*) and law (*nomos*) and literally means self-legislating, giving the law to one's self. Actions done through external or internal compulsion are, by contrast, "heteronomous" (the law being given by something *hetero* or "other"). In this way autonomy differs from, though also presupposes, *metaphysical* freedom, which is commonly defined as acting independently of the causal order of nature. *Political* freedom, of course, has to do with people's relationship to government and other people regardless or their relationship to systems of cause and effect. But theories of political freedom also draw upon the concept of autonomy.

Politics

Conceptions of autonomy are important politically, because one's ideas about politics are often bound up with one's ideas about what people are and what they're capable of doing or not doing. Those who think that people are not capable or little capable of self-legislating, self-regulating action are not likely to think that people are capable of governing themselves.

Liberal democratic theory, however, depends upon that ability. The authority of government in liberal democracies draws its justification from the consent of the governed. Through systems of elections and representation the people of democracies give the law to themselves. Liberal democracies are also configured to develop certain institutions (like the free press) and to protect political and civil rights (such as the rights to privacy and property) toward the end of ensuring people's ability to act autonomously and effectively. In this way, liberal democrats recognize autonomy not only as an intrinsic human capacity but also as a political achievement and an important element of human well-being.

The legitimacy of liberal democracy is therefore threatened by claims that human beings are not the truly autonomous agents we believe ourselves to be. And there is no shortage of people prepared to argue this view. Many critics maintain that people really can't act independently of their passions, of their families, of the societies in which they live, of customs, conventions, and traditions, of structures of privilege, exploitation, and oppression, including internalized oppression. Some go as far as to claim that the sort of autonomy liberal democrats describe is the fantasy of wealthy, white, European and North American males – or, worse, a privilege they enjoy only because they deny it to others. Still other critics regard the idea as a mystifying ideology through which the ruling class deludes people about the exploitive system under which they labor.

Medical ethics

The concept of autonomy has become increasingly important, however, in medicine. Many medical ethicists have effectively argued that because human beings are autonomous, no medical treatments ought to be administered to patients without their informed consent to any procedures or therapies – unless they're not competent to make informed choices (e.g. perhaps because of mental illness). That is, patients must both: (1) understand what is to be done to them, what risks are entailed, and what consequences may follow; and (2) agree to the treatment in light of that understanding. When they fail to acquire informed consent, medics are said to act paternalistically, invasively, and disrespectfully, deciding what's best for an adult who really should be allowed to make such decisions for him or herself.

Problems, however, with the requirement to respect autonomy arise in trying to determine precisely when a patient is incompetent, as well as when a patient is sufficiently well informed. Just how much mental impairment is too much; just how much information is enough? Living wills are intended as one way to get around at least some of these problems.

See also

1.2 Agency, 2.4 Deontological ethics, 4.18 Universalizability

Reading

Gerald Dworkin, *The Theory and Practice of Autonomy* (Cambridge: Cambridge University Press, 1988)

Catriona Mackenzie and Natalie Stoljar, eds., *Relational Autonomy: Feminist Perspectives on Autonomy, Agency, and the Social Self* (New York: Oxford University Press, 2000)

★"Autonomy," special issue of *Social Philosophy & Policy* 20.2 (2003)

1.5 Care

In Victor Hugo's *Les Misérables* (1862), the hero Jean Valjean is sent to prison for stealing a loaf of bread to feed his starving sister and her seven children. Valjean is not a bad man, but he believes the need to care for his poverty stricken family is more pressing than his duty to obey certain fixed moral laws concerned with the purchase of commodities. In making this decision, Hugo's character anticipates the arguments of recent moral thinkers who've advocated what's come to be called the "ethics of care."

Care vs. justice

The notion of care ethics originated when psychologist Carol Gilligan (b. 1936) began to question the theories of moral development produced by Lawrence Kohlberg, for whom she had worked as a research assistant. Gilligan concluded that Kohlberg's theories were flawed in two ways: (1) they were based only upon the behavior of boys; and (2) they regarded as inferior the forms of moral deliberation Gilligan would find to be common among girls. Central to girls' ways of deliberating, Gilligan found, were idiosyncratic considerations that emerged through caring relationships. Boys, by contrast, seemed to appeal more often to general rules, principles, duties, and rights – in her rubric, "justice" – in determining what ought to be done.

Gilligan argued that girls' (and by extension women's) ways of moral deliberation are not and should not be thought of as inferior. Instead women's and girls' ways of deliberation should be thought of simply as different from (and perhaps superior to) those of boys (and men). These conclusions were published in Gilligan's 1982 book, *In a Different Voice: Psychological Theory and Women's Development*, a text that's become central to care ethics and has added theoretical weight to "difference feminism."

Difference feminism commonly holds that there are essential differences between men and women. In the light of these differences, it works to promote an understanding and appreciation of those characteristics distinctive among women, rather than to establish a simple equality between the sexes. (Seeking equality rather than valorizing difference comprises what many call "equality" or "equal rights feminism.")

Care ethicists maintain that ethical decisions arise through caring in a way that's different from the way they arise when rules and principles decide things; and they hold that care isn't just another virtue but that instead it's basic to ethical reflection itself. Because of this, care thinkers have little use for the abstract (and perhaps absurd) hypothetical examples to which other ethicists often appeal. Decisions about allocating resources or about healthcare or about punishment cannot, care ethicists say, be resolved by considering what "one" (that is, some abstract person) would do if "one" were stuck in a hypothetical cave or out in a hypothetical lifeboat with no hypothetical food or if "one" woke up to find a hypothetical cellist and his life-support equipment hooked up to "one's" hypothetical body. (All of these are examples that prominent ethicists have actually used.)

Moreover, it's not sufficient in determining whether some act is right or wrong to show that it either breaks or doesn't break some rule, law, principle, or set of rights. Instead, for care ethicists, ethical determinations flow more or less naturally from the unique and particular features of individual caring relationships. Jane might, for example, come to a settled decision about maintaining life support for her father through discussions and interactions with those directly involved, rather than by appealing to a law, a rule, a deduction, or an abstract, purportedly universal example. Her friend Aisha, her family, and her community might come to a different conclusion. Like Valjean, residents of New Orleans who were left homeless, isolated, starving, and thirsty by Hurricane Katrina might have been in violation of legal and other principles prohibiting theft when they looted grocery stores for food and water; but when considering their conduct through the lenses of care and compassion, it's hard to blame them.

Problems

There is, however, considerable difference of opinion about both (1) whether the claims regarding sex difference are factually true as well as (2) whether or not males can and should themselves adopt ethics of care. Many men, in fact, do claim to have incorporated care ethics into their moral lives, and feminist thinkers like Nell Noddings and Virginia Held have endorsed their doing so. Others are dubious about men's capacity to deliberate in the caring way possible for women.

Care ethics has also been criticized as an oppressive wolf in sheep's clothing. That is, while purporting to raise the status of things female, critics argue that it actually defines women essentially as caregivers – thereby recycling the sex-roles, the oppressive pedestal, the separate spheres, the self-effacement, and the self-sacrifice that have for centuries, perhaps millennia, helped keep women in subordinate, diminished positions.

Questions also arise concerning the ability of care ethics to resolve conflicting claims and decisions. Suppose two individuals (say, two lesbian parents), both involved in a caring relationship with one another and some third party (perhaps their child), find themselves coming to contrary ethical conclusions – for example, whether or not the child should be subjected to some risky medical procedure. Can the conflict be resolved without appealing to rules, principles, and abstract examples?

Perhaps the best ethical deliberation considers both care and justice. That is, perhaps rather than thinking about them as competitors, the two approaches ought to be regarded as complementary.

See also

3.22 Prudence, 4.9 Justice and lawfulness, 4.15 Sex and gender

Readings

*Rosemarie Tong, *Feminine and Feminist Ethics* (Belmont, CA: Wadsworth Publishing Co., 1993)
*Virginia Held, *Justice and Care: Essential Readings in Feminist Ethics* (Boulder, CO: Westview Press, 1995)
Daryl Koehn, *Rethinking Feminist Ethics: Care, Trust, and Empathy* (New York: Routledge, 1998)

1.6 Character

Tabitha is taciturn, rude, miserable, and reclusive. She has few friends because she is such poor company. Samantha, in contrast, is friendly, cheerful, and gregarious. She has many friends who are drawn to her warmth and wit. But although Samantha is generally seen as a "nicer" person, some other facts about the two women suggest she is not necessarily a better one. Samantha is good to her friends, and on a day-to-day basis she is kind to them. Other than that, she leads a simple life in which her needs are put first. She is not especially generous and takes no interest at all in the hardship of strangers. Tabitha, on the other hand, may not be good company, but she devotes her free time to the welfare of others. She avoids working with people, which she dislikes, but she spends 12 hours a week working for voluntary organizations and donates 15 percent of her income to good causes.

The philosopher Iris Murdoch (1919–99) wrote a novel, *The Nice and The Good* (1968), that makes a telling moral observation relevant to these two women. The title itself captures the point: there's a difference between possessing genial character traits and true moral goodness. Indeed, it's a truism "that one may smile, and smile, and be a villain" (*Hamlet* I. v).

Nevertheless, it would seem odd to conclude that the social functions of character have nothing to do with moral goodness at all. Aristotle (384–322 BCE), for example, believed that cultivating a good character (*ēthos*) was essential to our moral development. Human beings are creatures of habit (*ethos*) who don't and can't sit down and deliberate about the rightness and wrongness of each and every action as its possibility presents itself to us. That's just as well: making correct judgments in many situations is very difficult, and if people had to decide how to act on a case-by-case basis, they'd surely make many mistakes. It's therefore terribly important to develop a virtuous character, which means becoming the kind of person who is disposed to good deeds and to make good judgments generally.

Character and virtue

Good character could be seen merely as a means to the rather intellectual end of good decision-making. But for Aristotle, it's more than that. Acquiring a good character is important to an individual's happiness and well-being all by itself. Being good, for Aristotle, is about living well, becoming fulfilled, complete, content, and happy. Only a person of good character can achieve this, because it's the very qualities of good character themselves that compose much of what counts as human happiness (*eudaimonia*). Happiness, from this point of view, is more about one's internal constitution than one's external possessions or circumstance. Character, therefore, is crucial both to (a) being a complete, happy human being and (b) discerning and making the right decision.

The idea of moral character can enable us to make sense of the contradictions in Tabitha's and Samantha's make-up. First, contrary to appearances, in many ways it's Tabitha who has the better character, for it's she who characteristically thinks of others. Samantha's charms are more superficial.

That is, however, not the whole story. Tabitha clearly doesn't have many of the fully developed virtues of character Aristotle would consider essential for the good life. She serves the good of people, but in direct interactions people find her unpleasant. Moreover, her own life isn't fully flourishing: she's simply too miserable and solitary for that. Samantha may, overall, be a less virtuous person, but her capacity for sociability and its pleasures is nevertheless truly a moral virtue. Samantha and Tabitha, then, each lack precisely those virtuous traits the other possesses. The person of thoroughly good character in Aristotle's sense, however, must combine the virtues of both.

See also

1.10 Flourishing, 1.20 Sympathy, 2.16 Virtue ethics

Reading

*Thomas Aquinas, *Commentary on Aristotle's Nicomachean Ethics* [1271–2], edited by Ralph M. McInerny (Chicago: Dumb Ox Books, 1993)
Alasdair MacIntyre, *After Virtue* (Notre Dame, IN: University of Notre Dame Press, 1981)
Philippa Foot, *Moral Dilemmas* (Oxford: Oxford University Press, 2002)

1.7 Conscience

When someone is about to do something wrong in a film or cartoon, sometimes a little angel of conscience appears on the character's shoulder and whispers some admonition in his ear that reminds him of the moral impropriety of his act, stopping him before he goes through with the misdeed.

The personification may be just a cute device, but the idea of a voice of conscience is one with a long philosophical history.

Grasping that something is factually the case seems to be different from grasping that some act ought not to be done. The first sort of apprehension starts from knowledge about "what is" (the ancient Greeks called this *episteme*) and leads to theoretical wisdom (*sophia*). The second sort, by contrast, results from practical reasoning and comprises understanding "what should be," and in particular circumstances understanding whether or not a particular act should or should not be performed. It leads to practical wisdom (*phronesis*). Human reasoning, then, by this classic account, possesses the capacity to determine not only the "true" but also "the good." How is it that we can accomplish this grasp of moral truth? One of the most important answers given has been: through conscience. Without the capacity for conscience, many have held, moral reasoning would not be possible.

Early debates

The word "conscience" derives from the Latin word, *conscientia*, which means both (a) consciousness and (b) conscience as an inward consciousness that something is morally wrong. Its component parts mean "knowledge with," and in this it seems to correspond fairly closely to the probably older Greek term, *syneidesis*, which means much the same thing.

St Jerome's (d. 420) interpretation of Ezekiel 1.4–14 is (in)famous for having connected (possibly through a mistranslation) conscience not with *syneidesis* but with a related term, *synderesis* (insight). Following Jerome, medieval and early modern Christian thinkers expended a lot of effort trying to determine the role of *synderesis* in practical reasoning and its relationship to conscience, as well as to our mental faculties.

Thomas Aquinas (1225–74), for example, saw *synderesis* as simply an act of intellect by which we know the good (*Summa Theologica* I, Question 79, Articles 12–13). Bonaventure (1221–74) thought it did more, and through feeling gave us a little shove in the direction of doing good. Duns Scotus (1270–1308) thought it did much the same thing, but through will rather than feeling. Some came to see *synderesis* not as conscience itself but as something like the "spark" that gives rise to conscience. Other controversies about conscience also emerged, such as whether it can err; whether it can ever tell us what to do, rather than just what not to do; and what role it plays in relating general moral principles to particular situations.

The voice of God

Like many religious philosophers, Joseph Butler (1692–1752) regarded conscience as somehow manifesting God's moral guidance; God made us, and in making us God provided us with the ability to discern moral goodness, right and wrong. Call it the "inner light" (as Quakers did) or simply conscience, one of the most salient things about this power is that we have it despite the Fall from Eden and whether or not we've ever been exposed to any religious instruction, sacrament, scripture, or prophetic revelation. Because of this, conscience offers us something we "know with" others, a common ground or a shared court of appeal in moral conversation and controversy. Crucially, conscience offers a common ground not only to those of a given culture, religion, or legal system but also to all people and (perhaps more widely) to all moral beings (natural and supernatural).

Contemporary conscience

One hears little of conscience among academic philosophers today, though one does often hear reference to our moral "intuitions." In fact, for many contemporary philosophers, if a moral claim is inconsistent with our moral intuitions, we have good reasons to question it. "Intuition" in this sense is thus in some ways the contemporary remnant or cognate of older appeals to conscience. So, in assessing a set of claims about, say, abortion, war, euthanasia, or corporate ethics, one may appeal to conscience or intuition as a kind of test.

The notion of conscience also functions to mark profound moral limits – that is, as a concept to use when signaling a point at which one cannot compromise. Martin Luther's remark – as it is traditionally recounted – when he appeared in 1521 before the Diet of Worms to answer for his deviance, exemplifies this way of using conscience. In reply to his accusers, Luther is said to have said finally, "Here I stand. I can do no other." Similarly, "conscientious objectors" use an appeal to conscience in justifying their refusal to take part in war; and this appeal (when determined to be sincere and consistent) is as a matter of law often honored. As both a matter of law, then, and as it continues to appear in moral discourse, conscience or something like it is often given the final say.

See also

1.13 Intuition, 1.15 Natural law, 3.22 Prudence

Readings

*Samuel Butler, *Five Sermons*, edited by Stephen L. Darwall (Indianapolis, IN: Hackett Publishing, 1983); from *Fifteen Sermons Preached at the Rolls Chapel* (1726)

Douglas C. Langston, *Conscience and other Virtues: From Bonaventure to Mac-Intyre* (University Park: Pennsylvania State University Press, 2001)

Timothy C. Potts, ed., *Conscience in Medieval Philosophy* (Cambridge: Cambridge University Press, 2002)

1.8 Evolution

At a meeting of the British Association for the Advancement of Science in 1860, a year after the publication of Darwin's *On the Origin of Species*, Bishop Samuel Wilberforce (1805–73) mocked the scientist T. H. Huxley (1825–95) for his adherence to the new theory of evolution, asking if he was descended from the apes on his mother's side or his father's side. In so doing, Wilberforce mainly exposed his ignorance of Darwin's theory. Had he properly understood it, he would have realized his question simply does not arise.

But Wilberforce also makes a more subtle and interesting mistake. Underlying his question is the assumption that the dignity of humankind would somehow be undermined if it could be established that humanity's origins are to be found in a sub-human ancestor shared with other primates (assuming for the moment that it's meaningful to describe such a being as "sub-human"). In other words, the force of Wilberforce's remark depends upon the idea that out of base origins nothing noble can grow.

This is a false assumption, but it often prejudices the way in which people respond to attempts to explain the origins of morality in evolutionary terms. Evolutionary psychologists believe they can explain how basic moral feelings and principles could have emerged out of the amoral struggle for survival. Natural selection is value-free, but values nonetheless can arise out of it. Moreover, explanations of the origins of moral propensities are in no way evaluative judgments about them. It's one thing to explain; it's quite another to assess or justify.

The origins of virtue

In broad terms, many recent evolutionary accounts of ethics draw upon the work of game theory to show that populations are more stable and tend to grow more effectively over the long run if their members adopt strategies of the form "tit-for-tat." In other words, they start from a cautious assumption of trust and forgiveness and then repay the goodwill afforded them; but if their trust is betrayed too often or too deeply, goodwill is withdrawn. In contrast, populations whose members start from an aggressive, distrusting position do not flourish, because they cannot reap the benefits of cooperation. On the other hand, populations whose members are too trusting also fare badly, as they become easy pickings for predators.

In other words, cooperation as well as other-regarding feelings evolved because they made organisms fitter for survival. Many find this idea strange because they confuse the idea of natural selection or "survival of the fittest" with selfishness. "Fitness" is not just a matter of a brute strength; nor does it imply anything selfish, nasty, or brutish. It means nothing other than the ability of the organism (or perhaps more accurately, the gene) to "fit" with its environment in such a way as to maximize its chances of replication. Human genes, it's argued, are more likely to survive if the organisms that carry them possess some of the traits or at least capacities associated with moral goodness, such as empathy, affection, trust, and cooperation.

Although not just any evolved behavior would count as moral, it does seem to be the case that, had we evolved in a different way, with different traits and different capacities, different things would count as moral and immoral, assuming morality existed at all. For instance, if the sight of people being hurt caused us real, intense physical pain, the moral case for banning violence in films would be much stronger than it is.

The genetic fallacy

Some retort that this sort of account debunks ethics. Ethics, say the critics, if nothing else is about altruism and considering the welfare of others; but evolutionary theory reduces morality to nothing more than a set of purely pragmatic rules that serve the selfish interests of genes (as if molecules could be selfish). This line of reasoning, however, is flawed. Just as Huxley isn't a monkey even if he and monkeys share an ancestor, so ethics need not now be purely a question of gene selection just because in the past gene selection was the mechanism by which moral feelings first emerged.

Philosophers know this common mistake as the *genetic fallacy*: confusing the origins of a belief with its justification. Ethics can be justified in many ways – with appeals to duty, the welfare of others, the demands of consistency and so on, even the will of God. All these justifications are compatible with the view that the human capacity for moral thinking has its origins in the brute and amoral machinations of nature.

In order to show that the evolutionary account does debunk ethics, it would be necessary to argue that all the justifications people give for ethical decisions are *only* a veneer, and that, in fact, ethics is still no more than the selfish playing of tit-for-tat for personal or genetic gain. People do advance such arguments, and indeed they seem to appeal to the cynicism of contemporary minds. We moderns, especially those of capitalist societies, seem amenable to the suggestion that at bottom people are selfish, that our true motives are hidden from us, and that we shouldn't trust the reasons our conscious minds give for our actions. In this intellectual environment, the idea that morality simply masks naked self-interest born from the struggle for survival can itself easily thrive. One might even expect such a society to advance ideas like this.

Of course, it may be true. The plausibility, however, of the debunking account is not in itself an argument for it. In and of itself, explaining the origins of ethics in evolutionary terms neither vindicates nor debunks ethics.

See also

1.10 Flourishing, 2.7 Egoism, 2.9 Naturalism, 3.9 Facts/values, 5.3 Bad faith and self-deception

Reading

Jerome H. Barkow, Leda Cosmides, and John Tooby, eds., *The Adapted Mind* (Oxford: Oxford University Press, 1992)
*Matt Ridley, *The Origins of Virtue* (London: Viking, 1996)
Peter Singer, *A Darwinian Left: Politics, Evolution, and Cooperation* (London: Weidenfeld and Nicolson, 1999)

1.9 Finitude

Consider an imaginary world called Plentos. In Plentos people live forever, or at least as long as they wish. There are no shortages of any kind. Every kind of nourishment, excellence, and pleasure is available in limitless supply. Land of every description is available to all at no cost or effort. No one wants for love, or companionship, or for speedy, effective care. Everyone is omniscient, and nothing frustrates anyone's will. What would ethics be like in such a world? Would ethics even be necessary?

Just consider matters of property. As the Scottish philosopher David Hume (1711–76) argues, the rules of justice concerning property arise only because human desires for it surpass the quantities available. Because more than one party may desire the same parcel, some set of procedures must be implemented to determine who gets it. But if there were more than enough of the objects of desire, as it is with the air around us (at least for now), no conflicts over them could arise. Would rules prohibiting injury be meaningful if injuries were impossible or even if they were always promptly healed and didn't diminish the possibilities of life? If one lived forever and if injury were brief and without lasting effect, would it really matter if one's body or feelings were hurt? If perfect substitutes could always be had for whatever might be lost, would anyone care about loss, would the concept of loss be at all meaningful?

In short, it seems that there would be no reason for ethics in Plentos. Ethics emerges because of human finitude – because conflicts over finite resources and because some harms do impair our lives in ways that cannot be perfectly rectified. Finitude therefore seems to be a condition of ethics. It is only because our possibilities for flourishing are limited that people can harm or benefit us, and so be good or bad. And if we were finite in different ways from the ways we happen to be, then different things would count as good and bad.

The inescapability of finitude

Of course, finitude is inescapable for human beings. The objects of our desires as well as our needs are and will remain terribly limited. Natural resources, food, medicines, information, artwork, mates, friends, children, and many, many other things of human desire, need, and possibility are often in painfully short supply. We are vulnerable in countless ways. Our property and possessions are often irreplaceable and can be taken permanently from us. Our minds can be wounded and deranged irreparably. Our children can suffer and die. Our friends and companions can be lost, leaving us desolate and alone. Our will and our projects are often frustrated. Our knowledge and understanding are partial and incomplete. We can, in short, be harmed in countless ways that render our lives really and irremediably diminished.

Perhaps most importantly we all will die, each and every one of us. That is, we ourselves are finite. For philosophers like Søren Kierkegaard (1813–55) and Martin Heidegger (1889–1976) our mortality is the most important feature of human existence, requiring us to make existential ethical choices about what we will be, what we will value, and what will concern us. Human beings care because we are finite, and ethics is about managing our caring about things in a world where both we and what we care about will perish.

So, although it would be wrong to say that ethics is only about dealing with our finitude, it wouldn't be wrong to say that doing so is a mighty large part of it.

See also

3.13 Injury, 4.9 Justice and lawfulness, 4.14 Restoration

Reading

Søren Kierkegaard, *The Sickness Unto Death: A Christian Psychological Exposition for Upbuilding and Awakening* [1849] (Princeton, NJ: Princeton University Press, 1983)
*Albert Camus, *The Myth of Sisyphus* [1942] (New York: Vintage International, 1991)
*Lawrence J. Hatab, *Ethics and Finitude: Heideggerian Contributions to Moral Philosophy* (Lanham, MD: Rowman & Littlefield Publishers, 2002)

1.10 Flourishing

It's a commonplace to say about people living at little more than subsistence level – with scarcely enough food to live, and barely adequate shelter – that they aren't living but merely existing. The distinction doesn't need to be explained because people have a general sense of what it means: living a full human life requires more than just surviving from day to day in a biological sense. It's not just *that* we live; *how* we live matters.

Aristotle (384–322 BCE) developed this truism into a more complete ethical concept: *eudaimonia*, a word that literally means something like good-spiritedness but more properly translates as *happiness, well-being*, or *flourishing*. Although Aristotle's particular take on *eudaimonia* may be rooted in an outdated conception of human nature, there's much in his account that's still relevant today.

How to flourish

Aristotle's account of *eudaimonia* emerged from a discussion about the highest or most perfect good for humankind. He observed that people do many things for the sake of something else (as *means* to other ends), but the highest good must be something that is valuable in its own right, something that's an *end in itself*. But in what does this highest good consist, and why is it an end in itself?

For Aristotle, every kind of thing has its own proper function (*ergon*; *Nicomachean Ethics*, 1097b). That function distinguishes a thing from others. Living things, for example, are distinguished from inanimate things by virtue of their capacities for growth and nourishment. Animals are distinguished from other living things, like plants, by their awareness of their environments as well as by their capacity for desire and emotion. Human beings are distinguished from all other animals by their capacity to reason abstractly and act on the basis of rational principles.

To flourish, according to Aristotle, everything must live in accordance with its own distinctive nature and do so in a way that most perfectly realizes that nature. Functioning or acting in this way achieves a thing's excellence (*aretē*). A healthy plant that feeds from the sun and soil grows and flourishes. A healthy cat, hunting and reproducing successfully, also flourishes. The flourishing of a human being, however, requires more than growing, feeding, feeling, being conscious, and reproducing; it requires engaging in the distinctively human *activity* of reasoning about eternal truths, something Aristotle calls theoretical contemplation (*theoria*). Only then does a human being fully achieve its nature.

This happy activity is not a means to something else; it is *complete*, an end in itself. People who ask what one can *do* with philosophical contemplation fail to grasp this. They presume that, like making money, one engages in philosophical contemplation as a means to something else. But, according to Aristotle, one contemplates simply for its own sake. One makes money to philosophize; one doesn't philosophize to make money.

Perversely, one might ask *why* one *should* flourish, why it's better to flourish than not to flourish, and why it's better to be happy than unhappy. An answer that repeated Aristotle's account of human nature and the content of flourishing might seem rather out of date and inadequate today. But he was surely correct to note that there is something good in itself about a life fully lived, and bad about one which is severely limited. To question why it is better to flourish than not is to fail to see the obvious. Arguably, such a question can only be disingenuous.

What flourishing means now

What's different now? Today some of the details of Aristotle's account appear unsustainable in the light of advances in science and psychology. His account of what makes each species distinct is crude, and indeed the very idea of species, as he understood it, has been discredited. The extent to which humans are in fact rational beings is now more questionable than ever. Nonetheless, *eudaimonia* remains a potent central concept for ethics, and understanding what's required for people to flourish remains a coherent and defensible project.

The concept of flourishing, indeed, suggests the possibility of establishing some cross-cultural and trans-historical moral criteria. So long as all (or even most) humans share certain capacities for flourishing, judgments about how particular governments or societies promote or inhibit flourishing become possible. If poorly nourishing the minds and bodies of people here prevents them from flourishing, then it's likely to do so there. If denying women an education in England thwarts their flourishing, then doing so in Afghanistan does, too.

But this is just where the concept of *eudaimonia* becomes more difficult for us than it was for Aristotle. It may not only be impossible but also undesirable to advance a single account of what human flourishing requires. Many today adhere to a more diverse and pluralistic understanding of human nature and human flourishing than Aristotle did, and so are reluctant to prescribe one way of life as *the* way of life for all. The aesthete, the athlete, the scholar, and the tradesperson may all achieve different ways of flourishing, different excellences. So too may the American, the Tibetan, the Inuit, the Hmong, the Saudi Arabian, the Rwandan, and the ancient Athenian. That doesn't mean anything goes, of course. But it does mean that explaining what *eudaimonia* is without resorting to vague generalizations is harder than ever. Perhaps, on this question, by helping to figure out what human beings need to flourish, psychology, sociology, history, anthropology, and biology can be of real assistance to ethics.

See also

1.17 Pain and pleasure, 2.16 Virtue ethics, 3.16 Intrinsic/instrumental value, 3.22 Prudence

Reading

Ellen Frankell Paul, Jr, Fred D. Miller, and Jeffrey Paul, eds., *Human Flourishing* (Cambridge: Cambridge University Press, 1999)
*Martha Nussbaum, *Women and Human Development: The Capabilities Approach* (Cambridge: Cambridge University Press, 2000)
Corey L. M. Keyes and Jonathan Haidt, eds., *Flourishing: Positive Psychology and the Life Well-Lived* (Washington, DC: American Psychological Association, 2002)

1.11 Harmony

According to Paul McCartney and Stevie Wonder, ebony and ivory live together in perfect harmony – on the piano keyboard that is. Their song contains an allegorical message of course: humans should learn from pianofortes and get along regardless of skin color.

The choice of metaphor reflects a widely held perception that what is harmonious is somehow right. There is harmony when the parts of something – usually some social group like a family, city, or state – stand in a certain kind of desirable or ideal relation. That relation is thought to be rational, balanced, orderly, stable, and free from conflict or strife. It is therefore perhaps not surprising that philosophers have looked to the idea of harmony as providing insights into the right way to live.

Ancient harmony

Pythagoras and the Pythagoreans who followed him taught that the universe exhibits harmonies that can be mathematically described. The ethical imperative of this metaphysic was to cultivate one's soul so that it would somehow come to mirror or resemble the harmony of the universe. The microcosmic harmony of the self was to imitate the macrocosmic harmony of the universe. Both music and mathematics were to play a role, according to Pythagoreans, in cultivating the soul's harmony.

Plato was deeply influenced by the Pythagoreans. Not only did he continue to regard both music and mathematics highly in education. His work, particularly the *Republic* and *Timaeus*, also exhibits the preeminence of unity and harmony among his ethical and political ideals (e.g. the *three waves* of *Rep.* Book V). Just as the parts of the soul are to be harmonized with one another, so must the *many* parts of the city be brought into a harmonious *one.* Principal among the threats to social unity and harmony are faction, ignorance, and irrationality.

Asian thinkers in the Confucian, Taoist, and Shinto traditions also position harmony among the most important characteristics of both individual and social life. Confucians cultivate *Li* – principles of order, harmony, and propriety that have been distilled through custom and tradition. In addition, with Taoists, they also attempt to discern the *Tao* – that more metaphysical principle of nature to which one can appeal for example and guidance (see Natural law, 1.15). Shinto thinkers emphasize maintaining the purity and harmony of self, society, and world by honoring and following the example of the *kami*, sacred spirits of the natural world and the ancestral order.

Modern harmony

In a similar vein, early modern thinkers as diverse as Montesquieu (1689–1755), Joseph Addison (1672–1719), David Hume (1711–76), and James Madison (1751–1836) regarded the development of *faction* as among the most serious threats to the peace and stability of a social order.

Modern rationalistic metaphysicians also found the concept of harmony compelling as an ethical *desideratum*. But for them harmony also served the purpose of trying to come to terms with the apparent contradiction between the evils of the world and the omnipotence–omniscience–benevolence of God.

In the view of Gottfried Wilhelm von Leibniz (1646–1716), there is a pre-established harmony among all things, and the harmony of things is also the perfection of things. Since God is perfect, his Creation must be the best, most perfect, and most harmonious world possible. Leibniz's conviction that a universal harmony exists was so strong as to persuade him that what we find to be evil must only be so from our limited point of view (*Monadologie*, 1714).

Similarly, humans are, Benedictus Spinoza (1632–77) says, like tiny worms in the circulatory system of some vastly larger animal (*Letter to Oldenburg* #15). Unable to experience more than their immediate surroundings, humans experience things as evil that would clearly be good if understood in the context of the whole of the universe and God's order. What looks evil in the part must not be so in the whole. That can sound reassuring, but it can also seem callous in the face of human evils like the Holocaust or the Rwandan genocides.

Harmony can thus have two very different functions in moral discourse. It can be something we aspire to, or it can be something that is already there. Put crudely, it is the difference between thinking we need to work to make the world a better place and thinking it's already as good as it can be.

See also

1.15 Natural law, 2.11 Perfectionism, 2.13 Rationalism

Reading

Gottfried Wilhelm von Leibniz, *Theodicy* [1710] (Peru, IL: Open Court Publishing, 1985)

Robert Lawlor, *Sacred Geometry: Philosophy and Practice* (London: Thames and Hudson, 1982)

*Charles H. Kahn, *Pythagoras and the Pythagoreans: A Brief History* (Indianapolis, IN: Hackett Publishing, 2001)

1.12 Interest

Most people have more moral concern for people and intelligent animals than they do for daffodils and rocks. Indeed, someone who seems to care more for inanimate objects than for flesh and blood creatures will usually be rebuked for his or her skewed moral priorities. But why?

One common answer is that any possible candidate for moral concern must have an interest of some kind in its own welfare. It must make a difference to that being whether it persists or ceases to exist, whether it remains intact or disintegrates, or more generally whether or not its good is served. Anything that doesn't have this sort of interest in itself possesses moral value only if it in turn serves the interests of things that do.

So, for example, an obvious reason why it is wrong to kill an innocent human being is that innocent human beings have an interest in staying alive. People have relationships, the capacity to enjoy life, projects with which they're engaged. All of these can be described as the person's interests, and to rob a person of life is to damage those interests. Joel Feinberg (1926–2004) goes so far as to define "harm" as the thwarting or damaging of interests.

Interestingly, if you'll pardon the pun, it's not necessary that one *desire* what is in one's interest, as any smoker who knows about smoking's pathological effects but still desires to light up will testify. And, perhaps, it might be said that one need not even be *aware* of one's interests. For example, it might be in one's interest to step out of the way of the car that's fast approaching from behind, even if tragically one is unaware of it.

Interests aren't always commensurable, and sometimes people face "conflicts of interest." Conflicts of interest arise when different interests are or are likely to become incommensurable. If, for example, a judge's son should appear as a defendant in her court, the judge would face a conflict between her interests as a mother in her son's welfare and the social-political interests of justice she is bound to serve as a citizen and judge. Of course, sometimes, in fact often, interests are complementary – as they are, for example, between a complainant's interest in recovering damages through a lawsuit and his attorney's interest in earning a living.

Do animals have interests?

One of the most vexing questions facing philosophers today is whether or not non-human animals have interests. Most, if not all, surely do have interests in the here and now. All animals have an interest, for example, in not feeling unnecessary pain; and an animal's attempt to avoid pain, its exhibiting distress, and its becoming incapacitated when suffering is evidence of that interest. One might argue that many animals have social interests so far as they are social beings with young to rear, companions with which to relate, and hierarchies to maintain. If one accepts that such interests exist, then moral grounds also exist for taking those interests into consideration and for preventing unnecessary harm to animals.

Whether or not non-human animals have an interest in their future, however, is a rather complex matter. How the issue is resolved may be important to determining one's stance on animal rights. It's been argued that most non-human animals seem to live in the moment and certainly don't have long-term projects like careers, political agendas, research, businesses, or artwork in the same way that typically humans do. (It has to be said, of course, that some humans also live in the moment.) On the other hand, it is clear that a domestic cat does have an interest in the future in one sense: if it stays alive it may have a pleasant life ahead of it.

Needlessly ending a cat's life therefore does seem to militate against the cat's interests, but still the difference in the scope of those interests from the scope of typical human interests for some remains sufficient to draw a moral line. That's why it can be perfectly consistent to be in favor of improved *welfare* for farmed animals yet not be a vegetarian or recognize certain animal rights. A farmed animal's interest for some extends only as far as not being made to suffer needlessly.

From this point of view, plants and inanimate objects don't seem to have any interests at all – except perhaps in a loose, metaphorical sense. It makes no difference to the stone composing a mountain whether or not it remains intact or is blown to smithereens. Nor does it matter to a daffodil whether or not it's picked. But that doesn't mean that it's permissible to damage things without interests at will. Damaging things with no interests of their own can very much harm the interests of humans and non-humans. A gardener has an interest in the cultivation of his flowers and vegetables, and one damages that interest if one damages his garden. Ecological damage in general can be considered wrong because it harms the interests of the sentient life, human and non-human, that inhabits the world.

Drawing the line

Since the boundary between beings that in some sense have interests and beings that don't is a rather vague one, a difficult problem arises concerning where precisely one draws the line between them. With shellfish? Finned fish (does a salmon have an interest in reaching the headwaters of a stream to spawn)? Social creatures like birds, cattle, wolves, and bees? Cetaceans? Primates? Indeed, can one exclude any non-human animal and not be guilty of "speciesism"? And what about the interests of what might be called *liminal beings* like embryos, fetuses, those in comas and persistent vegetative states, the severely retarded, the mentally ill, etc.?

There is also a question of whether non-sentient objects can have interests. "Deep green" environmental philosophers have argued that they can, but most who argue that something like the Grand Canyon should be valued for its own sake and not just as means to an end do not base their arguments on any assumption that it has interests.

Of course, it is also possible to argue that interests are not central to moral value. There's more to ethics than the fact that some beings have interests. But recognition of the interests people and other animals have might be enough at least to get ethics going.

See also

1.17 Pain and pleasure, 1.19 Rights, 3.21 Moral subjects/moral agents, 4.16 Speciesism

Reading

Peter Singer, *The Expanding Circle: Ethics and Sociobiology* (Oxford: Oxford University Press, 1981)

Joel Feinberg, *Harm to Others*, volume 4 of *The Moral Limits of Criminal Law* (Oxford: Oxford University Press, 1987)

*Tom L. Beauchamp, *Philosophical Ethics: An Introduction to Moral Philosophy*, 3rd edition (New York: McGraw Hill, 2001)

1.13 Intuition

To know most things one's got to do some thinking. Even basic facts, such as "chicks are yellow," require drawing some general inferences on the basis of a limited number of observations or the authority of others. But there are some things it seems one simply doesn't need to figure out. What yellow looks like is one of them. You *just know* what yellow looks like – to you at least – and you don't need to justify your claim to knowledge by appeal to rational arguments or authority.

Could some moral knowledge be like this? Consider the concept of "good," for example. Does anyone really need to work out what goodness is? How could one even set out to demonstrate what it means to be good? Isn't goodness rather something that we can just recognize when it's present in an action or a person?

The view that we can do just that is known as intuitionism. Intuition in this sense is the capacity to know or apprehend something directly, without any need for a justification, such as a rational argument, to support it. It's related to the popular sense of the term, such as when people talk of "women's intuition" but it should not be thought of as a kind of hunch. There is nothing flaky about this type of intuition: it provides a direct and unmediated route to truth.

Modern intuitionism is prefigured in some very old ways of thinking about ethical terms, such as the Platonic idea of intuiting or seeing the good itself (*noesis*); or the Stoic notion of cataleptic or indubitable moral impressions. One also finds accounts of intuition with regard to moral and metaphysical matters throughout the medieval and early modern era, for example the doctrine appearing in Spinoza's *Ethics* (1677) of "intuitive knowledge" (*scientia intuitiva*).

The idea that intuition underpins moral reasoning may seem strange because, as anyone whose been around a while will testify, humans don't seem to have a reliable capacity to know what is right. To say, however, that people have a faculty that can intuit moral properties is not the same as saying that this capacity is infallible or easily used. Just as people's eyes can deceive them, so can their moral intuitions.

Moore and modern intuitionism

G. E. Moore (1873–1958) argued that the concept of "good" either (a) stands in need of further analysis or (b) is complete as it is. According to him, option (b) is the right one. Let's say, for example, that someone claims that "good" should be understood as "happy" or "happiness-producing." That can't be right, said Moore, because the question of whether good really is happiness is an open and disputed one. (Some, for example, argue that being good often entails sacrificing one's happiness, even one's life; others, of course, disagree.) But if happiness were just what "good" meant, then the question would not be open in that way. The two terms would mean the same thing, just as "bachelor" and "unmarried man" do.

Moore argued that *any* analysis of what the term "good" means would remain open in this way. And this shows that "good" cannot be analyzed or defined in terms of anything else – particularly features of the natural world, such as pleasure, happiness, or welfare. The mistake of thinking that "good" could be analyzed in terms of natural things he called the *naturalistic fallacy*.

"Good," therefore, is a *basic* concept. But if "good" is not analyzable into other more basic terms or elements, how do people know what it means? They know, according to Moore, because they directly intuit the good. Just as yellowness is something one directly apprehends, so too is goodness. That doesn't mean there is nothing to say about goodness. It's just that what there is to say doesn't define what it is.

The comparison with yellow is instructive here. One can tell someone who doesn't understand the word that yellow is the color of chicks and that if added to blue it makes green, and so on. These elaborations may help people to recognize what yellow is; but when they do finally recognize it, they apprehend it directly. In the same way, one can say that goodness tends to promote well-being and not suffering, or that good people are not cruel, and so forth. All these things are true, but they just don't capture the essence or meaning of goodness. To do that, one simply has to apprehend it directly.

Moral intuitionism's biggest problem is that it leaves the process of knowing moral truths rather mysterious. It also seems to face problems explaining how it is that people can resolve moral disagreements. Is there anything more that can be done in cases of moral disagreement than argue about whose intuitions are correct? Intuitionism offers a fierce challenge to those who think basic moral concepts can be elucidated in other terms. But its own account of how we know those concepts can seem just as unsatisfactory.

See also

1.15 Natural law, 2.9 Naturalism, 2.13 Rationalism, 3.9 Facts/values

Reading

G. E. Moore, *Principia Ethica* (Cambridge: Cambridge University Press, 1903)

Philip Stratton-Lake, ed., *Ethical Intuitionism* (Oxford: Oxford University Press, 2002)

Robert Audi, *The Good in the Right: A Theory of Intuition and Intrinsic Value* (Princeton, NJ: Princeton University Press, 2005)

1.14 Merit

It's no secret that the good things of life are not equally distributed. Things like wealth, education, healthcare, housing, respect, and leisure accumulate in enormous amounts around certain individuals and collectives leaving others to do without. In some cases the unequal distribution is the result of an injustice – e.g., theft, dispossession, or coercion. But aren't some inequalities just? Isn't it sometimes right and proper that some people get more of the "goods" than others, that some lead lives of luxury and ease while others endure punishment, incarceration, poverty, boredom, and generally diminished circumstances? Many think so, and the reason most commonly advanced to justify such inequalities is "merit" or "desert." Some people simply merit or deserve more than others; some people deserve less. But what is merit, and can it really justify inequality?

The attribution of merit

While some conservatives argue that merit may be conferred simply by family, national, or ethnic membership, others – following Jean-Jacques

Rousseau's 1754 *Discourse on the Origin of Inequality* and Tom Paine's 1791 *Rights of Man* – view the idea that merit should flow from the accidents of birth and fortune with suspicion. Liberal ways of thinking conceive merit as something that's attributed to people on the basis of what they do or choose. Working hard, producing goods and services that others find pleasant and useful, and performing heroic or self-sacrificing acts (like risking one's life to save another's) are all generally thought to warrant merit. Merit and reward may be conferred for things already done or, in some cases, for the promise of things still to be done (for example university education and a measure of respect are offered to US students in exchange for the promise of future military service). One might say, then, that it's ethically proper for some to receive more goods than others because some people act, have acted, or will act differently from others, and some acts are meritorious while others aren't. Curing someone's cancer seems to merit more reward than cleaning someone's house. Obeying the law merits reward, while breaking it merits (or warrants) punishment. In this way, systems of incentive and disincentive are established that influence people to achieve and to act morally.

But are things really so simple? Consider how performing an extremely beautiful, difficult, and complex violin concerto merits praise and even reward. But people like Nicolò Paganini are to a significant extent just born with the dexterity, the pitch, and the sensibility – in short the talent – for such things, while others just aren't. The gifts of birth aren't acquired through one's choices and efforts. No amount of effort, for example, is likely to make the authors of this book into successful heavyweight boxers, ballerinas, or professional basketball players.

Besides natural genetic endowment, merit seems to be made possible by other things beyond an individual's control. Being born to parents who recognize and support their child's talent and have access to resources for the training necessary to develop that talent can hardly be thought to be the result of one's own actions. So, if what people do depends largely upon what they are born with and what's by chance available to them, and if these things are largely beyond their control, to what extent can what people do justify the attribution of merit – and inequality?

Meritocracy

The issue of merit is particularly important with regard to politics and social justice. A fair society, many argue, is not one in which wealth is distributed equally, or even according to need alone, but one in which hard work and accomplishment are rewarded. Why, though, should those who are gifted with intelligence, strength, supportive caregivers, psychological stability and drive, a safe and peaceful society, inherited wealth, and other unearned advantages get more of the good things society can distribute than other people? Are the privileged, the naturally strong, and the intelligent somehow superior beings in comparison to the disadvantaged, the weak, and the mentally impaired? Why should some people have to live in noisome and dangerous deprivation simply because they were born with fewer endowments while others live in palatial luxury, safety, and opportunity? Even more pointedly, why should those who make poor choices suffer such extreme deprivations? Don't fools have needs, too?

In any case, a genuine meritocracy might look rather less attractive than people are likely to think. Consider the parents of a sluggish, decidedly unaccomplished, and morally limited child. Let's call this child the "slacker." The slacker's parents possess enough wealth to help their ungrateful offspring acquire an advanced education, pay for medical bills, start a business, and then later inherit a considerable sum. Because of their support, the slacker lives a long life full of comfort, leisure, power, wealth, and privilege.

Across town lives another couple, parents who raise a rather different child – a virtuous, extremely talented, hardworking, charitable, and even heroic young citizen. The heroic child's parents, however, lack the wealth necessary to give much assistance to their child. As a result, the heroic child's parents are unable to help develop their child's potential. The heroic child's intellectual and artistic gifts are never fully realized, and, after contracting a crippling but preventable disease, the heroic child is rendered permanently impoverished and disabled.

Is this outcome morally defensible? In a pure meritocracy, the slacker's parents would have devoted their resources to virtuous children rather than to their own. In any society where merit is a necessary condition for getting the good things that life distributes, the slacker had better get ready to do without. But few people would think depriving the slacker an obviously proper policy. If the current majority is right, then even if merit is an important factor in distributing praise, rewards, and other goods, it can't be the whole story. While merit may be one factor in justifying inequality, other factors must be employed as well. Or could it be that many of the world's inequalities simply aren't justifiable?

See also

1.19 Rights, 4.9 Justice and lawfulness, 5.7 Free will and determinism

Reading

Anthony Ashley Cooper, Third Earl of Shaftesbury, "An Inquiry Concern-
ing Virtue and Merit" (1699, 1711), in *Characteristics of Men, Manners,
Opinions, Times,* new edition (Cambridge: Cambridge University Press,
2000)
Joel Feinberg, *Doing and Deserving: Essays in the Theory of Responsibility*
(Princeton, NJ: Princeton University Press, 1970)
*Louis Pojman, "Merit: Why Do We Value It?" *Journal of Social Philosophy*
30 (1999): 83–102

1.15 Natural law

In the debates today surrounding the issue of homosexuality, one is likely
to encounter the claim that homosexuality is immoral because it is unnatural. But what can this mean? Surely, the fact that something is natural
doesn't make it good? After all, bubonic plague is natural, as are tsunamis.
And surely being unnatural isn't enough to render something bad? Opera is
unnatural, as are computers, and football. Then, again, if we are to believe
many contemporary philosophers, in another sense everything is natural,
since everything takes place according to the natural laws of physics,
biology, and psychology, including human sexual conduct. Why, then, do
many find it meaningful to criticize homosexuality as unnatural?

Stoic natural law

Antecedents to the concept of natural law relevant to morality can found
at least as far back as Heraclitus of Ephesus (late sixth century BCE), who
spoke about a world-pervading *logos* (reason, law) that not only gave order
to the universe but also carried certain moral and practical implications.
The Pythagoreans taught that living properly meant achieving in oneself the
same harmonies, proportion, and rectitude found in the larger *cosmos*. Plato
followed them in this, maintaining in addition that goodness in human life
shares a deeper, independent, common ground with the goodness manifest
in the natural world.

None of these thinkers, however, explicitly discuss natural law *per se*.
Aristotle does mention it, and does advance claims relevant to natural law
theory – including claims that society has a natural basis, that the human
good is grounded naturally, and that we are capable of apprehending that

goodness through our natural reason. But it was Stoics like Zeno of Citium (333–264 BCE) who presented the first direct articulation of natural law theory. According to the Stoics, there is an immanent fire or breath (*pneuma*) that pervades the natural world and produces a rational and morally good order or *kosmos*. This immanent force defines a natural law that can be apprehended by right reasoning and underwrites the possibility of a universal community of moral beings, a *cosmopolis*.

The Christian development

This sort of universal society was important to Paul of Tarsus (d. 67 CE), who argued that the early Jesus movement should not be restricted to Jews but should include all people. For Paul, even those who had not known Jesus or Christian Scripture were still capable of living rightly because the fundamentals of moral law are "written in the hearts" and "conscience" of all people (Romans 2:11–15). The notion of a natural law, then, made it possible for Christianity to expand beyond the parochial society and culture in which it originated.

The work of Thomas Aquinas (1225–74), however, presents perhaps the most famous exposition of natural law theory. Aquinas holds that the natural is the "eternal law" of God as it is manifest in the natural world. (Natural law by itself, of course, is according to Aquinas incomplete and must be complemented by "divine law" acquired by humanity through revelation.) Rather than grounding the natural law in an immanent power, however, as the Stoics did, Aquinas locates the natural law in the activity of natural human reasoning. Whenever, therefore, people reason well about moral questions, the conclusions they reach will be consistent with the natural law. This points to the two basic ways one might think about natural law: (1) as somehow evident in the natural non-human, extra-social world; and (2) as naturally somehow rooted in the human mind, either as an intrinsic feature of practical reason or in human conscience – whether some divine being designed it that way or not.

There is political import to this, whichever way you follow: the natural law (*jus naturalis*) transcends all conventional civil law (*jus civilis*) and underwrites good civil law. When human or civil law is consistent with the natural law, society is governed well and different societies will be in agreement. When human law is inconsistent with the natural law, society is governed badly and discord ensues. The concept of "natural rights" stems from the natural law tradition, and hence the contemporary doctrine of universal human rights ultimately finds it source here, too.

The appeal of natural law

One of the principal attractions of natural law theory is that it offers the hope that we can define a common or universal moral ground to which people can appeal across cultures, times, and places. Natural law would make it possible to distinguish what is just by nature from what is just merely by convention, and it serves as a limit or bulwark against cultural relativism. If humans all share a natural capacity for reason, and if natural reason leads to a common or convergent set of moral conclusions, a more or less universal moral framework for human beings is possible.

Natural law would also enable criticism of existing society. If the laws of society are morally wrong or corrupt, then it makes no sense to look to them to settle questions of justice or good. One requires something beyond the social order in order to criticize it. This was just the strategy adopted by Martin Luther King, Jr, when he criticized the then legal and constitutional institutions of racial segregation in the United States. King's 1963 "Letter from Birmingham Jail" is a modern classic in its appeal to "natural law" as a way to legitimate his claim that the laws underwriting racial segregation were "unjust" laws.

It is, however, far from clear whether or not there is such a thing as natural law, and even if there were, whether anyone can divine it. Aquinas's claim that the natural law can simply be apprehended by human reason seems naively optimistic in light of the persistent fact that different competent thinkers find their way to very different moral conclusions.

See also

1.7 Conscience, 1.13 Intuition, 1.19 Rights, 3.24 Stoic cosmopolitanism

Reading

*Thomas Aquinas, *Treatise on Law*, edited by Richard J. Regan (Indianapolis, IN: Hackett Publishing, 2000); cf. *Summa Theologica* (1266–73) I-II, Questions 91–5

Samuel Pufendorf, *The Political Writings of Samuel Pufendorf*, edited by Craig L. Carr (Oxford: Oxford University Press, 1994); cf. *The Law of Nature and Nations* (1672)

Malcolm Schofield, *The Stoic Idea of the City* (Chicago: University of Chicago Press, 1999)

1.16 Need

What does one really need? How much can one do without? It's a deceptively simple question but perhaps an important one in this extraordinary
age of fabulous accumulation and devastating poverty. Most of us can easily
do without fancy clothes, frivolous electronic toys, ornaments and decora-
tions. It would be tough for some to do without a phone, but most could
manage. People don't strictly need refrigerators or air conditioning. But
could one do without family? Friends? Sunlight? Memory? Perhaps one
must first ask: "need" in what sense?

What is necessary?

It is characteristic of needs that one can always ask: "What do you need
it for?" One might need a certain word to finish a crossword puzzle. One
might need an egg to complete a recipe. One needs nourishment and oxygen
to remain alive. One needs human contact and society for sound mental
health. The ability to read is needed to become generally well educated.

But some of these needs seem to be of a different order from others. The
economist and social theorist Joan Robinson (1903–83) argued that at the
most basic level of society humans exist in what she called the "realm of
necessity," where certain physical and perhaps psychological needs must be
met simply to sustain life. Basic societies spend most of their time in efforts
to satisfy these necessities. As societies grow more productive, however, the
basic needs of life are quickly secured, freeing up time to produce surpluses.
These surpluses permit humans to enter what she called the "realm of
freedom," where humans may freely create, produce, and consume a countless variety of goods and services, things that they don't really need but
that enrich, expand, or waste their lives nonetheless. Artwork, scholarship,
entertainment, luxury, sport, society, contemplation, and leisure activities
are things that aren't necessary to basic human survival; but they still contribute quite a lot to human life.

Thinkers as diverse as Aristotle (384–322 BCE) and Abraham Maslow
(1908–70) have noticed that there's a lot more to being fully human than
staying alive. In order to become who we really are – who we most completely or most excellently are – we may need many of the things Robinson
associated with the realm of freedom. If to flourish more or less fully as
human beings requires thinking in complex ways, then things like literature
and philosophy may be human needs. If becoming fully human requires
expressing our selves through material objects, then art may be a human
need. Perhaps a free and good society itself is a human need. Outside of

human society, says Aristotle, one would become an inhuman animal – unless one is a god (*Politics*, Book I, 1253a27–33). Speaking of which, some would argue people need a conscious relationship with the divine.

The creation of needs

One of the thorniest issues in this regard involves determining just what sorts of things humans actually do need (or ought to need) beyond the maintenance of life. Perhaps these needs vary from culture to culture. And perhaps this is so because some societies actually create new needs. Karl Marx (1818–83) and others have maintained that one of the characteristics of capitalist, commercial societies is that they must continually create new needs in order to sustain and expand markets. So, while people lived very happily and very well for centuries without electric lights or televisions or cell phones, many today in the world's wealthy capitalist societies have come to believe that they absolutely must have these things. In the parlance of some philosophers, people exhibit "adaptive preferences" – preferences that adapt to or are even distorted by social circumstances.

The Greek philosopher Epicurus (341–271 BCE), like many Hellenistic thinkers, concluded that people ought to resist the vain, empty, artificial, and unnecessary desires produced by society and cleave instead only to those that are "natural and necessary" to human beings. Doing so leads people to tranquillity (*ataraxia*) and to real happiness (*eudaimonia*), while satisfying unnecessary, artificial desires doesn't really leave us content at all. For Epicurus human beings naturally desire friendship, society, and intellectual conversation.

It's not clear, however, which needs are truly natural and which are merely artificial. In fact, one might say that the distinction is a false one, as it seems natural for human beings to produce artificial things. Epicurus's distinction, therefore, leaves it unclear whether people need things like great libraries, publishing houses, universities, theaters, operas, films, and the economic means necessary to produce them. Even if the natural can be distinguished from the unnatural, how should we rank or establish the priority of some needs over others? When needs compete, how should we choose among them?

The existence of real and compelling need is one of those dimensions of our lives that makes ethics both possible and, well, necessary. Understanding that people have needs and reflecting upon what they are help us understand that certain ways of behaving or not behaving really matter. Because of this, one might say that what makes some practices wrong is that they improperly deprive people of what they need. And discerning more basic and less basic needs helps us rank things that are more or less important to prohibit and more or less important to endorse.

See also

1.6 Character, 1.12 Interest, 1.14 Merit, 2.16 Virtue ethics

Reading

Aristotle, *The Politics and The Constitution of Athens*, revised standard edition (Cambridge: Cambridge University Press, 1996)
Epicurus, "Letter to Menoeceus" in *The Epicurus Reader: Selected Writings and Testimonia* (Indianapolis, IN: Hackett Publishing, 1994)
*Joan Robinson, *Freedom and Necessity: An Introduction to the Study of Society* (New York: Pantheon Books, 1970)

1.17 Pain and pleasure

While making an online donation of rice to a famine-ravaged corner of the world, you discover that consumer choice now even extends so far as to include the rice variety to send. Three options are presented. The first is bland, the second is known for its delicious flavor, while the third gives most people who eat it stomach ache. In all other respects – cost, nutritional value, method of production, country of origin, and so on – all three are the same. Which should be chosen?

It seems to be a no-brainer. Of course, it's better to send the tasty rice, and of course one would never send the kind that gives people stomach ache. But why is this choice so clear? Because pleasure is *in itself* good, and pain is *in itself* bad. To put it another way, all other things being equal, pain makes people worse off and pleasure makes them better off. So, since there's no additional cost, financial or otherwise, in choosing the rice that gives pleasure, it's obviously better that the recipients of the aid eat that type rather than a less pleasurable variety. Likewise, since there's no compensating benefit for the pain caused by the third variety, there's no reason to choose it over the bland or tasty alternatives.

Intrinsic goods

This may not seem to be a very profound point. Its significance, however, becomes more evident if one tries to think of any other things that are good in themselves. Knowledge? Surely not – no one is rendered better off simply through knowing more things. If that were the case, individuals could improve their lot simply by memorizing entries from the phone book. Money? If it's a good at all, money's not good in itself but only for what can be done with it. Life? Many people actually would prefer a shorter and fuller life to a longer, miserable one. Many would also prefer a human life, even a short one, to that of a vegetable. Mere life, therefore, doesn't seem to be something people value greatly.

It's seemed to many people, including Aristotle (384–322 BCE), Jeremy Bentham (1748–1842) and John Stuart Mill (1806–73), that the list of things that really are *intrinsically* good – clearly valuable in themselves – is a very short one: pleasure or happiness. These two perhaps aren't quite the same, but both relate to the subjective welfare of sentient creatures. Similarly, the list of things that are clearly bad in themselves boils down to pain and unhappiness. Everything else is good or bad only in relation to these. If art is good, it's because it's a form of higher pleasure. If lying is bad, it's because it tends to cause distress. If life is good, it's only because it's a precondition for happiness. A life that is incapable of experiencing pleasure or happiness has little value at all.

To test the plausibility of this argument, imagine a planet were discovered that was inhabited by intelligent beings unable to feel pleasure or pain. Would it be possible for them to have morals, or at least the idea of something good in itself? Our intuitions are unclear on this. Indeed, it's a challenge to see why it would be right or wrong to "harm" beings who never perceive anything as a harm, never feel any distress, even at their own extinction, or any pleasure in staying alive. On the other hand maybe things like life and intelligence are good in themselves, even if their goodness is sometimes masked or overridden by bads or even other goods.

Pleasure principles

For Bentham, the fundamental importance of pain and pleasure led him to formulate a moral theory known as "hedonic utilitarianism," the main plank of which was the "greatest happiness principle": *The morally right action is the one that yields the greatest happiness to the greatest number.*

Some have complained that this principle legitimates the oppression of minorities, so long as it pleases the majority to do so. Others have criticized its failing to distinguish among types of pleasure. Bentham's successor, John Stuart Mill, answered this last criticism by arguing that the *quality* of pleasure is more important than its *quantity*. More specifically, he argued that there are *higher* and *lower* pleasures, those of the mind and those of the flesh, respectively. Maximizing happiness requires maximizing both forms of pleasure, not just those that are most intense. Of course, the higher pleasures surpass the lower; or, as Mill famously put it, "better to be a human being dissatisfied than a pig satisfied."

In a similar vein, Epicurus (341–271 BCE) distinguished *static pleasures* (those of serenity, tranquillity, repose) from *active* or *kinetic pleasures* (which include the pleasures of satisfying desire, principally physical desire, and excited pleasures like those of dancing and sport). Pleasures may also be distinguished by: intensity, duration, and purity (freedom from admixtures of pain). Others have distinguished between *natural* and *artificial* as well as *healthy* and *perverse* pleasures in making moral distinctions among various types of pleasure.

However pleasure is understood, hedonic utilitarianism has been very popular, though perhaps more as a principle to guide government policy than personal morality. It has, nevertheless, also attracted plenty of critics, all of whom in various ways claim that there's more to the good life (and so more to being good) than just happiness or pleasure. Robert Nozick (1938–2002), for example, argued that we would not choose to enter a machine that gave us only pleasurable experiences or made us completely happy if doing so meant removing ourselves from real life. That doesn't mean pleasure isn't good in itself, it just means that there are other goods of this sort – for example, living an "authentic" or true life, or being an autonomous agent capable of making meaningful choices for oneself. The 1999 film *The Matrix* famously plays on this critique in its depiction of a choice presented to the characters between living in a difficult and often painful reality (achieved by taking a red pill) or in a more pleasant delusion (via a blue pill). Which would you choose?

The measure of pleasure

Another problem facing hedonic utilitarianism is the extent to which it's possible to measure pleasure. If one can't precisely determine how much pleasure different alternatives produce, how can one choose among them? Similarly, to what extent is it possible to compare the pleasures one person enjoys with those of another (making what's called an "interpersonal utility comparison")? Giving Rupert Murdoch £100 may result in a negligible increase in his happiness, while giving that same amount to a poor man may yield a great deal more. But perhaps the poor man is a very anti-materialistic religious mendicant; while Murdoch is so acquisitive that every acquisition yields tremendous joy. In that case, giving the money to Murdoch would produce more happiness than giving it to the poor man. Who can know the subjective responses of others?

Indeed, for these and other reasons, many regard the attempt to reduce morality to considerations of pain and pleasure as a failure. Nevertheless, it's hard to see how pain and pleasure could not but have some role to play in our moral thinking. All other things being equal, they do seem to be good and bad in themselves. But all other things are rarely equal, and there are other elements of morality out there for us to take into account, as well.

See also

1.10 Flourishing, 1.20 Sympathy, 2.1 Consequentialism, 5.3 Bad faith and self-deception

Reading

Jeremy Bentham, *An Introduction to the Principles of Morals and Legislation* [1789] (Oxford: Oxford University Press, 1996)
*John Stuart Mill, *Utilitarianism* [1863] (Indianapolis, IN: Hackett Publishing, 2002)
Robert Nozick, *Anarchy, State, and Utopia* (New York: Basic Books, 1974)

1.18 Revelation

Extraterrestrials who had only read humanity's corpus of moral philosophy would be forgiven for thinking that human beings based their values on rational reflection and argument. Were they actually to land on Earth, however, they would be in for a great shock. For they would find huge numbers of people who take their lead not from reflection and reason but instead from revelation.

"Revelation" may be defined as the reception of knowledge, moral imperatives, or even a sense of certainty from a divine source through a process distinct though perhaps not entirely separate from natural reasoning. God speaking directly to Moses from a burning bush (Exodus 3:4) and Moses' receipt of the Ten Commandments on the summit of Mount Sinai on two tablets of stone "written by the finger of God" (Exodus 31:18) are two of the world's most famous examples of revelation.

Revelation may also be conveyed through a "messenger" (which is the literal meaning of the Greek *angelos* from which "angel" is derived) or some other intermediary, even a natural object or event like a storm. God, for example, is said to have communicated the Qur'an to Muhammad (570–632) not directly but through the angel Gabriel. Revelation may even be unaccompanied by observable signs or visions, as for example when the Pope is guided to make infallible pronouncements or when prophets and theologians learn the truth regarding vexing theological issues like the nature of the Trinity.

Revelation therefore offers an account of ethical reasoning and deliberation in which its starting points, its procedures and processes, and the manner in which its conclusions are assessed, rest ultimately not upon our reason, our cognitive faculties, our emotions, passions, and feelings, or our place in society, but rather somehow upon something supernatural.

Relation to reason

Different traditions and thinkers have offered different accounts of the relation of revelation to reason. Thomas Aquinas (1225–74) maintained that revelation can never contradict the findings of reason. Ibn Rushd (1126–98), by contrast, argued that the truths of reason and revelation are two different and incomparable discourses. Francis Bacon (1561–1626) argued that revelation has no bearing on natural science, whereas many modern day creationists argue that any scientific theory that contradicts the Bible must be false.

With regard to ethics, one must decide whether or not the findings of revelation are relevant to civil law or general ethical theory. For example, if the Torah be thought of as revealed, then should civil law prohibit homosexuality or homosexual marriage (Leviticus 20:13), or permit the acquisition of "male and female slaves from the pagan nations that are around you" (Leviticus 25:44)?

Traditionalism

Some have held that revelation isn't just a personal affair but rather takes place through a larger community or institution, such as the Roman Catholic Church, the Religious Society of Friends (Quakers), or European culture. Augustine in his *Confessions* (fifth century CE) had maintained that the hand of Providence is discernible only retrospectively, through memory (*memoria*). Louis de Bonald (1754–1840), a conservative Christian opponent of the French Revolution, argued that revelation is manifest in the traditions of society. Others with more mystical inclinations – like René Guenon (1886–1950) and Ananda Coomaraswamy (1877–1947) – describe a perennial, universal, and primordial tradition that can be apprehended through something like continuing revelation and mystical experience.

Problems

Contemporary philosophers, however, often reject revelation as an element of ethical reasoning because it's unreliable. For one thing, the content of supposed revelations are often contrary to one another, and it just is not logically possible for all of them to be true. Appeals to revelation, then, fail to achieve the universality, generality, and agreement they purport to provide and to which ethical inquiry commonly aspires.

For those who are satisfied with provincial or localized ethics, this may be of little consequence. But complacently settling for a provincial ethics may be seriously wrongheaded, for when revelations clash there's likely to be no deliberative way to reconcile them – which may in part explain why religious differences proliferate. But when there's no way to reconcile ethical differences, no way to reason or talk things out, social and political trouble is likely to follow, as perhaps it does today among some adherents of Christianity, Islam, Hinduism, and other religions which base their teachings on supposed revelations.

See also

1.7 Conscience, 1.13 Intuition, 1.21 Tradition and history

Reading

Immanuel Kant, *Religion within the Boundaries of Mere Reason* [1793], *and Other Writings*, edited by Allen Wood and George di Giovanni (Cambridge: Cambridge University Press, 1998)

Etienne Gilson, *Reason and Revelation in the Middle Ages* [1938] (New York: Scribner, 2000)

Ronald Michael Greene, *Religion and Moral Reason: A New Method for Comparative Study*, new edition (Oxford: Oxford University Press, 1988)

1.19 Rights

Thomas Jefferson (1743–1826) famously wrote in the US Declaration of Independence (1776) that: "We hold these Truths to be self-evident, that all Men are created equal, that they are endowed, by their Creator, with certain unalienable Rights, that among these are Life, Liberty and the Pursuit of Happiness." Similarly, Tom Paine (1737–1809) argued in *The Rights of Man* (1791–2) that the French Revolution was fought to secure something very much like those same rights. What on Earth were these men talking about?

Natural rights

Jefferson's view of rights comes largely from the theory laid out in John Locke's (1632–1704) *Two Treatises of Government* (1680–90). Locke's theory in turn is rooted in what's known as the "natural law" tradition. In terms of "rights," this tradition underwrites the strange and powerful idea that people are entitled to certain treatment and consideration by virtue of extra-social dimensions of the natural order – that is, features of reality that aren't the invention of societies, cultures, or individuals. By turns drawing upon Abrahamic, Stoic, and deist conceptions of nature, natural law theory portrays these entitlements as divinely ordained. While the origin of natural law, both physical and moral, is divine, human apprehension of it is quite ordinary, relying upon the exercise of the natural capacity to reason.

Because these rights are grounded in an independent, extra-social order, no human government can modify or override them and no individual can give them away. This is what makes them crucial for Locke, Jefferson, and Paine (who wrote to justify the Glorious, American, and French Revolutions, respectively). When government fails to honor these rights, people are justified in resisting or even rebelling against it. Natural rights, then, make legitimate disobedience to the state and even revolution.

This is a terribly important entitlement, one not generally recognized until modern times. And it requires something extra-governmental to justify it; for unless one can appeal to something beyond the government and what it declares to be legitimate, there can be no basis for a right of rebellion. Accordingly, Martin Luther King, Jr, in his famous "Letter from Birmingham Jail" (1963) appeals to extra-social and divine moral principles in justifying both (a) his claim that the US regime of racial segregation was wrong and (b) his disobedience to the demands of that regime.

But where are they?

The problem with natural rights, however, is that it seems impossible to find them in nature – which is strange, given that Jefferson claimed they're self-evident. Look yourself over and you're likely to detect limbs, skin, hair, and the belly button that philosophers spend so much time contemplating. But you won't see any rights.

This is because, some say, rights aren't natural but are instead social-political artifacts. They're the creations not of God but rather of legal and extra-legal institutions (like churches and families). For example, when those in the United States wish to determine the character and scope of their own rights, they commonly turn not to God or nature but to the US Constitution (1787). The Constitution, however, doesn't even mention natural rights, God, or any other supra-social grounding for rights. Its very human authors did, however, stipulate rights through the articles and amendments it contains, articles and amendments that were invented by human beings through a social-political institution, the Continental Congress.

Conceptualizing rights as non-natural is an appealing alternative to natural rights and natural law theory because it frees us from the metaphysical and epistemological problems of finding them in natural reality. But perhaps there's a cost to this strategy. If rights are socially constructed, on what basis can anyone argue with governments or societies that don't recognize what others believe to be fundamental human rights? If rights are simply social artifacts, then did the Jews of Nazi Germany actually have a right to life?

Negative and positive rights

Rights are often categorized as either negative or positive. Negative rights are rights to act, think, and speak free from interference, in particular government interference. Hence negative rights are also called "rights of non-interference." We might, then, describe negative rights as establishing the freedom *to* do certain things and to be free *from* interference while engaged in those practices. So, for example, people are often said to possess a negative right to free speech – that is, to expressing themselves as they wish without government hindrance, obstruction, or reprisal. Privacy, the right to deny others or the government knowledge of certain conduct or information, is another popular negative right. Negative rights then typically imply obliging others, especially the state, *not to do* certain things, namely not to interfere with those who possess negative rights.

There is, of course, another kind of right, a category that's frequently a matter of political controversy – "positive" or "claim" rights. These are rights that legitimate making *claims* upon the state or upon others to actually do certain things. Correlatively, positive rights establish *duties* obligating those upon whom the claim is made to provide something to those making the claim. For example, children generally have the right to make claims upon their parents or custodians for food, shelter, education, and care of various sorts. These claims, then, correlate with duties obligating parents or state to provide these goods. Legitimate heirs, similarly, have a right to claim their inheritance.

Sometimes negative and positive rights are intertwined with one another in ways that make them virtually inseparable. For example, the negative rights to free speech and to the security of property in our social order are connected to the positive right of citizens to make claims upon the state for protection from assault, interference, theft, and invasion of privacy.

What is to count as positive or claim rights remains a controversial topic. Should people have the right to make claims upon society for paid employment? Should those whose ancestors have faced historic injustices like slavery or dispossession have the right to advance claims for reparations upon the descendents of those who perpetrated the injustices?

The appeal and problem of universality

"Human rights" has become one of the most powerful concepts in politics, informing the discourses and practices not only of international legal institutions but also organizations committed to social-political reform and transformation. Like Locke's conception of natural rights, human rights are powerful in part because they are taken to be universal; hence from them can be derived criteria for evaluating political events anywhere in the world – Kosovo, Iraq, China, Chechnya, the United States, Pakistan, or Rwanda.

The United Nations' Universal Declaration of Human Rights (1948) establishes various human rights as matters of international law, but some have argued that much of what goes under the guise of human rights is western political ideology. Demanding of non-western and non-capitalist societies, then, that they observe these rights amounts to imperialism. The Chinese government, for example, has advanced arguments along these lines when criticized for its response to the 1989 demonstrations in Tiananmen Square and elsewhere. Others argue that the practices of covering women in public and cutting genitalia (male and female) are not violations of human rights but legitimate expressions of different cultural traditions.

There is, however, a risk in overplaying the empirical evidence for this doubt. As a matter of fact, when the UN Universal Declaration of Human Rights was being drafted, it was often representatives from the non-western nations who were most keen to include various rights in the list; and it's often activists within non-western states who clamor most vigorously for the defense of those rights. The idea that the document is simply a white-western imposition is historically inaccurate, even if the contemporary discourse of rights emerged first in the western traditions.

Responsibilities

It's often said that with rights come responsibilities. This generally means that receiving benefits from the civil and social order obligates one to return certain goods and services to it (taxes, military service, etc.). Philosophically, one might also argue that the very thing that entitles certain beings to rights also makes them the sort of beings that have duties.

Although rights may in general imply responsibilities, the claim that they must always do so is harder to maintain. Rights are granted to all sorts of things that have no way of taking on any concomitant responsibilities – such as non-human animals, the unborn, the comatose, and even eco-systems. To make the rights–responsibilities link even plausible in such cases, it is necessary to talk of rights only being conferred on those with the potential or impaired ability to meet responsibilities. But clearly, that's not possible in every case.

See also

1.15 Natural law, 2.16 Virtue ethics, 3.1 Absolute/relative, 3.24 Stoic cosmopolitanism

Reading

H. L. A. Hart, "Are There Any Natural Rights?" *Philosophical Review* 64 (April, 1955): 175–91

Ronald Dworkin, *Taking Rights Seriously* [1977] (Cambridge, MA: Harvard University Press, 2005)

*Micheline R. Ishay, ed., *The Human Rights Reader: Major Speeches, Essays, and Documents from the Bible to the Present* (New York: Routledge, 1997)

1.20 Sympathy

David Hume (1711–76) writes in *A Treatise of Human Nature* (1739) that "the minds of men are mirrors to one another" (Book II, Part ii, §5). By this he means that we feel the emotions and sentiments others feel. Being around a cheerful person can lift one up. The presence of a depressive can be depressing. When people observe others in pain, they feel a kind of pain, too – in a sense feeling another's pain. It's this capacity for sympathy that arguably not only binds us together socially but also makes possible our moral life. Indeed, the absence of a capacity to sympathize with others' pain is a pathology characteristic of sociopaths.

Consider an imaginary world where people couldn't sympathize with one another at all. Let's call it "Asympasia." Would it be possible for the people of Asympasia to care whether or not their actions harmed one another? Would family and friends take regard for each other's interests? Would compassion, concern, worry, consolation, solicitude, or love be possible without sympathy?

Contra rationalists and egoists

The doctrine of sympathy was developed to answer certain shortcomings its proponents found in competing moral philosophies. The ancient Stoics maintained that the rule of reason and the suppression of sentiment (*apatheia*) establish the conditions necessary to live morally. Legions of philosophers – Plato (427–347 BCE), René Descartes (1596–1650), Benedictus Spinoza (1632–77), Samuel Clarke (1675–1729), and Immanuel Kant (1724–1804) – in various ways agree. According to thinkers like these, reason is able to grasp moral truths built into the natural or divine order, the metaphysical foundations of reality, the relations among ideas, and the nature of reason itself.

A competing view has been advanced by philosophers like Thomas Hobbes (1588–1679) and Bernard Mandeville (1670–1733), who maintained that people are exclusively selfish creatures who act only in ways they believe will serve their selfish desires. Reason from this point of view is relevant only to the extent it can determine through calculation the means of satisfying egoistic objectives.

But "moral sentiment" theorists found both of these accounts unsatisfactory. Thinkers like Francis Hutcheson (1694–1746), Adam Smith (1723–90), and David Hume, rejected both the claim that reason grounds morals and the contention that people are simply egoists. The rationalists are wrong because reason alone doesn't establish right and wrong; it plays into our moral life only to the extent it affects emotion and sentiment, determines the means of acquiring what we desire, and discloses the consequences likely to follow upon our actions. The egoists are wrong because sympathy gives us real regard for others. Morality ultimately, then, is based upon sympathetic feeling guided by reasoning.

A common ground

One of the features of moral sentiment theory that makes it attractive to people is its ability to navigate the difficult waters of nature and nurture in a satisfying way. Because moral sentiments, or at least the capacities for them, are found more or less universally among people, they provide a common ground for a universal or common morality stretching across cultures, geography, and history. Moreover, since it's a natural feature of human beings, moral sentiment is consistent with evolutionary and sociobiological theories of morality.

Although the idea of "moral sentiment" has much in common with that of "conscience," it differs in that moral sentiment is malleable. Different environments, different societies, and different systems of moral education shape it differently. Moral sentiment theory, then, also accounts for the variability of moral values both within and across cultures; and it does so without the cost of eliminating the possibility of finding a common ground in cross-cultural moral and political conversation.

If ethics is grounded in sentiment, then moral discourse must not only present sound arguments, it must also affect people's sentiment. Images, narratives, examples, and literary tropes, as well as considerations of custom and tradition, will therefore have a place in moral discourse every bit as important as the analysis of concepts.

See also

1.7 Conscience, 2.7 Egoism, 2.13 Rationalism

Reading

Bernard Mandeville, *Fable of the Bees* [1714] *and Other Writings* (Indianapolis, IN: Hackett Publishing, 1997)
David Hume, *Enquiry Concerning the Principles of Morals* [1748], edited by Tom L. Beauchamp (Oxford: Oxford University Press, 1998)

Adam Smith, *Theory of the Moral Sentiments* [1759] (Indianapolis, IN: Liberty Fund, 1982)

1.21 Tradition and history

"Would you tell me about your mother?" the therapist said to her client. Freudian psychology may be wrong about the "Oedipal complex," but it was surely right to hold that to know a human being one must know his or her past.

Among the important things one must consider in ethical deliberations, too, is that human beings, like human societies, each have a history, not just a past. Inanimate, non-historical objects like stones relate to the past in a way different from the way humans do. A stone may have been mud or lava or stellar gas, but it's unaware of these past states and is related to them simply in unconscious causal ways. But conscious humans face a past of meanings they inherit, to which they must refer consciously in their current lives. For human beings, the past as history affects the present in very important ways – including present ethical deliberations and ways of feeling. As William Faulkner said, "The past isn't dead – it isn't even past."

A tradition of thinking about tradition

The German philosopher Martin Heidegger (1889–1976) called the quality of being born into a world of meanings and practices that are not of our own making but that we must take over our "thrownnesss" (*Geworfen-heit*). Unlike stones, which simply exist across "time" (*Zeit*), human beings and their existence are characterized by "temporality." We are "temporal" (*gezeitlich*) and "historical" (*geschichtlich*) beings, thrown into history in such a way that we must define our present and project ourselves into the future in relation to that history.

Heidegger was certainly not the first philosopher to have noticed this. In the nineteenth century, German thinkers like G. W. F. Hegel (1770–1831) as well as, later, British thinkers like F. H. Bradley (1846–1924) and R. G. Collingwood (1889–1943) speculated about the importance of history in human life. Earlier Europeans like Giambattista Vico (1668–1744) were also sensitive to the way in which human life is deeply and essentially historical.

Among the historical dimensions of human existence one might iden-tify specific, customary lines of meaning and practice called "traditions."

Traditions may be relatively unreflective – such as the traditions of speech and ornament. Or they may be more consciously developed – such as the traditions of theology. Tradition has also, of course, been very important to the Asian philosophical traditions. Confucius (551–479 BCE), for example, rooted *Li* (proper conduct) and *Jen* (benevolence) in an appreciation of traditions and customs.

The critique of rationalism and modernity

An important critique of modernity holds that many have forgotten that humans are creatures of history, custom, habit, and tradition. Philosophical critics like Michel de Montaigne (1533–92), Edmund Burke (1729–97), Michael Oakeshott (1901–90), and Chantal Mouffe (b. 1943) pursue, in various ways, this sort of line.

They point out that many philosophers speciously claim to have achieved, usually through what poses as reason, some sort of transcendence beyond, independence from, and authority over customs, opinions, and traditions. These "false philosophers," as Hume (1711–76) called them, claim in other words to have achieved a God's-eye, absolute point of view on reality. Benedictus Spinoza (1632–77) called this point of view approvingly, "a view from eternity" (*sub specie aeternitatis*); Thomas Nagel (b. 1937), by contrast, called it critically "a view from nowhere."

Nagel's point is well taken, for how is it possible for humans to become independent of their histories, cultures, customs, and traditions when humans are inescapably historical, cultural, and customary beings? The concepts people use, the languages they speak, the architecture and disposition of their feelings, their attitudes, beliefs, and habits are informed by history and tradition – ethical concepts, beliefs, feelings, and habits among them. Indeed, for many, history calls upon us to fulfill historical obligations that bind individuals, families, movements, peoples, and nations.

That's not to say that criticism, novelty, and change are impossible. People aren't stuck in the past, and traditions aren't strictly speaking always conservative. There are, after all, traditions of resistance. But attending to history and tradition does mean that the instruments of change must be grown in the soil of history, custom, and tradition. To persuade others of the need for moral change, one must begin where people are – and where they've been. To present meaningful forms of persuasion and argument one must speak in recognizably meaningful ways, one must sympathize with certain habits of feeling, and one must understand the resonance ideas, words, and images carry for people. Doing all this requires knowing and appreciating their histories. Moral commitments don't fall from the sky.

Moral critics must also reflexively think about their own embeddedness in history, taking care to realize that whatever criticisms they develop do not originate in some transcendent realm where reason or divinities float above the world. Rather both custom and criticism are elements of the ordinary, historical, and common life all people share.

Now, about your mother . . .

See also

2.13 Rationalism, 3.22 Prudence, 5.15 Standpoint

Reading

Edmund Burke, *Reflections on the Revolution in France* [1790] (Oxford: Oxford University Press, 1999)

*Michael Oakeshott, *Rationalism in Politics and Other Essays* [1962] (Indianapolis, IN: The Liberty Fund, 1991)

Georgia Warnke, *Gadamer: Hermeneutics, Tradition, and Reason* (Palo Alto, CA: Stanford University Press, 1987)

Part II

Frameworks for Ethics

2.1 Consequentialism

In March 2004, a drunk driver in Rolling Meadows crashed his friend's Mustang, killing the two back-seat passengers. At his trial, he said in his defense, "I was only trying to help him because he was drunk – more than I was." The judge was not impressed and sentenced him to 16 years in prison for his offense.

In so doing, the judge was thinking like a good, though perhaps simplistic, consequentialist. In general "consequentialism" refers to a family of moral theories that assert that the wrongness of actions is determined entirely by the consequences. One kind of consequentialism takes the pivotal comparison to be between the consequences of the act itself and the consequences of other acts the agent could have done instead. Another kind of consequentialism takes the pivotal comparison to be between the consequences of a rule forbidding this kind of act and the consequences of alternative rules. An action that makes things better is good; an action that makes things worse is bad. The intentions or motives of the agent are in themselves neither here nor there (unless, as we'll see, they affect the consequences). The fact that the drunk driver was "only trying to help" does not make his actions right.

The case for consequentialism

Consequentialism has an attractive neatness, and its basic claim – that what our actions yield is crucial to their morality – surely must contain at least a kernel of truth. But it does not always account for our intuitions as easily as it might in this case. For example, let's say the drunk driver didn't crash and didn't cause any harm. Had he been stopped by the police, he would still have been punished, albeit more lightly. Yet, his act had no bad consequences.

The consequentialist can argue that the law is therefore wrong to punish people for reckless behavior that actually caused no harm. Alternatively, she could claim that drunk driving is wrong because it *tends to cause* bad consequences. If it did not, there would be no reason to think it wrong. Judging the consequences this way focuses not simply on the individual act but on the *practice* in general or the *rule* that describes the practice. A consequentialist who takes this line can explain why cases of successful drunk driving and other acts that luckily don't cause harm are nevertheless wrong. It also explains why, when no actual harm is caused, people consider the offense less serious than cases where harm actually results. *Deontological* theorists, in contrast, for whom the nature of the act itself determines its moral standing, are going to have a tough time explaining why all instances of drunk driving, whether the driver killed someone or not, aren't equally bad.

Although our drunk driver's judge may not have realized it, more sophisticated consequentialists can even explain why people are right to take account of intentions and motives. It is actually the case that people often get much lighter sentences if they can show benevolent, or at least no malevolent, intent. And this practice is defensible on purely consequentialist grounds. Having good intentions can count for something because, as a matter of fact, intending good things does produce more good consequences than intending bad things.

Versions of consequentialism

Consequentialist theories vary according to how one understands what makes consequences good or bad. The most significant consequentialist positions are forms of utilitarianism:

- *Hedonic (or hedonistic) classical utilitarianism*: Actions are right in so far as they promote the greatest happiness of the greatest number and wrong in so far as they diminish that happiness. Different types of pleasure or happiness may be valued differently.
- *Welfare utilitarianism*: Actions are right in so far as they promote the welfare of the greatest number and wrong in so far as they diminish that welfare, well-being, or flourishing.
- *Preference utilitarianism*: Actions are right in so far as they allow the greatest number to live according to their own preferences and wrong in so

far as they inhibit their doing so, even if those preferences aren't in fact what will make them experience the most pleasure.

Each of these positions can be construed as forms of either act or rule utilitarianism, depending upon whether one assesses the effect of either (a) individual acts or (b) general practices upon people's happiness, welfare, or ability to live as they prefer. These different types may also be structured in various combinations in order to achieve what's been called *pluralistic utilitarianism*. On this view, each type has something compelling about it, and the best moral reflection is pluralistic, combining different principles in different ways in different circumstances.

Criticisms

One general criticism to which most utilitarian ethics are susceptible is that they tend to deal in an unacceptable way with *aggregates*: the total amount of happiness, welfare, preference, satisfaction, etc. In doing so it's argued that they are indifferent to the rights of individuals. For example, it may be possible, say the critics, for a utilitarian to justify violating the rights of a minority in order to increase the general good. Isn't this just what slave-holders might argue?

In addition, it can be objected that sometimes the liberty and privacy rights of individuals demand that the majority sacrifice some of its happiness. The majority might feel more secure if the police and other agents of the state could engage in preventive detention, searches of people's homes and mail, wire taps whenever they wished, the monitoring of Internet activity, racial profiling, and torture. But this increase in security, or at least the feeling of security, would come at the expense of individual rights. To answer this problem, the utilitarian must, on pain of abandoning individual rights, find a way to justify in consequentialist terms limiting the majority and even sacrificing some of its happiness, welfare, and preferences.

Consequentialism also faces additional problems. The future is uncertain and notoriously hard to predict; and, moreover, there are a lot of ways to define the notion of "consequences." In launching a military operation, for example, its consequences are largely unknown, and the *actual consequences* often don't resemble the *expected consequences*. Would the invasion of a "rogue state" produce a "quagmire" of Vietnam-like proportions? Would it provoke more attacks than it prevented? Would it instead establish liberty, peace, justice, and prosperity in the region? Are the *direct consequences* of the invasion the only relevant factors, or should one also consider *indirect consequences* that may occur through, for example, the agency of third parties, such as other nations, private militias, or international institutions? Are *unknowable consequences* as important as those that are reasonably *knowable*? In addition to appreciating the differences between expected/actual, direct/indirect, and knowable/unknowable consequences, one may also need to balance the *immediate consequences* of an action against the *distant consequences* that lie farther off in space and time.

Across all these different binary oppositions cut different *categories of consequence* – economic, political, religious, individual, etc. The consequences of various categories might need to be weighted and ranked, as the negative consequences of one category might override the positive consequences of another, and vice versa. Finally, any of the consequences we already mentioned should be evaluated in light of what philosophers call *counterfactual consequences* – that is, consequences that would have followed (a) had different courses of action been taken or (b) had no action been taken at all. Figuring out what would happen counterfactually, however, is notoriously difficult, often impossible.

Simply saying that actions should be evaluated by their consequences, therefore, isn't enough. One has to possess a very precise understanding of what sort of consequences should and shouldn't count, as well as how they should count. Otherwise, one's judgments will be little better than those of a drunk driver.

See also

3.2 Act/rule, 3.7 Commission/omission, 3.14 Intentions/consequences, 5.8 Moral luck

Reading

J. J. C. Smart and Bernard Williams, *Utilitarianism: For and Against* (Cambridge: Cambridge University Press, 1973)
Samuel Scheffler, ed., *Consequentialism and Its Critics* (Oxford: Oxford University Press, 1988)
*Julia Driver, *Ethics: The Fundamentals* (Oxford: Blackwell, 2006)

2.2 Contractarianism

The signatories to the International Criminal Court (ICC) have explicitly entered into an agreement to be bound by international law and to be subject to punishment for breaking it. Explicit consent to be bound in this way is, however, rare. For example, the Nuremberg Principles were established to punish crimes against peace, war crimes, and crimes against humanity committed during World War II. But the Nazis prosecuted under them never agreed to be bound by their terms. Similarly, the International Criminal Tribunal for the Former Yugoslavia prosecutes people like Slobodan Milosevic and Radovan Karadzic when neither had signed the UN Security Council Resolution 827 establishing it.

Can we be bound by agreements, treaties or contracts to which we haven't explicitly consented? The question isn't just pertinent to war crimes. It also arises in relation to social contract theories, which seek to justify the moral standing of the state and its laws generally.

Social contracts

Early modern theorists like Thomas Hobbes (1588–1679), John Locke (1632–1704), and Jean-Jacques Rousseau (1712–78) speculated about what humans were like before they entered into societies or recognized state authority. According to their story, given the facts of human nature and the infelicities of life in what these philosophers called the "state of nature," people found it preferable to enter a contract that established state authority.

Hobbes's story is particularly well known. For Hobbes human nature renders people entirely selfish atoms of desire. Life, however, for such beings in the state of nature is terribly difficult. It is, in Hobbes's famous formulation, "solitary, poor, nasty, brutish, and short," a war of all against all (*Leviathan*, Chapter 13).

People eventually figure out that they have something to gain by entering into agreements (a) to recognize the authority of a government over them and (b) to respect moral principles regarding one another's conduct. In return, of course, people give up the freedom to do whatever they wish.

It's this combination of consent, benefit, and sacrifice that gives contractarianism its strength. Moral principles are binding because we agree to them; or at least they are the sorts of things to which it would be rational or reasonable to agree. And it's rational to agree to them, honor them, and to make sacrifices in ways they demand because doing so benefits us individually and collectively.

Moreover, contractarianism explains why it's justifiable to punish wrong-doers. People who have violated the law or engaged in immoral acts have broken the contract. They have therefore forfeited at least some of their rights; and to the extent that punishments are reasonably part of the contract, one might argue that they have actually consented to be punished.

What consent?

Contractarianism, however, makes it more difficult to speak meaningfully about universal human rights or about duties we owe to all human beings. If people outside our societies are not "signatories" to our contract, we have no obvious duties or obligations to them – nor they to the requirements of our society's demands. Perhaps that is why most actual political contracts are transnational: the relationship among societies and nations would risk being a very real "war of all against all" without them.

Others worry that the social contract tradition is little more than a myth which is unable to do the justificatory work required of it. It's unlikely that Hobbes's state of nature ever really existed, and the "original position" of John Rawls's (1921–2002) modified version of contractarianism is only hypothetical. The contract itself is pure metaphor. The worry is that states and laws cannot be properly justified by appeal to fictitious things.

Understanding this problem, contractarians have appealed to a notion of *implied consent*. That is, while no one has explicitly agreed to a contract, our conduct in paying taxes, obeying and calling upon police, voting, and participating in war all implies consent. If people didn't consent, they wouldn't do such things. Since, however, there is no realistic way of opting out or withholding consent, it seems strange to interpret doing what you have no choice but to do as being a sign that you consent to the demands made of you.

Other contractarians respond by arguing that these objections miss the point. The social contract tradition isn't premised on any historical or sociological facts. Rather, it simply aims to show why or how things make sense or are justifiable, rather than how they have in fact been justified.

See also

1.19 Rights, 4.5 Fairness, 4.9 Justice and lawfulness

Reading

Thomas Hobbes, *Leviathan* [1651]: *With Selected Variants from the Latin Edition of 1668*, edited by Edwin Curley (Indianapolis, IN: Hackett Publishing, 1994)

David Gauthier, *Morals by Agreement* (Oxford: Oxford University Press, 1986)

Thomas Scanlon, *What We Owe to Each Other* (Cambridge, MA: Harvard University Press, 1998)

2.3 Culture critique

Lipstick is ideology! The way it's produced, advertised, packaged, and promoted sets the rules concerning what we desire, how we should think of ourselves and the world, how we should obsequiously fall into line behind its sleek, stylized, industrialized, body-altering, only-money-can-buy techno sheen. The lips of the advertisement become more real and more desirable than real lips. They tell us not only what we should be, but also what we are.

This is an example of a form of criticism that has developed under the rubric of "culture critique," a term originating in "The Culture Industry," the celebrated chapter four of Max Horkheimer (1895–1973) and Theodor W. Adorno's (1903–69) book, *Dialectic of Enlightenment* (1944). Having experienced the rise of National Socialism in Germany, Horkheimer and Adorno became acutely troubled by what they saw as the oppressive dynamics of late capitalism and totalitarianism. They were not, however, satisfied with the critical instruments developed by preceding thinkers. Together with Walter Benjamin (1892–1940) and others, they would found the Frankfurt School. Frankfurt School thinkers developed in culture critique a hybrid form of critical theory that aimed at synthesizing the insights of Marxism and Freudian psychoanalysis while engaging more penetrating and complete analyses of the workings of language, iconography, and culture. Horkheimer and Adorno's work was especially influential on succeeding theorists such as Herbert Marcuse (1898–1979) and Jürgen Habermas (b. 1929).

A growth industry

One of the most provocative claims of culture critique is that oppressive and manipulating forces are to be found not only in the laws and policies of states or great commercial institutions. The work of oppression and manipulation also takes place to a large extent in music, architecture, advertising, film, and the technological consumer society in which people have become increasingly immersed. In the way wants are created, in the way lives and products are standardized and regulated, in the fetishizing and the sexing-up of mechanical, mass-produced, trivializing products, the culture industry has rendered people unable to resist the demands of power and even blind to both its existence and its exercise. Mass culture is an impediment to resistance; its most consistent product is passivity and obedience.

Since the early days of the Frankfurt School, culture critique has burgeoned into something of an intellectual industry of its own. One finds now disciplines like critical race theory, queer theory, cultural theory, critical science studies, media studies, women's studies, post-colonial theory, et al. While thinkers involved in these fields tend to draw on the work of continental philosophers (Marx, Freud, Jean Baudrillard, Jacques Lacan, Gilles Deleuze, Gayatri Spivak, Slavoj Žižek), they certainly don't always do so (e.g. Stuart Hall, Terry Eagleton). While it would be wrong to say that any particular interpretive framework unites them, perhaps it wouldn't be wrong to say that they hold this in common: a conviction that culture is a powerful but also knotty and complex affair that needs to be decoded, unraveled, closely read, scrutinized, and subjected to sustained critique in order to understand how it plays upon our lives.

Culture critique is not so much a set of principles as a habit of asking a set of related questions about the ideas, words, images, or texts that surround us. How do they manipulate people and make them more manageable and responsive to different kinds of power? How might they affect people in ways concerned with race, sex, class, gender, the body, obedience, hierarchy, authority, capitalism, and desire? Are we using culture, or is it using us?

See also

4.15 Sex and gender, 5.6 False consciousness, 5.11 Power

Reading

Theodor W. Adorno, *The Culture Industry* (New York: Routledge, 1991)
*David Morely and Kuang-Hsing Chen, eds., *Stuart Hall: Critical Dialogues in Cultural Studies* (New York: Routledge, 1996)

Slavoj Žižek, *Interrogating the Real: Selected Writings*, edited by Rex Butler and Scott Stephens (London: Continuum, 2005)

2.4 Deontological ethics

Fazeena is an expert in disaster relief. She has, however, taken time off work because her family needs her. She is a widow, her elderly father suffers from the early-stages of Alzheimer's, and one of her children is seriously ill. But when a devastating earthquake strikes, her employer implores her to help out. "We need you," he says. "Thousands of lives are at risk, and without your experience we'll be much less efficient." Fazeena thinks for a short while, but replies, "I'm sorry. I have to put my family first. It is to them that I am duty-bound."

Fazeena's decision is more than understandable. It's probably the one most people would take in her position. Her choice, however, also reveals something fundamental about her ethical framework. Clearly she does not think that to do the right thing she must consider the effects of her actions on everyone, irrespective of their relationship to her – for quantitatively more people would be helped if she went to help the earthquake victims. Her moral duties are narrower than this and are concerned primarily with a limited number of people to whom she has a special, overriding relationship.

The call of duty

This way of thinking exhibits features typical of the deontological approach to ethics. On this view, morality is concerned with *duties* and *principles* that require moral agents to behave in specific ways *regardless of the consequences*. As such, the claims of these duties and principles may trump those of the greater good or the good of the majority. Moreover, for deontologists, duty rooted in principle must be the sole source of moral action, not feelings of happiness or satisfaction (including the feelings of the moral actor). The world as a whole may be a much better place if Fazeena leaves her family for a while and helps with the relief efforts. But as a mother and daughter, her duty is not to those earthquake victims but to her sick family members. Her deontological approach contrasts sharply with a consequentialist view, which is likely to require a broader consideration of people's welfare when making a moral decision.

Because the deontological approach typically narrows the scope of ethics and leaves agents with a fairly limited number of duties, it often requires that one say, "That's simply not my responsibility," in the face of suffering. If that sort of response seems harsh, keep in mind that any moral system that doesn't limit the scope of our moral responsibility in some ways will be unrealistically demanding. Since no one can possibly address every need or wrong, an unlimited ethic will simply ask what's not possible. Deontology, it may be argued, simply accepts the truism that everyone occupies a different place in the world and has moral duties particular to that place.

Of course, deontological frameworks can be very demanding, too. Pacifists who refuse violence for deontological reasons may have to face rather unpleasant experiences and even accept death. Telling the truth isn't always easy either and sometimes requires the sacrifice of personal gain and advantage. Caring for family members in need is likely to be no picnic.

But, on the other hand, deontological ethics do recognize that there are limits to our duties. Not requiring us to do any more than duty demands, they acknowledge that some acts are *supererogatory* – going beyond what we are obliged to do. Heroism is to be admired, but it's not a duty.

Critique

The most common criticism of deontological ethics is that there are times when duties should be abrogated in the name of a higher good. If one can only save a life by breaking a trivial promise, surely it's morally permissible, even required, to break the promise. If Anne Frank were hiding in one's attic, surely it would be permissible, even required, to deceive the Nazis who have come to the door looking for her. If something as devastating as HIV/AIDS could be cured by putting family second for once, surely that would be the right thing to do. If, however, the deontologist accepts this, then she risks admitting that ethics is not based (entirely) on duties but (also) on something else, such as the general welfare.

The deontologist would reply by arguing that in all such cases where there seems to be a moral demand to relinquish our duties, what's really going on is that there is a conflict of duties and one simply has a greater claim on us than the others. The deontologist need not claim that our duties are always clear or are never in tension.

Not so clear cut

Although it is fairly simple to differentiate deontological from other approaches to ethics in general terms, it's not always neat and easy to define deontology. For example, it is just not true that deontologists take no interest in consequences. Indeed some duties – to cause no harm, for example – are defined in terms of consequences. Nor do non-deontological frameworks have no place for duty. Indeed, hedonic utilitarianism – a consequentialist ethic – commands a single overriding duty, the happiness principle: to maximize the greatest happiness of the greatest number. The characteristics of the deontological approach – notably stressing duties rather than consequences and acknowledging the relevance of the agent's particular situation rather than requiring an impartial viewpoint – are simply more pronounced in deontological than in other moral frameworks. But that doesn't mean that deontology has a monopoly on the considerations it takes as paramount.

See also

3.4 Beneficence/non-maleficence, 3.14 Intentions/consequences, 3.17 Legal/moral, 5.16 Supererogation

Reading

Immanuel Kant, *Groundwork for the Metaphysics of Morals* [1785] (Cambridge: Cambridge University Press, 1998)
Thomas Nagel, *Equality and Partiality* (Oxford: Oxford University Press, 1991)
*Stephen Darwall, ed., *Deontology* (Oxford: Blackwell, 2002)

2.5 Discourse ethics

Ethics committees and commissions are an increasingly normal part of modern political life. But sitting around the tables of these bodies are men and women with very different sets of moral commitments. How can they find enough common ground to engage in meaningful discussion, let alone agree?

The answer that would reflect the mainstream of thinking in the western ethical tradition is that participants should aspire to an impartial or objective point of view. Impartiality is taken to be important in morals because when it's achieved one is able to make moral judgments in a way that responds to the moral qualities of the situation rather than to one's self-interest.

Various philosophers have explored different methods of achieving impartiality. Reason has often been taken to be essential to this process. Plato seems to have regarded the rational process called *dialectic* as up to the task. Dialectic, on his model, requires the interaction of at least two people engaged using reason (*logos*) and also desire (*eros*) to grasp independent moral standards.

Immanuel Kant's (1724–1804) method of impartial moral reasoning is perhaps the strictest of all. Kant's *universalizability* test not only requires adherence to universal rational norms (like non-contradiction); it also requires a complete separation of rationality from feeling and sentiment. Adam Smith (1732–90), by contrast, believed that one could make judgments from the point of view of an *impartial spectator* only through the cultivation of moral sentiment. More recently, John Rawls (1921–2002) argued that individuals are capable of imagining themselves behind a "veil of ignorance" that places them in an "original position" where they may formulate fundamental moral and ethical principles without knowing what attributes they would have or what their position in a society which followed those principles would be.

The discourse solution

Frankfurt philosopher Jürgen Habermas (b. 1929) has responded to these predecessors by advancing an influential alternative known as "discourse ethics." Habermas agrees with Kant et al. that *reason* offers the way to impartiality and even universality. But Kant's method, says Habermas, is too individualistic; it doesn't adequately attend to the way that impartiality must be validated or justified through rational communication with others. Habermas, then, follows Plato in construing reason as an interactive *process*. Unlike Plato, however, for Habermas, impartiality and universality are not defined by the grasp of an independent standard. The standard for Habermas is bound up with the process itself.

Similarly, Habermas regards Rawls's view as insufficiently social, insufficiently procedural. Moreover, there seems something suspiciously artificial in Rawls's imaginative fantasy, rendering it perhaps little more than an intuition pump. Habermas's theory, by contrast, seems to promise the possibility of concrete *practical discourse*.

Habermas's understanding of the validation of ethical judgments rests on social *agreement* more than abstract norms of rationality. In this, his theory contains a powerful democratic dimension, one that depends upon the ability of participants in a discourse to be open to the arguments of others so that what Habermas calls the "unforced force of the argument" may lead to agreement. He writes: "Only those norms can claim to be valid that meet (or could meet) with the approval of all affected in their capacity as participants in a practical discourse."

Habermas's discourse ethics leads those engaged in ethical reflection to criticize and regulate their reflection: Have alternative resolutions and conceptions of this issue been explored? Have participants assessed the way in which the consequences of alternatives will affect every participant, and has everyone potentially affected been able to participate? Have participants engaged in the practical discourse in a free and open way?

The hope – and some say it is no more than that – is that if ethics committees, and other public moral discourses, proceed in this way, moral agreement will eventually become possible, even for a world characterized by substantive moral disagreement.

See also

1.20 Sympathy, 2.7 Egoism, 4.18 Universalizability

Readings

Jürgen Habermas, *Moral Consciousness and Communicative Action* [1983] (Cambridge, MA: MIT Press, 1990)
Seyla Benhabib and Fred R. Dalimayr, eds., *The Communicative Ethics Controversy* (Cambridge, MA: MIT Press, 1990)
*William Rehg, *Insight and Solidarity: The Discourse Ethics of Jürgen Habermas* (Berkeley: University of California Press, 1994)

2.6 Divine command

Angel Maturino Resendiz (or Rafael Resendiz-Ramirez, aka the "Railroad Killer") was a serial killer and rapist who over a period of two years brutally murdered nine people. But like many killers and rapists before and since, Maturino Resendiz believed that he was a force for good, not evil. According to Dr Larry Pollock, a psychiatrist working for his defense, Maturino Resendiz felt he had been directed "to people who were evil and deserved to be dead, and as an angel of God he was doing God's will."

Of course, almost everyone believes that Maturino Resendiz was not doing God's will at all, but was mentally ill and deluded. His case, however, does reveal some of the central problems faced by divine command theory – the theory that morality has its source in God, and the moral law is what God commands. People generally may believe that murderers who claim divine command are mistaken, but according to Scripture, people generally thought (and still think) that Noah and the Apostles were mistaken, too. Many have also regarded the claims of Muhammad, Martin Luther, Joseph Smith, and the Pope to be falsehoods. Then there's the provocative example of Abraham, whom God commanded, according to the story, to kill his son, Isaac (Genesis 22). Why believe the authors of Genesis but not Resendiz? If one ought to do what God commands, how is one to *know* what God commands? There are so many contrary candidates, and unlike disputes in the natural sciences, there seems to be no generally agreed-upon set of procedures for settling the disagreement. If divine command theory is true, then one must accept that Maturino Resendiz may have made an understandable mistake, acted conscientiously, with good intentions, or even properly followed God's instruction all along.

Divine command theory is and has been common sense for many. That's why people are so quick to agree with Dostoevsky's Ivan Karamazov, who said "If there is no God, everything is permitted" (*The Brothers Karamazov*, 1879). After all, in the Abrahamic faiths, the moral law does come directly or indirectly from God. The tablets of stone delivered on Mount Sinai to Moses are just the best-known example of the moral law being decreed by the deity for us to follow (Exodus 20, 34; Deuteronomy 5).

The Euthyphro *dilemma*

The durability of divine command theory strikes many as puzzling, however, given what seems to be a decisive refutation of it by Plato (427–347 BCE) in his dialogue *Euthyphro*. Plato puts his objection in the form of a question Socrates asks of the young Euthyphro, a purported expert on matters divine: Do the gods love what is holy (or pious) because it is holy; or is what they love holy because they love it (10b–11c)? Correlatively, one might ask: does God command the good because it's good; or is it good because God commands it?

If God commands what is good because it is good, then things are already good or bad irrespective of what God commands. This position would mean that God's command is not the source of morality, after all. The same conduct would be good or bad independently, whether or not God commanded it.

But then what of the alternative, that what God commands is good because God commands it? That route doesn't seem very promising either.

The problem here is that, because things are only good or bad because God commands them, it simply becomes a matter of God's will to determine what is good or bad. That means God could by an arbitrary act of will reconfigure things so that what's now good becomes instead evil and what's now evil becomes instead good. If God commanded murder it would be right. If God commanded rape, pillage, torture, and genocide, then it would be the duty of every moral agent to obey. William of Ockham (1287–1347) bit the bullet and affirmed that God could do just that, and do it at any time. Not many, however, are able to follow him in this view.

The position that what's moral or immoral is based ultimately in the commands of God's will has come to be known as *voluntarism*. Many find it a dissatisfying position because, at least on the face of it, voluntarism seems not only absurd because it makes morality arbitrary; it also seems to strip morality of its authority, or at least its power to motivate. Why believe that one should do what's good, why actually do the hard work of being good, if what's good could just as easily be bad? Duns Scotus (1265/66–1308) answered this objection by arguing that while God's commands are the source of morality it's not possible for God to command otherwise. But if God is so constrained, it seems it is not *just* God's saying so which makes things right or wrong after all.

The two possibilities together therefore suggest that either divine command theory is false and we don't need the divine as the source of morality; or morality is arbitrary, and what is good could just as easily be bad and vice versa. Divine command theory is either false, or it debases the very idea of morality.

Disobedient sons and interracial couples

Even if this dilemma can be resolved, the epistemological problem remains concerning how anyone is to know what God commands. You don't need to hear voices to be confused about this. Jews and Christians take the book of Deuteronomy to be the word of God, for example, but if anyone were to follow its commands he or she would soon be placed under arrest for some pretty serious crimes – like murder, for having stoned a disobedient son to death (21:18–21). Radical Christians calling themselves "Phineas Priests" in fact believe that a few passages of the Book of Numbers (25:6–18) command the faithful to kill interracial couples. Even many conventional religious leaders have commanded at least one thing that others believe to be seriously immoral.

Fortunately, people like Angel Maturino Resendiz will always be relatively rare. Yet the worry remains that their actions are entirely consistent with the truth of divine command theory. Accepting divine command theory, therefore, runs the risk of making the same kind of mistakes he did, even if they are not so serious.

See also

1.3 Authority, 1.18 Revelation, 2.1 Consequentialism

Reading

Janine Marie Idziak, *Divine Command Morality: Historical and Contemporary Readings* (New York: Edwin Mellen Press, 1978)
Paul Helm, ed., *Divine Commands and Morality* (Oxford: Oxford University Press, 1981)
*Philip L. Quinn, "Divine Command Theory," in *The Blackwell Guide to Ethical Theory*, edited by Hugh LaFollette (Oxford: Blackwell, 2000), 53–73

2.7 Egoism

"All sensible people are selfish," wrote Ralph Waldo Emerson (1803–82). Nowadays, conventional wisdom is that one doesn't even have to be sensible to selfish – because in fact everyone is always selfish. In some circles, a belief in genuine altruism is taken as a sign of naivety.

Emerson's line, however, need not inspire cynicism. The question, "Can egoism be morally justified?" is clearly not self-contradictory and needs to be answered. Furthermore, if being good and being selfish happen to require the same things, then selfishness would be something to celebrate.

Psychological egoism

First, however, something must be said about the view that, as a matter of fact, everyone is at heart an egoist. People may not do what's in their own best interests, but they will, according to the psychological egoist, only do what they *believe* is in their own best interests. Apparent counterexamples are just that – apparent. Take the sentiments expressed in Bryan Adams's soppy ballad, "(Everything I Do) I Do It For You." Echoing countless other love songs, Adams sings "Take me as I am, take my life. / I would give it all,

I would sacrifice."Yet even this extreme profession of selflessness can easily be seen as masking a deeper selfishness. Why, after all, is he saying this? For the purposes of seduction, of course. He may believe he is sincere, but then perhaps this is one of nature's tricks: only by fooling the seducer can the seduction be successful. Besides, even if he's telling the truth, what does that show? That he would rather die than be without his love? Selfishness again! Death is better than being miserable *for him*.

This view – known as psychological egoism – can be very persuasive. But although you can always explain away altruistic behavior in selfish terms, it's not clear why we should prefer a selfish explanation over an altruistic one simply because it's possible to do so.

From a logical point of view it's important to see that from the fact that the act is pleasing it doesn't follow that the act was done *for the sake of* the pleasure. From the fact that saving a drowning swimmer makes one feel good, for example, it doesn't follow that the saving was done *for the sake of* the good feeling. Pleasure may be a happy result of an action while not being the reason for the action.

There's also an objection that can be brought against the egoistic hypothesis from the point of view of scientific method – it can't be tested. If every act can be interpreted as selfish, it's not even possible to construct an experiment that might falsify the hypothesis. If someone saves a drowning swimmer, he did it for selfish reasons. If he doesn't save the drowning swimmer, he didn't do it for selfish reasons. Admissible hypotheses must, at least in principle, be somehow testable. And since every possible act can be interpreted as selfish, no observation could ever in principle test psychological egoism.

Ethical egoism

Even if psychological egoism is true, however, it only says something about the facts of human psychology. It doesn't say anything about whether or not being egoistic is rational or moral – whether one *ought to be* selfish. In short, it leaves all the big ethical questions unanswered. Ethicists cannot avoid the question of whether egoism is morally justified.

Adam Smith (1732–90) took a stab at an answer, at least in part, by arguing that selfishness *in economic affairs* is morally justified because it serves the common good in the most efficient way: "It is not from the benevolence of the butcher, the brewer, or the baker, that we expect our dinner," he wrote, "but from their regard to their own interest. We address ourselves, not to their humanity but their self-love, and never talk to them of our own necessities but of their advantages."

Smith's argument in *The Wealth of Nations* does not, however, justify what is known as *ethical egoism*: the view that it's *always* ethical to act in one's own interests. Even though it may be true that egoism is an efficient route to the common good in certain contexts, it's implausible that it's *always* so. Contrary to popular conception, Smith's general moral theory is, in fact, decidedly not egoistic, grounding morality instead in sympathy, moral sentiment, and an unselfish "impartial spectator." Smith does not defend ethical egoism as a *universal* or even *general principle*. To do that, one needs to argue that egoism is *itself* morally justifiable, that it's justifiable even if it doesn't serve as a means to some other good.

Rational egoism

So, how might one argue that egoism is ethically justified? Well, many believe that ethics must be rational. Moral laws might not be entirely derived from rational principles, but at the very least ethics must accord with reason, and not command anything contrary to reason – that is, anything that's inconsistent, self-contradictory, or conceptually incoherent. So, if ethics must be rational, and one may rationally (consistently, etc.) act for the sake of self-interest, then acting selfishly meets at least a rationality test for morality.

It's not at all clear, however, how acting rationally for the sake of self-interest is in any ethical sense decisive. Helping oneself seems no more or less rational than helping someone else. Might one not act rationally for the sake of immoral aims? Indeed, many would argue that aims or goals cannot be established by rationality alone.

Perhaps the most important question with regard to this issue is whether there's any conflict between self-interest and altruism anyway. Many ancient Greek philosophers, including Plato and Aristotle, wouldn't have seen any conflict between egoism and altruism because they thought that if one behaves badly one ultimately harms oneself. The greedy man, for example, is never at peace with himself, because he is never satisfied with what he has. In contrast, as Plato had Socrates say before his own execution, "a good man cannot be harmed either in life or in death." That may be too optimistic a view. But the idea that being good is a form of "enlightened self-interest" is plausible.

But does enlightened self-interest give people a reason for being altruistic, or does it show genuine altruism isn't possible? Some would argue that any act that's in one's self-interest cannot be called altruistic, even if it helps others: the concept of altruism *excludes* self-interested actions, even those that coincide with the interests of others. An alternative view holds that altruism and self-interest are compatible: the fact that do-gooders know that doing good helps them in no way diminishes the extent to which what they do is done for others. The dilemma can be posed with regard to the Bryan Adams song. Is he lying when he says everything he does, he does it for her, if he *also* does it for himself? Or has he just conveniently neglected to point out that his altruism requires no self-sacrifice?

See also

1.20 Sympathy, 2.15 Subjectivism, 3.22 Prudence, 5.14 Skepticism

Reading

*Bernard Mandeville, *The Fable of the Bees* [1714] *and Other Writings*, edited by E. J. Hundert (Indianapolis, IN: Hackett Publishing, 1997)
Adam Smith, *The Wealth of Nations* [1776], edited by Edwin Cannan (New York: The Modern Library, 1994), Chapter 2
*Robert Shaver, *Rational Egoism: A Selective and Critical History* (Cambridge: Cambridge University Press, 1998)

2.8 Hedonism

Why be moral? One way to try to answer this question is to consider why it would be a good thing if every moral problem were actually sorted out. What would everyone being good actually lead to? World peace. No one dying of hunger. Everyone being free. Justice reigning supreme. And what would be so good about that?

The obvious answer is that then everyone would be happy – or at least, as happy as is humanly possible. So, the point of being good is that it would lead to a happier world.

If this is right, then the basis of morality is hedonism: the view that the only thing that is of value in itself is happiness (or pleasure, though for simplicity we will talk only of happiness for now), and the only thing bad in itself is unhappiness (or pain). This might seem a surprising conclusion. After all, hedonism is usually associated with the selfish pursuit of fleeting pleasures. So, how can it be the basis of morality?

Happiness as the ultimate good

The answer to this question must start with an explanation of why happiness is the only good. Aristotle (384–322 BCE) thought this was evidently true, because there are things done for their own sake and things done for the sake of something else. Things done for the sake of something else are not valuable in themselves, but only *instrumentally valuable*, as *means to an end*. Those things done for their own sake, in contrast, are *intrinsically valuable*, as *ends in themselves*. Of all the good things in life, only happiness, it seems, is prized for its own sake. Everything else is valued only because it leads to happiness. Even love is not valued in itself – a love that makes us permanently miserable is not worth having.

There is, however, nothing in this conclusion that entails pursuing selfish, fleeting pleasures. Epicurus (341–271 BCE), one of the first hedonic philosophers, understood this well. He thought that no one could be happy if he or she permanently sought intense pleasures, especially of the fleeting kind (what he called *kinetic* or active pleasures). Rather, to be truly happy – or, perhaps better, "content" – one needs a certain calm, tranquillity, and peace of mind (*static* pleasures). And if we see that happiness has value in itself, then we have reason to be concerned with the happiness of others, not just our own. Hence, Epicurus concluded, "It is impossible to live a pleasant life without living wisely and honorably and justly, and it is impossible to live wisely and honorably and justly without living pleasantly."

One of the most important hedonic ethics of the modern era is the utilitarianism of Jeremy Bentham (1749–1832) and John Stuart Mill (1806–73). From the same premise – that pleasure and happiness are the only goods, and pain and unhappiness the only evils – they concluded that actions are right in so far as they promote the greatest happiness of the greatest number and wrong in so far as they diminish it.

Precisely what?

One of the recurring problems for hedonic philosophies is pinning down just what it is that is supposed to be intrinsically valuable. Is it pleasure – by which we mean pleasant sensations? Or is it happiness, in which case what is that? A stable state of mind? A temporary feeling of well-being? Objectively flourishing? Or are each of these good in themselves?

The problem is a persistent and serious one, for if we understand happiness and pleasure in conventional senses, it becomes far from clear that they are intrinsic goods, above all others. Moreover, philosophers' attempts to precisely define the crucial qualities of pleasure (as Bentham did, for example, by pointing to properties like "intensity" and "duration") are notoriously slippery. Critics of Mill's work argue that, if he were serious, he would have to admit that the life of a contented pig is better than that of a troubled philosopher. Mill tried to reply to this by distinguishing between *higher pleasures* of the mind and *lower pleasures* of the body (*Utilitarianism*, 1859).

But what makes higher pleasures higher? Mill thought "competent judges," who had experienced both, would prefer a life with some higher pleasures than one with only lower ones, but not vice versa. Yet, even if this were true, it doesn't seem to be the case that the higher pleasures are preferred simply because they are more pleasurable. If, however, there are other reasons for choosing them, then hedonic considerations are not the only important ones after all.

Robert Nozick made an even stronger argument against hedonism in a thought experiment in which he asked if one would choose to live happily in a virtual world or less happily in the real one. Almost everyone, he suggested, would prefer the real world, which suggests people prefer reality to happiness. If that's right, then happiness is not the only thing that's good in itself. It seems that truth and authenticity are, as well.

See also

1.10 Flourishing, 1.17 Pain and pleasure, 3.19 Means/ends, 5.13 The separateness of persons

Reading

Epicurus, *The Epicurus Reader: Selected Writings and Testimonia*, edited by Brad Inwood and Lloyd P. Gerson (Indianapolis, IN: Hackett Publishing, 1994)
Robert Nozick, *Anarchy, State and Utopia* (New York: Basic Books, 1974)
*Fred Feldman, *Pleasure and the Good Life: Concerning the Nature, Varieties and Plausibility of Hedonism* (Oxford: Oxford University Press, 2004)

2.9 Naturalism

Since the publication of Charles Darwin's *The Origin of the Species* in 1859, the claim that human beings are a full part of nature has become more and more accepted. With the success of modern science, we have also seen the placing of nature at center stage in human understanding. There is no widely accepted supernatural science or supernatural medicine. So, why should there be a supernatural ethics? Surely what we now need is for ethics to be naturalized, just as science has been.

It's not easy, however, to say what counts as "nature" or the "natural order." Some have defined it in terms of the observable *causal orders* discovered and explained through the natural and social sciences. Others, like G. E. Moore (1873–1958), have described nature as whatever exists in time. Whatever "nature" and the "natural" are, though, naturalistic ethicists wish to distinguish them from the metaphysical, the divine, the supernatural, and the theological. That is, naturalistic ethics works to construe ethics in a way that makes no reference to things like God, soul, revelation, Platonic forms, metaphysical "essences," "substance," the "One" (Plotinus), "monads" (Leibniz), a self-positing metaphysical "I" (Fichte), "*Geist*" (Hegel), "Will" (Schopenhauer and Nietzsche), or even "freedom" (Sartre).

Ethical naturalists think it better that we turn to the language and to the reality described by sciences like biology, psychology, chemistry, physics, cognitive science, and perhaps also social sciences like sociology. There are two principal reasons for this: (1) the sciences seem to have been remarkably successful; and (2) over time philosophical scrutiny has for many (though not all) produced trenchant criticisms of the reliability, the political import, and even the very meaningfulness of metaphysics, theology, and religion. Actually naturalizing ethics will mean that we alter both the meanings of ethical terms and the way ethical prescriptions are made.

Naturalizing ethics

Ethics requires distinctive terms like, "good," "bad," "right," and "wrong." Ethical naturalists have tried to understand these terms in purely natural ways; that is by defining them solely in terms of things found in the natural world or the natural order of things. So, the meaning of "good" for a naturalist can be understood only in terms of the material, biological, psychological, or physical characteristics of things. Saying "sexual abuse is bad" then is saying something like: "sexual abuse causes physical and psychological pathologies in those who are subjected to it."

But how can ethical prescriptions by naturalized? The sciences, after all, only tell us *what is*, not *what ought to be*. Sociology can describe and explain how people do in fact act; it does not and *cannot* say how they *should* act. Psychology and cognitive science can explain how people do in fact think and feel; it cannot say how they *should* think and feel. "What is," critics say, is the domain of the sciences. "What ought to be" is the domain of ethics and moral philosophy.

Defenders of ethical naturalism might respond by saying that moral judgment is a natural activity among human beings. Moreover, the groundwork of human ethics is the result of natural selection. Evolution has selected for ethical traits because they serve as an effective means of perpetuating our genetic lines. Had we evolved differently, we might judge morality different. Perhaps we wouldn't have the natural conscience to which Bishop Butler pointed, or the moral sentiments described by Adam Smith and David Hume, or even the capacity for rational moral judgment at all, a capacity Aristotle thought was deeply characteristic of our species. As things stand, however, we do by nature possess such capacities, and for us judgments concerning ethical issues are as natural as judgments about the various factual states of affairs that make up the world.

Philosophical ethics acts, like logic and the philosophy of science, as a way to clarify basic concepts, to explore their implications and coherence, and to formulate methods for making moral judgments in meaningful ways that achieve more agreement, more stability, and more systematic organization. After that, nature will take its course, and humans will judge. Just as the great naturalizer W. V. O. Quine (1908–2000) argued about the relationship between philosophy and physics, there isn't an absolutely clear line differentiating ethics from the sciences. The sciences depend upon philosophy for conceptual clarification and method. Ethics depends upon the sciences for the information on the basis of which moral judgments are best made.

Whether this answer, or others like it, is good enough to assuage doubts about the ability of naturalized ethics to yield true moral prescriptions is the key bone of contention between ethical naturalists and their opponents.

See also

1.8 Evolution, 1.20 Sympathy, 3.9 Facts/values, 4.8 The "is/ought gap"

Readings

Larry May, Marilyn Friedman, and Andy Clark, eds., *Minds and Morals: Essays on Cognitive Science and Ethics* (Cambridge, MA: MIT Press, 1996)

William A. Rottschaefer, *The Biology and Psychology of Moral Agency* (Cambridge: Cambridge University Press, 1998)

William D. Casebeer, *Natural Ethical Facts: Evolution, Connectionism, and Moral Cognition* (Cambridge, MA: MIT Press, 2005)

2.10 Particularism

Some people are trapped in a burning building, and there's only enough time to get one more out using the escape helicopter before the building collapses. There are three people left: a 60-year-old, unmarried, childless senior cancer researcher; a 14-year-old child; and a stay-at-home mother of three children. Who should be saved?

Many people react to such questions by saying it's impossible to tell without knowing more information. Is one of them more willing to sacrifice his or her own life for the others? How dependent are the mother's children on her? Does she have close relatives who are willing and able to care for the children? Will the 14-year-old grow up to be a physician or a crack addict? Is the cancer researcher in love? Why is each of them in the building, anyway? Is one of them an arsonist who set the fire?

One might try to get around these difficulties by declaring *ceteris paribus* – all other things are equal. In this case *ceteris paribus* means assuming that the only relevant differences between these people are those specified. But the nagging doubt remains: in real life other things are never equal. Every case is different. Even if one could decide who should escape the building in this *particular* situation, no *general* lesson could be drawn from it because the next time a similar circumstance arises, crucial details will again be different.

It is partly for reasons like these that moral particularism has become more important in recent years. Moral particularists argue against the centrality of general principles in morality. More radical particularists even claim that there are simply no defensible general moral principles at all. Moderate particularists, on the other hand, argue that at best one can make use of some principles as general rules of thumb, though they should never provide the last word against which the morality of particular actions are judged.

Particularism flies in the face of almost the entire history of ethical thought. All moral systems operate according to principles. That's why moral individuals are commonly described as being "principled." What specific moral principles are actually held varies according to the moral theory that defines them, but the importance of principle itself seems to be universally acknowledged. So, why should one reject such a central plank of moral thinking?

The case for particularism

Particularists are impressed by the fact that, despite numerous attempts to formulate general moral principles, at some point they always seem to break down. Debate among moral philosophers often takes the form of raising objections to a moral theory by finding a counterexample that shows an action to be either (a) wrong but consistent with the principles under consideration or (b) right but inconsistent with them. Given this repeated failure of moral principles to stand trial by counterexample, one can either conclude that philosophers just haven't formulated the right principles yet or that the entire project of so doing is doomed.

Particularism provides an *error theory* for this history of apparent failure: it explains why it is that no general moral principles hold without exception. The reason is actually quite simple: the factors that inform moral consideration are infinitely variable, whereas general principles are fixed or at least finite and limited. To put it another way, real life is finer-grained than any general moral principle could ever be, and therefore no general moral principle can ever do justice to all the complexities of real life. "There are more things in heaven and earth," says Hamlet, "than are dreamt of in your philosophy" (*Hamlet* I. v).

That doesn't mean that moral reasoning is impossible. On the contrary, for particularists moral reasoning is possible in just the same way that general practical problem-solving is possible. Consider how one decides where to buy a house. One may have a few general preferences, but there's no rule that can be applied to determine exactly which house to buy. Of course, to help decide people often start out with a list of general *preferences* or *rules*. But these are constantly revised as they confront realities on the ground. So, it's common to hear people say things like, "I said I'd never buy a house that needed a lot of work, but this one was so adorable I had to get it." In the same way, when people begin moral deliberations they may start with some general preferences or rules (no war, no lying, and so forth), but these don't determine the final conclusion they reach.

It's sometimes said that moral judgments have to be constrained by rational consistency, and without general rules consistency isn't possible. But it's not clear this follows. The consistency constraint still applies to particularism: to justify making a different judgment in apparently identical situations, the particularist just has to explain what the morally relevant differences between the two circumstances are.

Particularism shares some features in common with situation ethics, the Christian ethic developed by the theologian Joseph Fletcher (1905–91). Although there are important differences in detail, both are attempts to reject a morality guided by fixed rules without collapsing into an amorality where no moral reasoning or judgment is possible at all.

See also

3.22 Prudence, 4.3 Consistency, 4.18 Universalizability, 5.12 Radical particularity, 5.15 Standpoint

Reading

Joseph Fletcher, *Situation Ethics* (Philadelphia, PA: The Westminster Press, 1966)

Odo Marquard, *Farewell to Matters of Principle* (Oxford: Oxford University Press, 1989)

Brad Hooker and Margaret Olivia Little, eds., *Moral Particularism* (Oxford: Oxford University Press, 2001)

2.11 Perfectionism

We live in officially egalitarian times. We grant the equal dignity and worth of all human beings and like to knock our heroes off their pedestals. Yet, it's hard to go all the way with this approach. After all, surely it's just true that Albert Einstein and William Shakespeare had minds that approximated more closely to human perfection than we humble authors of this book. To deny that seems crazy. Yet to accept it requires the belief that objectively speaking, there are more or less excellent examples of human beings. What does this mean, and how are such objective standards possible? Moral perfectionists think they have the answers.

Human nature and nature's perfection

If there is such a thing as human nature, and if that nature can be more or less perfected or blunted, then there may be something like objective standards for moral choices, character, and conduct. For moral perfection theorists, the very meaning of what's morally "good" is whatever helps us to realize a more perfect nature. The problem is in identifying what human nature is, and what it means to perfect it.

Virtue ethics provides one possible answer. Theorists like Plato and Aristotle wrote about human excellence (*aretē*), specifically the excellences of the human soul or mind (*psychē*). Different parts of the soul have different excellences. So, there are accordingly excellences or virtues of (1) the intellect, (2) the passions and desires, and (3) ambition and spiritedness – as well as (4) the relations among them.

One might of course speak of other human perfections, as well. For example, consider the perfections of the body. Surely, one might say, an Olympic decathlon winner, a world-class ballerina, or a concert pianist has achieved the perfections of the body better than a couch potato who sits all day in front of the television.

Perhaps one might also speak of perfections concerning one's relationship to the divine (*theological virtue*), to one's family, to one's society (*civic virtue*), to other living things, and even to the natural world (*ecological virtue*). Perhaps one may speak meaningfully of a more or less perfect political order (*political virtue*).

Having identified these various perfections, the next question is what need we do to foster them, since only by fostering them will we live moral lives.

Roads to perfection

Reason – in the form of the natural and social sciences – can provide information about health and illness, pathology and healing. Practice can provide a means to improve physical skill and dexterity. So it is that we can readily explain what one should do to make more perfect the excellences of the body and the technical arts. Doing this is relevant to moral perfectionists, for improving ourselves in such ways is indeed an ethical matter.

But can reason adequately formulate moral or intellectual ideals, as well? Theories of moral perfection often reject the notion that unambiguous rules can be formulated for what is and is not perfect. If reason depends upon rules, but rules can't formulate perfection, then perfectionism can't be the business of reason.

On the other hand, perhaps reason includes something more. Philosophers like Stanley Cavell (b. 1926) and Alasdair MacIntyre (b. 1929) have emphasized the importance to reasoning about moral perfection of ongoing conversations among friends, or at least members of shared communities, in struggling to make one's moral claims and moral self intelligible to others. Along these lines, MacIntyre has famously said that people need a new St Benedict to define a new community through which new norms and criteria may be established for reasoning about morals (*After Virtue*, 1981).

But can adequately objective standards emerge through such a process? History suggests the ideals set out by moral perfectionists are far from being universal and objective. Roman thinkers adopted the Latin concept of masculine *vir* (from which the word "virility" derives) in defining virtue and perhaps with it a rather unrepresentative ideal of human perfection. Aristotle is notorious for having fleshed out the content of virtue in the form of an Athenian male aristocrat, and in fact moral perfectionism has often been criticized as the ethical theory of elitists and aristocrats who are drawn by their vanity to a theory that flatters them as examples of human perfection. On the other hand, isn't the notion of moral perfection also important to the conversation animating a democratic and egalitarian society as it searches for ways to improve itself and better realize the ideal of a more perfect society or commonwealth?

Perfectionism in practice

Although perfectionism can sound very elitist, in some ways it's much closer to the normal concerns of ordinary people than many other moral theories. After all, we all want to know how we can make our lives go better, as the burgeoning shelves of bestselling self-help books attest.

Moral perfectionism itself offers a kind of self-help guide. Many people must make choices about how much time to devote to earning money, to children and family, to political or social service, to recreation, or to intellectual pursuit. It's tough to find the proper balance and mix, but an ideal of human perfection may help. On grounds of human perfection, one might choose a lower paying job in order to spend more time with one's children, one's books, and with the needy of the world. The accumulation of wealth, after all, by most accounts doesn't characterize human perfection. But still, how much should be sacrificed? The data of psychology, history, anthropology, and sociology can help. Conversations with friends and mentors, and even novels, poems, films, and paintings, may be important, too. Perhaps so will time spent in the natural world. In any case, finding answers will require an ongoing conversation about how best to lead a human life. That's what it means to be a reflective moral being.

See also

2.16 Virtue ethics, 3.12 Individual/collective, 3.22 Prudence

Readings

Alasdair MacIntyre, *Whose Justice? Which Rationality?* (South Bend, IN: University of Notre Dame Press, 1988)

Stanley Cavell, *Conditions Handsome and Unhandsome: The Constitution of Emersonian Perfectionism* (Chicago: University of Chicago Press, 1990)
Thomas Hurka, *Perfectionism* (Oxford: Oxford University Press, 1993)

2.12 Pragmatism

The development of new technologies of political violence in the world has provoked a great deal of moral deliberation about how to deal properly with them. This has led to some governments abandoning long-held principles that govern the legitimacy of self-defense. Among these is what many call the "imminent threat" or "clear and present danger" test.

For many ethicists and jurists, violently acting in self-defense, preemptively or otherwise, is warranted only when there is a "clear and present danger." It's a doctrine that, at least with regard to customary international law, gained currency after an 1837 naval incident between the US and Great Britain. Articles 2 and 51 of the United Nations Charter follow this doctrine by legitimating acts of self-defense only where there is an "imminent" threat.

But perhaps things are different today than they were in 1837. Today weapons of then unimaginable destructive power may be delivered to their targets so swiftly and secretly that perhaps it's unreasonable to think that those targeted will even have a chance to detect them and respond with any sort of effective self-defense. Perhaps new developments in communication, transport, and the technologies of killing render the clear and present danger or imminent threat tests outdated. If so, then maybe violent preventative measures have become morally permissible where in the past they were not. How are we to decide?

Let's be pragmatic

While some would look to unchanging or singular principles, pragmatists have no qualms about regarding moral principles in a sort of evolutionary way – that is, as guiding rules that must adapt to new conditions.

On this view there are no such things as "moral facts," if what is meant by the term is a moral truth that exists independently of moral practices and moral actors, applies to everyone, and doesn't change over time. Rather, morality is something dynamic and inextricably bound up with actual, concrete social practices, discourses, and problems.

Determining which action, way of life, or policy is right or wrong does not then require that one grasps some independent or logically prior truth. It does not require discovering something that is "out there," independently – be it what God commands, reason authorizes, or natural law prescribes. Pragmatism holds that a better way to think about moral determinations, rules, principles, laws, etc., is as the best ways we've figured out so far for ordering our lives, given our interests, beliefs, histories, and the problems we face.

Coming to pragmatic determinations, then, doesn't rule out reasoning and theorizing; but it does hold that reasoning and theorizing about ethics cannot be divorced from actual practices, conditions, and problems. Reasoning does not transport us to some independent point of view where we see things as God sees them or, in Benedictus Spinoza's (1632–77) phrase, *sub specie aeternitatis* (under the view of eternity). Properly understood moral reasoning is always (whether it admits it or not) directly connected to social, concrete and practical life. It grounds itself in the experience, history, and habits of those who engage in it.

Another useful example in understanding moral pragmatism may be found in disputes over the right to possess firearms. In the United States, many defenders of that right appeal to the Second Amendment of the US Constitution and what they believe to have been the *original intent* of its authors. For pragmatists, the assumption that the moral conclusions reached by a group of men two hundred years ago will necessarily continue to work forever afterwards is just silly. It's perfectly possible that the world has changed so much since then that new moral and political rules are needed. Only careful reflection on the experiences people have accumulated and the concrete effectiveness of various alternatives can say.

What pragmatism is not

This way of thinking about moral reasoning, since it rejects moral absolutes, may be thought of as having relativistic implications. But if relativism implies that cultures, societies, time periods, or individuals are unable to judge or even understand one another, then pragmatism is not relativistic. Like the principles of international law and commerce, moral judgments concerning others will develop through deliberation upon the actual experience of cultures, nations, and societies with one another. Different cultures can criticize one another's morals just as well as they can criticize one another's technologies.

Nevertheless, pragmatism is both tolerant and pluralistic. Employing various moral principles is pragmatically possible, and different societies may well face different problems, have different needs and sensibilities, and hold different values. So, pragmatism is not staked upon the claim that morality must be reduced to a single principle that completely defines morality and that never needs to be complemented or even supplanted by others.

Some moral systems are called *consequentialist*, in the sense that they contend that moral rules or actions are to be judged by their consequences. Other moral systems are called *deontic* because their assessments are generally centered on features of the rules and actions themselves, rather than their consequences.

Pragmatism fits properly into neither of these categories since it rejects the idea that there is a fundamental distinction between acts and their consequences, at least in a morally significant way. Both actions and their consequences are to be considered morally relevant. In fact, they must be, because they cannot be fully extricated from one another.

See also

2.1 Consequentialism, 2.14 Relativism, 3.19 Means/ends

Readings

John Dewey, *Human Nature and Conduct* [1922] (Carbondale: Southern Illinois University Press, 1988)
James S. Gouinlock, *Rediscovering the Moral Life: Philosophy and Human Practice* (Amherst, NY: Prometheus Books, 1993)
Hugh LaFollette, "Pragmatic Ethics," in *Blackwell Guide to Ethical Theory* edited by Hugh LaFollette (Malden, MA: Blackwell, 2000), 400–19

2.13 Rationalism

"Welcome to your ethics class. So far, you have learned the basic moral axioms and formulae, and you have learned how to use your pocket moral calculators. In this lesson we are going to use these principles to solve some moral dilemmas. I will chalk the facts on the board. Please work out your conclusions and remember – show your calculations!"

Many have been frustrated that while the conclusions of mathematics seem so definite, indisputable, and clear, those of ethics seem so indeterminate, controversial, and vague. But although it may seem absurd to imagine people solving moral conundrums as they do mathematical problems, the dream that this may indeed be more or less possible has inspired the work of rationalists.

During the seventeenth and eighteenth centuries, thinkers like René Descartes (1596–1650), Benedictus Spinoza (1632–77), Gottfried Wilhelm von Leibniz (1646–1716), and Samuel Clarke (1675–1729) looked for a way to determine moral truths rationally through the content and relations among ideas. They argued that the mind or soul could apprehend principles through reason, intuition, or the intellect and then reason out moral conclusions.

For the rationalists, reasoning from moral first principles to moral judgments is deductive, in just the same way as mathematics or formal logic is. This allows morality to be determined with the same degree of certainty. Feeling or sentiment, unsurprisingly, has no place in this sort of moral deliberation. Instead, rationally discernible harmony, balance, lawfulness, and a kind of Stoic restraint characterize sound moral truth.

Turning to reason in this way promised early modern and Enlightenment thinkers not only a more certain and universal morality. It also promised an alternative to religious dogmatics. Rationalism isn't, of course, entirely antithetical to religion. Those rationalists who remained religious simply held that reason complements revelation through the rational apprehension of divine law, often, as in the case of the deists, in the form of natural law.

The term "rationalism" also has a broader ethical meaning, one that characterizes much of western philosophy – namely, the idea that the very activity of reasoning about things, especially moral matters, cultivates a kind of moderation and even mastery of the passions, emotion, and feeling. For rational thinkers, then, not only does reason apprehend moral truth. It also disciplines, orders, and habituates feeling and structures character. Even philosophers of moral sentiment like David Hume share in this view.

How is rationalism possible?

For the narrower version of rationalism to work, you first need to be able to establish what the first principles of ethics are. Ancient Stoics, for example, argued for the existence of *cataleptic impressions*, indubitable ideas or phenomena upon which the mind can with certainty base its beliefs. Later, Descartes argued that there are "clear and distinct" *innate ideas*, and Spinoza described *common notions* that give a kind of ballast to moral (and other) claims not possible through ordinary experience or empirical science.

Having established this, you then need to explain how mathematical rigor is possible in the reasoning that follows from these principles. To do this, many rationalists maintained what later became known as the doctrine of *internal relations*. This is the idea that the moral relations among ideas, or things themselves, are intrinsic to those ideas and not brought to them *extrinsically* by contingent and variable things like custom, socialization, habit, or feeling. Like the relations of numbers, rationalists needed to hold that these relations were essential and intrinsic so that moral claims could achieve the certainty, invariability, and universality of mathematics and deductive logic.

Getting everything in place for rationalism of this sort to fly is therefore something of a tall order, and these days strict ethical rationalists are decidedly in the minority. Philosophers are generally skeptical of all the key planks of rationalism: the possibility of establishing certain first principles, the possibility of reasoning deductively from moral principles, and the possibility that the moral relations among things and ideas are fixed and internal. Nevertheless, something of the rationalist impulse surely remains in any theorist who seeks to establish order and general principles in the field of moral deliberation.

See also

1.20 Sympathy, 3.22 Prudence, 4.18 Universalizability

Readings

René Descartes, *The Passions of the Soul* [1645–6], edited by Stephen H. Voss (Indianapolis, IN: Hackett Publishing, 1989)
Samuel Clarke, *A Demonstration of the Being and Attributes of God* [1704] *and Other Writings* (Cambridge: Cambridge University Press, 1998)
Scott MacDonald, ed., *Being and Goodness: The Concept of the Good in Metaphysics and Philosophical Theology* (Ithaca, NY: Cornell University Press, 1991)

2.14 Relativism

Relativism is often thought of as an "anything goes" ethic which denies that anything is right or wrong, except in the mind of the person who thinks it is. Since this makes it impossible to say that the Holocaust, mass rape, or ethnic cleansing are wrong more generally, it's easy to see why relativism is seen by many as the great threat to human decency. For instance, Pope Benedict XVI, in his last few days as Cardinal Ratzinger, said:

> relativism, which is letting oneself be tossed and "swept along by every wind of teaching," looks like the only attitude (acceptable) to today's standards. We are moving toward a dictatorship of relativism which does not recognize anything as for certain and which has as its highest goal one's own ego and one's own desires. (*National Catholic Reporter*, April 22, 2005; quotation from Ephesians, 4:14)

Being a relativist, however, is a bit like being a post-modernist: plenty of people are accused of being relativists, but very few describe themselves in that way. It's probably true to say that there's not a single moral philosopher of repute who would maintain simply, as relativists are thought to do, that no moral judgments are superior to any others. Nevertheless, what they say is often close enough to confuse those not prepared to attend to the details.

What is moral relativism?

In its broadest sense, a moral relativist is anyone who rejects the view that moral rules and principles are absolute and universal, applying to all persons, in all places, and at all times. Note that it is not contradictory to hold that relativism is itself absolutely and universally true. Moral relativists need not think that everything is relative, only that normative moral rules and principles are.

Relativists can reject absolutism on any number of grounds. Non-cognitivists who criticize absolutism focus on questions of knowledge and intelligibility arguing that moral rules are not the sort of things that can be meaningfully said to be known. Non-realists hold the metaphysical thesis that moral facts, at least objective moral facts, simply don't exist. Others argue that morality changes and evolves over time and place, and that moral codes appropriate for one set of circumstances may not be appropriate for another.

All these non-absolutist positions can be described as relativist, since they maintain that morality isn't timeless, universal, and independent of context. Rather, morality is rooted in particular cultures, histories, species, social groups, religions, or even individuals. One can only make sense of "right" and "wrong" relative to these particularities.

And note that these particularities aren't always subjective things. So, it's wrong to identify, as so many do, relativism with subjectivism. Different objective features of different societies may yield different objective moralities. Therefore, any description of morality is incomplete until one specifies not only "what it's relative to" but also "what determines it." Morals may, for example, be "relative to" societies and "determined by" the objective conditions of scarcity, the distribution of wealth, or, as some have argued, even the climate of that society.

One consequence of this is that, inevitably, there will be competing and incompatible moral standards. And because there is no objective or independent moral standard by which to judge them, it cannot be maintained that one is objectively superior to another. Indeed, when moralities collide, there may be no way to resolve the differences between them rationally. This is what irks realists. They find intolerable the idea that comprehensive or universal moral uniformity or at least agreement may be impossible.

Is relativism amoral?

Critics claim that relativism has to collapse into an abandonment of morality altogether. Their argument can be summarized thus:

1   If relativism is true, then there is more than one set of moral principles, and none of these sets of principles is objectively superior to any other.
2   If no set of principles is objectively superior to any other, then it makes no sense to talk about some moral values being better or worse than others.
3   But morality is not possible without judgments of better or worse.
4   Therefore, relativism, if true, makes morality impossible.

The argument has intuitive appeal, but arguably begs the question against relativism. The key is the second premise: for the absolutist, it makes no sense to talk about some moral values being better or worse than others if there are no objective standards. But this premise is precisely what many relativists dispute. They would argue that people can make sense of moral terms like right or wrong, better or worse, but only if they do so without the illusion that these are objective judgments. To use the terms properly people must acknowledge their finitude, their limits. The absolutist claim that "only objective judgments carry any weight" is precisely what's at issue, and so cannot be taken as a premise in an argument against relativism.

Indeed, there's no logical contradiction in vigorously asserting specific values without a commitment to universalism. Take, for example, a relativist faced with the rise of Soviet repression in the 1930s. The fact that she has no absolute basis for the judgment that gulags are immoral may have no practical import, at all. For the opponent of Soviet repression, it may be, no more than a philosophically interesting point about the nature of moral reasoning. The idea that she *should* be less committed to the moral values that animate her opposition is therefore far from self-evident. Moreover, if one believes that morality springs from, for example, subjective human sympathy rather than objective truth, it's hard to see why the lack of moral absolutes should have any effect on moral motivation at all.

See also

1.21 Tradition and history, 2.15 Subjectivism, 3.1 Absolute/relative, 5.10 Pluralism

Reading

Martin Hollis and Steven Lukes, eds., *Rationality and Relativism* (Cambridge, MA: MIT Press, 1982)
*Richard Rorty, *Objectivity, Relativism, and Truth* (Cambridge: Cambridge University Press, 1990)
*Maria Baghramian, *Relativism*, revised edition (New York: Routledge, 2004)

2.15 Subjectivism

On February 15, 2003, an estimated one million people took to the streets of London to urge the British and US governments not to go to war with Iraq. Some of the protestors shouted, "Tony Blair: murderer. George Bush: murderer." Others chanted "One, two, three, four, we don't want your bloody war."

The two chants represent two characteristic features of how people understand moral judgments. The first – "Tony Blair: murderer" – is an example of a moral judgment as a factual claim. According to this statement it was just true that Blair was a murderer, perhaps because he had clearly violated objective laws concerning legitimate and illegitimate killing. The second – "We don't want your bloody war" – is an example of a moral judgment as expressing something more subjective, namely an attitude of strong disapproval. To many it seems that both the *factual claim* and the *attitude* need to be in place for a moral judgment to carry any weight. In other words, to say something is wrong is not just to state a fact but also to reveal a disapproving attitude toward it. Merely to disapprove of something only shows a personal preference, and cannot by itself constitute a moral judgment.

That, at least, is the "common sense" understanding. Subjectivists, however, claim it's a fundamentally misguided view. As evidence, they might ask for a second look at the mass of humanity that poured its way through the streets of London in 2003. It may appear that certain factual claims were being made about the morality of war, but the overwhelming sense one would have got from being there was of the deep disapproval – to put it mildly – of the impending invasion. That, a subjectivist might claim, reflects the reality that moral judgments are, most basically, about our affective attitudes toward actions, not about dispassionate reasons and logical arguments.

Varieties of subjectivism

The godfather of subjectivism is David Hume, who argued that rationality by itself is entirely incapable of producing reasons for action. As he famously put it, "'Tis not contrary to reason to prefer the destruction of the whole world to the scratching of my finger" (*A Treatise of Human Nature* [1739–40], Book II, Part iii, §3). By this he meant that in order to prefer one thing to the other, humans must in some way feel differently about them; and rationality cannot be the source of any feelings because it's only about truth and falsity and the relationship between statements. Reason, therefore, can operate in the service of feeling or even affect feeling, but reason cannot itself produce feeling: "Reason is, and ought only to be, the slave of the passions, and can never pretend to any other office than to serve and obey them" (*Treatise*, II, iii, §3).

Note that to the extent that the idea of a collective or group subject makes sense, it may be possible to speak of a subjectivism that's collective or social. For this reason many conflate social relativism with social subjectivism. But while different social subjects are likely, according to subjectivism, to yield different moralities, relativism is possible even if subjectivism is wrong. Different societies might have different moralities for different objective reasons.

In its most extreme form, subjectivism becomes *emotivism*, the theory championed by A. J. Ayer. It's sometimes known as the "Boo! Hoorah!" theory, since it claims that when people say something is "right" or "wrong," they are doing no more than emoting their subjective feelings. Language misleads us, says Ayer. "Abortion is wrong" looks like a factual claim that's either true or false. But really, the logical grammar of such a statement is better captured by a phrase such as "Abortion – yuck!"

which is neither true nor false but is merely an expression of emotion or feeling.

Critique

The major objection to emotivism is that, if it were true, then there could be no moral debate between people who disagree; and all moral reasoning would be a sham. Emotivists reply by saying that there is still some room for discussion, just as there is when people disagree about a piece of music they like. They would, however, accept that the room for discussion is narrower than is commonly supposed. Many find this position troubling. What can one say, for example, to those who do not disapprove of torture, ethnic cleansing, or dictatorship?

Less extreme forms of subjectivism claim that although morality is rooted in what we might call human sentiment and sympathy (general feelings of benevolence, empathy, and so on), that doesn't mean there is nothing to be said about it. For one thing, emotions are informed by rational and conceptual considerations. One reason why people are racists, for example, may be that they have false and confused ideas about the differences between people of varying skin color. So, at the very least, reason has a role in getting right the facts that inform our feelings. Reasoning well can also include certain habits of restraint, moderation, and openness that can cultivate certain types of character and therefore certain habits of feeling.

Subjectivism can even lead to a broader range of moral discourses. Not only does philosophy have a role to play, but subjectivism also recognizes roles for poetry, fiction, photography, painting, film, and music. Does anyone really think that photographs of the Holocaust have no moral effect on people? Indeed, it's often the non-theoretical portions of moral conversations that have the greatest effect. Nevertheless, critics insist that if the buck stops with what people feel rather than with reasons and facts, morality cannot have a secure base and slides into a vapid, permissive relativism.

Subjectivism has a complicated relationship with non-cognitivism – the view that moral judgments are neither true nor false. Many subjectivists are non-cognitivists, but one could also claim that moral judgments *are* true or false, in so far as they accurately describe subjective states, dispositions, or attitudes relevant to moral judgment. Conversely, non-cognitivists may not be subjectivists. One can hold that moral judgments are not true or false, but nor do they describe attitudes of moral agents. And, of course, many cognitivists are anti-subjectivists.

See also

1.20 Sympathy, 3.6 Cognitivism/non-cognitivism, 4.18 Universalizability, 5.13 Skepticism

Reading

A. J. Ayer, *Language, Truth and Logic* (London: Victor Gollancz, 1936)
J. L. Mackie, *Ethics: Inventing Right and Wrong* (London: Pelican Books, 1977)
Simon Blackburn, *Ruling Passions* (Oxford: Oxford University Press, 1998)

2.16 Virtue ethics

To many Europeans, the furor surrounding the impeachment of US President Bill Clinton in 1998 was mystifying. And the two major traditions in moral philosophy would have supported that view. Consequentialists would focus our attention on the outcomes of his actions, and probably conclude that they had no bearing on his work as president. Deontologists would note that he had failed in his duty as a husband, but not as a major world leader.

A large swath of public opinion, however, was persuaded that his conduct was morally serious, because of the important "character question." More philosophically, one might say that Clinton's affair with Monica Lewinsky exhibits his lust, intemperance, and weakness of will. His deceptive statements under oath perhaps indicated excessive ambition, pride, and a poor sense of justice. In short, the affair showed that Clinton lacked the virtues required of a great leader.

This line of thought echoes an old stream in ethical reasoning that doesn't focus on how one should act, but on what kind of person one should be. According to this approach, right actions are defined according to the virtues of those who perform the actions, not the other way around. This stream of thinking has become known as "virtue ethics." In addition to consequentialist and deontological theories, virtue ethics is commonly identified today as the third principal way of thinking about ethics.

Excellence

Virtue ethics began in ancient Greek discourses about *aretē* or *excellence*, which the Romans translated later with the Latin word *virtus*. The basic thought is that humans, like all things, have a specific nature or essence. As acorns develop into mighty oaks, humans begin in the womb and realize their full or complete being, becoming excellent, when fully mature. With the achievement of excellence comes happiness (*eudaimonia*).

More accurately, one should say that it's *possible* for humans to realize or actualize their full potential. The realization of human nature can be more or less complete, more or less perfect. Just as disease, insects, fire, and poor soil may stunt or distort the development of an oak, illness, war, and famine may stunt or distort the development of human nature. Individuals don't control where they're born, whom they're born to, or a lot of other things about the world that matter to human (or arboreal) development. Because of this, actually achieving excellence may depend in part upon good fortune or what's called "moral luck."

There's something else, however, involved in the development of humans that's not relevant to the development of oaks – society. Humans are, according to Aristotle anyway, social beings, and their nature must be cultivated socially. Humans, unlike oaks, don't just grow; they are raised, educated, socialized, and informed by customs, conventions, and traditions. When raised properly, humans not only realize strong, healthy bodies, they develop certain traits of character. *Character* comprises a certain set of emotional traits or dispositions. When the emotions, desires, and passions are cultivated in an excellent way, people achieve not just biological excellence but also moral virtue.

Sexual desire, for example, is from this point of view neither good nor bad in itself. One can desire virtuously (perhaps desiring one's spouse or companion in appropriate ways) or viciously (desiring inappropriate partners in inappropriate ways). Similarly, anger is in itself neither good nor bad. One can feel anger virtuously (righteous indignation for a grave injustice), or one can feel anger viciously (flying into a rage in reaction to a trivial slight). As Michael Oakeshott put it in *On Human Conduct* (1975), ethics is not so much about doing or not doing as it's about the *way* we do things.

Reason and habit

The words "ethical" and "moral" derive from words that mean "arising from character" – the Greek *ēthikos* or *ēthikē* and the Latin *moralis*. But *ēthikos* and *moralis* both also carry the connotation of arising from habit or custom. There's good reason for this, for as virtue ethicists understand it, habits play a crucial role in the formation of character. It's through habit that emotional and even intellectual dispositions are shaped, reinforced, disciplined, and moderated. It's in the soil of habit that moral excellences or virtues develop and stabilize. Habits are nurtured socially, through family, community, religious ritual, and education, perhaps even through public policy.

Habit even affects the intellect. Aristotle famously called humans the "rational animal," but while perhaps in some sense humans reason naturally, the techniques of logic, science, analysis, etc. must be inculcated through education and practice. So, virtue ethicists commonly speak of *intellectual virtue* as well as moral virtue.

Not all virtue ethicists attribute so much importance to habit. The Stoics, in particular, instead focus almost exclusively on reason in the establishment of virtue. Some readings of Plato see him as doing the same. Reason, by these accounts, to establish and enforce virtue must dominate feeling and act according to an independent norm like the natural law or transcendent forms grasped by reason.

What is virtue?

Traditionally, virtue ethicists have collected the virtues together under four cardinal virtues:

1   Wisdom and prudence (*sophia* and *phronesis*, *prudentia*), the virtues of the intellect;
2   Courage or fortitude (*andreia*, *fortitudo*), the virtue of the spirited part of us;
3   Temperance or moderation (*sophrosyne*, *temperantia*, *moderatio*), the virtue of passion, emotion, and desire;
4   Justice (*dike*, *iustitia*), the virtue of harmonizing the first three, as well as the virtue of the civil and political order.

Christian philosophers like Augustine of Hippo and Thomas Aquinas add to these the theological virtues of faith, hope, and love (or charity, *caritas*). One curious contention of virtue ethicists is that there is an intimate link between what good actions are and what the good person does – this for the strange reason that only the good person can know what the good action in any given circumstance is (*Nicomachean Ethics* 1113a32–3). This could be taken to mean that what virtuous people do actually defines or determines what "good" and "bad" are. Or it could mean that only when people achieve sufficient intellectual skill and emotional maturity are they able to apprehend the objective, independent standards of morality. The difference is a significant one, which entails radically alternative metaphysical commitments about moral goodness.

See also

1.10 Flourishing, 2.9 Naturalism, 2.11 Perfectionism, 3.12 Individual/collective

Reading

Aristotle, *Nicomachean Ethics*, edited by Sarah Broadie (Oxford: Oxford University Press, 2002)

Roger Crisp and Michael Slote, eds., *Virtue Ethics* (Oxford: Oxford University Press, 1997)

*Stephen Darwall, *Virtue Ethics* (Oxford: Blackwell, 2002)

Part III

Central Concepts in Ethics

3.1 Absolute/relative

Female genital cutting is wrong. Discuss. But don't expect your discussion to be a calm one. This is one of the most controversial of subjects, to such an extent that it is hard to find a neutral way even to describe it, as many critics insist on referring to it as "female genital mutilation."

To many westerners, the practices of female genital cutting common in Africa and other parts of the world seem to be very, very wrong. Are there any practices that more clearly manifest the ingrained violence against women's bodies and women's pleasures that is pervasive in patriarchal societies – as well as the internalized oppression of the women who live in them?

People, however, also recognize that the practice has a traditional role in some other cultures, a role deeply rooted in cultural identity, aesthetics, coming-of-age rituals, and even resistance to western domination. Besides, who are westerners to judge others? Aren't westerners just cultural imperialists when they insist that because *they* think it is wrong, others must bow to their opinions and abandon their time-honored customs? One would think that in light of the long and bloody history of European and American abuse of Africans, westerners would resist meddling in their affairs.

Which side of the debate one falls down on may well depend on whether one thinks morality is absolute or relative. Morality is *absolute* if it applies to or binds all people or things universally at all times in all places. For this reason, many substitute "universal" for "absolute" when describing this view of morality. Morality is *relative* if it only applies to or binds specific people or things, perhaps only at specific places and times.

The rise of relativism

Sociologically, there's been a major shift over the last few hundred years away from absolutism to relativism. For much of human history, it would have been assumed that moral norms were absolute or universal, not least because most thought they came from an absolute authority: God or something like God. Right is right and wrong is wrong, period. (There is, however, an interesting way in which polytheism, with its acknowledgment that different people have different gods, functioned in a more relativistic way.)

With the rise of modern secular philosophies – like those of Montesquieu (1689–1755), David Hume (1711–76), and Adam Ferguson (1723–1815) – moral relativism has become much more popular, so much so that today people often take it as a truism that what's wrong for one culture or person may not be wrong for another.

The increased popularity of relativism, however, is in part down to a mis-conception. Many in the west value *toleration* and want to avoid anything with the taint of imperialism, and to say that values are relative seems to be one way of doing this. If one's values are relative or limited to his or her own culture, no one has a right to judge the values of other cultures. And, indeed, perhaps it's no accident that modern ideas of toleration and relativism developed simultaneously.

On the other hand, perhaps the relativist argument for toleration over-simplifies matters in more than one respect. First of all, logically speaking, toleration and relativism need not go together. Toleration may, for example, be better thought of as a universal and absolute moral value. Indeed, this is perhaps what many people who think they are relativists actually believe: everyone at all times and in all places should be tolerant. Furthermore, tol-eration need not be a value in a relativist morality. A group may without inconsistency decide that their relative values include a total disregard for the values of others. Might not a relativistically inclined Nazi argue that, "*For us Nazis* anti-Semitism is good, so quit with the criticism"? Then, of course, there's the problem Theodore Schick and Lewis Vaughan have called the "relativists' petard" – that is, the apparently self-contradictory and self-refuting way that relativists hold relativism itself to be an absolute truth.

In any case, it's important to see that moral absolutism and relativism are *metaethical* positions: they are about the *nature* of ethics and not the *content* of specific ethical judgments. That means that while they may be historically connected, there is no logical or necessary link between liberal or imperial-ist values and absolutism or relativism.

Objective and subjective

We should also distinguish between the absolute/relative and the objective/ subjective distinctions. Something is said to be *objective* when it can be said to be true, real, or meaningful irrespective of one's point of view, and *subjective* if it can be said to be true, real, or meaningful only from specific points of view, with reference to a subject. Absolute/relative by contrast has to do with the *range* of the truth, whether or not it holds universally across, geography, culture, history, and persons or is instead intrinsically restricted to some subset of them. It is easy to see why some take each term in the pairs objective–absolute and subjective–relative to be interchangeable, but they're not actually synonymous.

For example, whether or not it proves to be a sustainable position, there is at least sense in the idea that one might hold absolute values, subjectively grounded. You might, for example, believe that it's impossible to ground any moral values objectively, because morality isn't possible or meaning- ful without subjective moral sentiments, feelings, or choices. But you might also think that certain moral claims can be absolute. Not all societies may, for example, possess the institution of vow-taking. But once choosing to enter that institution and take a vow, isn't it absolutely wrong to break it? One might also argue that given the nature of human feeling, clitoridec- tomy is always and everywhere wrong for everyone – even though no moral claim is objective. For sure, that might be a tricky position to defend, but it is not self-evidently contradictory. Danish philosopher Søren Kierke- gaard (1813–55), or at least one of his characters, held that a subjectively grounded commitment to the absolute is just what real faith is about. It's a position deeply bound up with Christian existentialism.

More straightforwardly, it may be both absolutely and objectively true that *morality* is subjective – in the same way that it's absolutely and objec- tively true that preference for flavors of ice cream is subjective. Similarly, it may be absolutely and objectively true that *morality* is relative in the same way that it's absolutely and objectively true that grammar is relative. So, *moral* relativists may not be inconsistent at all in holding the *metaethical* position that moral relativism is objectively and even absolutely true; while ethical claims may be relative, metaethical statements about ethical claims need not be.

The absolute/relative and objective/subjective distinctions are used rather sloppily in public and popular discourses. To use them properly requires mindfulness of two things: first, their precise meanings; and second, the fact that they concern the nature of morality in general and so do not in them- selves tell us anything about how we should or should not behave.

See also

2.14 Relativism, 3.6 Cognitivism/non-cognitivism, 3.20 Metaethics/norma-tive ethics, 5.10 Pluralism

Reading

John Locke, "Letter on Toleration: Humbly Submitted" [1689] (Indian-apolis, IN: Hackett Publishing, 1983)
*Gilbert Harman and Judith Jarvis Thompson, *Moral Relativism and Moral Objectivity* (Oxford: Blackwell, 1996)
*Maria Baghramian, *Relativism* (London: Routledge, 2004)

3.2 Act/rule

As a moral vegan, Conchita thought it was wrong to eat any animal product. But here she was, in a remote part of South America, being offered a dish containing goat's milk from a very hospitable but poor family. And the goat the milk came from led as free a life as you could imagine. But if her self-imposed moral rule about her diet was to mean anything at all, surely she couldn't just ignore it for convenience?

Rules can make moral decision-making easier. But it's very hard to find any substantive moral rule that most of us wouldn't concede has some exceptions. Don't kill – but what if by doing so you could save millions of innocents? Don't lie – but even when national security is at stake? Don't cheat – but even when you are up against a malevolent cheat who will take you to the cleaners if you let him? Should people then just abandon rules, or is there some way of making them flexible enough to deal with the complexities of the real world?

The role of rules

What one needs to get clear about is the role moral rules play. Perhaps the most conventional model places rules between general principles and actions. At the basis of morality are one or more, but generally not many, *basic general principles*. They might, for example, include the golden rule of doing unto others only that which you would have done unto you, or the classical utilitarian principle that one should act in order to maximize the greatest happiness of the greatest number.

These general principles can then be used to generate moral rules. Don't lie, cheat or kill, for example, because doing so will decrease the general happiness, or because you would not have them done unto you. One then follows these rules in particular situations.

On this model, if a particular situation seems to require acting against the rule, the solution may be found by going back to the basic principles behind the rule. One might then find that the principle does not require the exceptionless rule you thought it did, perhaps because the principle generates a number of rules and, in this case, another rule trumps it. In the case of Conchita, it may be, for example, that her basic principle is respect for others and by refusing the meal she is showing less respect to her hosts than she would be to the perfectly content goat. Being a vegan is usually the right way to honor the principle of respect for life, but not always.

The problem for some with this solution, however, is that it seems to make rules no more than rules of thumb. If rules can be overridden by the general principles that stand behind them, then it is the principles that ultimately ground moral judgment and not the rules. In effect, each case must be judged on its own merits, and rules can offer us no more than general guidance as to what is usually the right thing to do.

This is seen as a particular problem for utilitarianism. Many critics say that applied consistently the principle would legitimate gross injustice for the sake of increased general happiness. One could, for example, convict an innocent scapegoat to appease a baying mob. Some defenders of the theory have replied by saying the utilitarian should follow the rules that *generally* promote the greatest happiness (they call this *rule utilitarianism*). That is, one should figure out which *rules* generally maximize happiness and minimize suffering and then stick to the rules, even when in particular cases happiness might have to be sacrificed. This, they argue, is the prudent thing to do since people tend to rationalize their behavior in particular cases, always finding some way to make it seem right. But, on the other hand, doesn't sacrificing happiness in particular cases undermine the very principle of utilitarianism? Perhaps, when deciding what the right thing to do is, one should judge by referring only to basic principles so that rules just drop out of the equation. Would that really pose a significant problem?

Acts first, rules later

A yet more radical response is to say that morality works precisely the other way around. Rather than deriving rules from principles and then assessing particular acts, really one should always judge what is the right thing to do by seeing what particular act is right in that circumstance. This view is called moral particularism, because it rests on the idea that each case is unique, and because of this the right thing to do can't be discerned simply by appealing to general principles.

In a similar way, act utilitarians say that one should judge simply whether or not the particular act at hand maximizes happiness and minimizes suffering. Like moral particularism, then, act utilitarianism restricts moral reflection to the particular situation under consideration. But the two views are very much unlike one another in that act utilitarianism says that there is always and only one thing that makes acts right, i.e., that the acts maximize utility. Particularism, by contrast, denies that there is anything that is always morally relevant, much less decisive.

Moral particularism seems counter-intuitive, but it can explain why it is that societies seem to have developed good moral rules and principles. It's not surprising that similar cases demand similar responses, and so patterns emerge in moral judgments. For example, if in 99 particular cases out of 100, lying is found to be wrong, it's easy to decide that "lying is wrong" should become a rule. At the level of the rules themselves similarities also become evident, and so it becomes possible to abstract from collections of rules to even more general principles. It becomes, then, helpful to formulate these rules and principles in theories, codes, and laws. But the important thing to remember here is that rules and principles originate in particular judgments about which individual acts are right or wrong; they do not themselves determine these judgments. Morality works from acts up, not principles down.

The act/rule distinction is most often invoked in the context of debates about utilitarianism. But as we have seen, it is actually a distinction with much wider significance for the nature of morality in general.

See also

2.10 Particularism, 3.19 Means/ends, 5.12 Radical particularity

Reading

John Rawls, "Two Concepts of Rules," *Philosophical Review*, 64 (1955): 3–32
*William H. Shaw, *Taking Account of Utilitarianism* (Oxford: Blackwell, 1998)
Stephen Darwall, ed., *Consequentialism* (Oxford: Blackwell, 2002)

3.3 Bad/evil

George W. Bush was ridiculed for characterizing three other nations as an "axis of evil." The ridicule was largely political, suggesting that the phrase was imprudent. But there was something more. Some of the criticism hinged upon the notion that the very concept of "evil" is somehow quaint, naive, or simple-minded. Was this criticism warranted?

When asking whether evil exists, it's necessary to distinguish between natural and moral evil. Natural evils include things like earthquakes, plagues, floods, tsunamis, and other natural events that cause tremendous suffering. Ancient Epicureans made much of this category of evil, while moderns like Voltaire (1694–1778) in his 1759 story, *Candide*, and Hume in his 1777 *Dialogues Concerning Natural Religion* argued that the existence of such evils made the existence of a good, all-powerful God deeply problematic, if not impossible. Religious thinkers, on the other hand, have often regarded natural evils as punishments for our sins.

Manichean dualism

Most of the time, however, when people talk about evil they're taking about moral evil – not bad things that "just happen" but bad things that are the result of human or supernatural agency. A striking example of using the concept of evil may be found in Manicheanism – named after the third-century Persian thinker Manes, who maintained that two opposing deities pervade the world, one good and one evil. Doing what's wrong, then, according to Manicheanism, is to align oneself with the dark in the cosmic battle. It's a stark and dualistic way of thinking about morality and the world, one where evil isn't simply a lack or a corruption of something good but is rather its own kind of being, an actual anti-good.

Evil or ignorance? Weakness or rebellion?

There's another tradition, however, different from Manichean dualism, that attributes wrongdoing not to positive evil, but negatively to ignorance or deficiency. In the *Apology, Symposium, Republic*, and elsewhere, Plato's Socrates, for example, argues that immorality is a species of error and ignorance. Knowing the good entails being good, and conversely being good entails knowing the good. If someone isn't good, then according to Socrates that person must be ignorant of the good. One reason to think this is true, according to Plato's texts, is that doing what's bad by its very nature actually harms the wrongdoer just as it harms others, and no one would knowingly harm him or herself. Therefore no one knowingly does what's bad.

Augustine (345–430) regarded the immorality-as-ignorance thesis as sheer poppycock. Augustine argued that people can and often do both (a) knowingly and (b) intentionally engage in conduct that's morally wrong, even when they clearly understand what's right and good. This intentional rebellion is different from what Aristotle called *akrasia* or moral weakness – that is, being overwhelmed and driven to do wrong by an impulse or desire despite knowing that the action is wrong. This rebellion, unlike *akrasia*, purposely acts against goodness (and for Augustine against God, too, the ultimate ground of goodness). Immoral rebellion is better described by a term with more gravity than "bad"; with rebellion, badness becomes "evil."

Immorality as diminished being

Bad or evil has also been understood to be what is degenerate or corrupt (by Plato and Augustine included). Morality on this account isn't simply about doing what's good; it's also about *being* good. Knowing, doing, and being good amount to realizing certain human excellences, perfections, or virtues; and realizing these perfections is realizing our very being. Immorality, then, means not only doing what's bad or evil or even being bad or evil. It actually means becoming less human. A bad man is in a very real sense less of a man than a good man. Even Satan is not an anti-God, the opposite of goodness. He is rather a degenerate form of something very good, a fallen angel. Neo-Platonists like Plotinus (third century CE), Proclus (*c.* 410–85), Pseudo-Dionysius (*c.* 500), and Boethius (*c.* 480–525/6) did much to advance this view.

Rethinking evil

Friedrich Nietzsche (1844–1900) believed that all this Christian-Platonic nonsense needed to be shaken off and replaced with "transvalued" values that retrieve the original meanings of moral terms. Nietzsche held that "good" originally referred to the strong individuals who created, led, and dominated a culture. "Bad" denoted the weak, the followers, the cultural subordinates of the strong and creative. It was Christian-Platonic culture that inverted these meanings, cleverly using them against the strong, so that "good" became abstract and metaphysical, associated with purity, the denial of the body and desire, humility, obedience, and sacrifice. "Bad" became "evil" under the slogan, "Blessed be the meek." Using these conceptual weapons, the weak had successfully seized the (moral) world from the strong.

In a different way, German philosopher Hannah Arendt (1906–75) tried to transform our concept of evil. If anything is evil, the Holocaust is evil; and if anyone is evil, Adolf Eichmann (1906–62), the architect of the Nazi *Endlösung* or Final Solution, is evil. Nazis like Eichmann are often thought of as monstrous, somehow non-human beings. But when Arendt (a Jew herself) finally laid eyes on Eichmann during his 1961 trial in Israel, she saw not a monster but an ordinary human being, a dull and commonplace bureaucrat whose everyday activities produced the murder, abuse, and impoverishment of millions of people. Hence she found in Eichmann what she called a "banality of evil." Part of the horror she confronted is the discovery that evil is today no grand, cosmic affair. None of us is terribly different from the worst among us, and the banal mechanisms of our ordinary lives can, if we aren't careful, give rise to the most hideous of crimes.

See also

3.4 Beneficence/non-maleficence, 5.1 *Akrasia*, 5.5 Fallenness

Reading

Augustine, St, *Confessions* [late fourth century], translated by Rex Warner (New York: Penguin, 1963)
*Friedrich Nietzsche, *On the Genealogy of Morals* [1887] *and Ecce Homo*, translated by Walter Kaufmann and R. J. Hollingdale (New York: Vintage Books, 1967)
Hannah Arendt, *Eichmann in Jerusalem: A Report on the Banality of Evil* [1963], revised edition (New York: Penguin Books, 1994)

3.4 Beneficence/non-maleficence

A woman is walking along the street, and her pocketbook falls out of her purse. Another woman sees this and just walks on by without saying anything. A third spots it, picks it up and gives it back to the woman who dropped it. But then the pocketbook falls out again. A fourth woman sees the pocketbook, picks it up and walks off with it.

The third woman has clearly behaved well. She has shown *beneficence* – kindness and goodness toward others, intentionally acting to serve the others' good. The fourth woman has clearly behaved badly. She has shown *maleficence* – unkindness, cruelty, or other wrongs toward others, intentionally acting to others' detriment. (Maleficence shouldn't be confused with *malfeasance*, a related term that means intentionally wrong or illegal conduct, but is generally restricted to contexts of politics, business, and public service.) But what of the second woman, the one who just walked on? She failed to be *beneficent*, but was she actually *maleficent*? After all, she didn't actually take the purse from the woman. Did she do wrong, or did she simply do neither right nor wrong? Is it possible to be neutral is such situations?

It seems that there are two ways of not being bad: (1) being good to others (beneficence) by positively acting in ways that serve their good and (2) simply not being bad to them (non-maleficence) by not acting, by neither positively serving their good nor negatively harming them, while perhaps allowing them to be harmed. But is there a difference between harming others and allowing others to be harmed? How do these two strands of acting and not-acting fit together? Is morality mainly about beneficence or simply non-maleficence? And is it good enough to just be non-maleficent?

First, do no harm?

The command, "First, do no harm" has been attributed both to the Roman physician, Galen of Pergamum (131–201 CE), and to the Greek Hippocrates (460–380 BCE). The imperative was directed at professional physicians, not the people at large. Nevertheless, it can be borrowed to suggest that avoiding harmful acts is the first priority of ethics. Only after achieving this should one worry about actively promoting good. That may seem rather negative, but there are plenty of moral systems that stress what to avoid rather than what to do. Of the Ten Commandments, for example, eight are prohibitions; the only two positive exhortations are to honor one's parents and to keep the Sabbath day holy.

Different moral frameworks tend to weight beneficence and non-maleficence differently. The ethics of the Pentateuch, for example, is based on the idea of a fallen humankind. As such, it's largely concerned with fighting the human tendency to sin. The morality of the Gospels, by contrast, seems more concerned with love of one's neighbor and actively showing kindness. Jesus of Nazareth, as he's depicted in the Gospels, seems less interested in chastizing sinners, such as prostitutes and adulterers, than in encouraging others to forgive and help them.

The difference in emphasis between beneficence and non-maleficence indicates something of the differences between *consequentialist* and *deontological* ethical systems. Deontological ethics focuses on our *duties* to others, and most such duties are negative: one should not harm, attack, slander, lie, or steal. Deontological ethics stipulate fewer duties to actually be nice, kind, caring, hospitable, or generous. So, deontological ethics tends to promote non-maleficence above beneficence.

Consequentialist ethics, on the other hand, is based on the idea that one should always do the act or follow the rule that leads to the best consequences (although what "best" means varies according to different consequentialist ethics). Doing good is better than both doing bad and doing neither good nor bad. So, consequentialist ethics promotes not simply non-maleficence but actual beneficence. Moreover, from a consequentialist point of view, one is culpable for failing to stop harm as well as for actually causing harm – so long as the causing and preventing were more or less equally within one's powers and the costs of prevention were not prohibitive. For the consequentialist one should not only *avoid causing suffering or harm*; one should also *reduce suffering or harm and promote happiness and flourishing*.

Do people have obligations to the hungry and poor?

To return to the woman and her dropped pocketbook, most people would conclude that the second woman behaved wrongly. The only disagreement would be how wrong she was. For a consequentialist, the failure to act benevolently when the opportunity to do so was so easy is a significant moral failing. The deontologist may still condemn her. But as she didn't engage in a *crime of commission* (actually steal, lie, or do any other wrong), her simple *crime of omission* would be less serious.

The disagreement, however, can be much more stark once one turns to situations where the opportunity to do good is not quite so immediate. Consider the plight of the world's hungry and poor, for example. If one thinks the positive obligation of beneficence is as important as that of non-maleficence, then it is a serious moral failing not to do a great deal to help feed them and relieve their poverty. But if one regards non-maleficence as more important than beneficence, then their plight, while pitiful and tragic, is not something one is duty-bound to relieve. This is a much more serious moral dispute than figuring out whether or not people should condemn someone who doesn't tell a passer-by she has dropped her pocketbook. It takes us to a core question concerning what it means to be moral.

See also

2.4 Deontological ethics, 3.7 Commission/omission, 3.13 Injury, 5.16 Supererogation

Reading

*Peter Singer, *Practical Ethics*, 2nd edition (Cambridge: Cambridge University Press, 1993)

Garett Cullity, *The Moral Demands of Affluence* (Oxford: Oxford University Press, 2004)

Tim Mulgan, *The Demands of Consequentialism*, new edition (Oxford: Oxford University Press, 2005)

3.5 Cause/reason

On the morning of June 28, 1914, Gavrilo Princip fired two bullets into the automobile carrying Archduke Franz Ferdinand and his wife Sophie, killing them both and igniting World War I. We can ask "What were the *causes* of Princip's conduct?" and "What were the *reasons* for Princip's conduct?"

We might say (hypothetically) that Princip's attack might have been *caused* by things like his having been abused as a child, a malignancy in his brain, his having been socialized to believe that violence is the way to resolve conflict, his suffering a schizophrenic delusion, his having been exploited by the ruling class, etc. His *reasons* for killing Ferdinand, however, may have been rather different, including things like: weakening the grip of the Austro-Hungarian empire on Serbia, sending a message to the aristocracy that its moment in history had come to an end, or fulfilling a perceived moral obligation (perhaps to keep a promise he made to avenge the death of a fallen comrade).

Cause and justifications

The distinction between asking about the causes of conduct and the reasons for conduct is related to the difference between "causal explanations" and "moral justifications." Causal explanations attempt to understand human conduct as the effect of some causal order, an order that can be described by various scientific laws (the *ordo essendi*). This entails conceiving of human conduct as part of the natural order or some other causal order, something many wish to resist. Moreover, causal explanations do not entail moral assessment. To explain someone's conduct is not necessarily to make a moral judgment about it.

Moral justification, by contrast, involves presenting reasons that demonstrate that the conduct under scrutiny is morally permissible or even obligatory. Moral justification and *excuse*, then, involve making ethical claims. Appeals to reasons can also be made in explanation, but to explain is not to justify or to excuse.

Some hold that reasoning that leads to moral action is part of a distinct kind of order (the *ordo cognoscendi*). The things that happen in causal orders happen in a necessary and deterministic way, but orders of reasoning and reflection from this point of view don't. It seems to be one thing to say: given (a) all humans are mortal and (b) Socrates is a human, it necessarily follows as a matter of logic that (c) Socrates is mortal. It seems quite another thing to say: given social conditioning, chemical brain processes, my contingent psychological make-up and so forth, I am caused to think that Socrates is mortal. Indeed, for thinkers like Immanuel Kant (1724–1804), moral acts by definition can't be the necessary effects of causes; it only makes sense to call acts moral when they are freely done on the basis of reason (see 1.2 Agency).

Not so distinct?

The boundary between explanation and moral justification can, however, become rather vague. For example, someone's reasons can be cited in explanations of behavior, such as when someone demands, "Explain yourself!" Reasons can be seen as causes at least in the sense that they serve as motives which move us to act.

Some philosophers have worked against the distinction between reasons and causes. Benedictus Spinoza (1632–77) thought that reasons and causes are actually the same things understood in different ways (see his *Ethics*, 1677). Similarly, G. W. F. Hegel (1770–1831) and Arthur Schopenhauer (1788–1860) postulated a common basis for causes and reasons, while still maintaining their difference. In a strange way, for Hegel, in fact, reasons and causes are both rooted in a deeper metaphysical reason he calls "*Vernunft*." Schopenhauer rooted them both in something called the Will. More recently, naturalistically inclined philosophers (and there are a lot of them) have tried to understand moral reasoning in naturalistic, causal terms – that is, as a strictly natural process. For example, Paul Russell (b. 1955) has interpreted David Hume's (1711–76) work this way.

Final cause

A more ancient conception of cause (*aitia*) is also relevant to ethics, namely what Aristotle called the "final cause" (*Metaphysics* I.3). The final cause is not a cause in the contemporary sense at all, but is the end (*telos*), purpose, or fullest realization of something. The final cause of an acorn is the mature, healthy oak. The final cause of an infant is the human adult contemplating eternal truth. The ethical dimension of final causes is this: in evaluating the moral propriety of an action or policy, one must judge whether it inhibits or encourages or is consistent with the achievement of a relevant final cause. If it isn't, it can't be morally proper.

See also

1.4 Autonomy, 2.9 Naturalism, 2.13 Rationalism

Reading

*Immanuel Kant, *Groundwork for the Metaphysics of Morals* [1785], edited by Allen Wood (New Haven, CT: Yale University Press, 2002)
Arthur Schopenhauer, *The World as Will and Representation* [1819, 1844], 2 vols., translated by E. F. J. Payne (London: Dover, 1996)
Paul Russell, *Freedom and Moral Sentiment: Hume's Way of Naturalizing Responsibility* (Oxford: Oxford University Press, 1995)

3.6 Cognitivism/non-cognitivism

Is God a trinity? Set aside for one moment what the answer to this question is and consider instead what *kinds* of answers are possible. One kind of answer, for example, would be to make a claim stating what the facts are. But is it possible to state answers to such questions as matters of fact? Even if there are actually "facts" about such things, can anyone know them? Might the answers instead be mere matters of opinion, so that saying God is a trinity is sort of like saying strawberries are delicious – it's just what people who share that opinion think? And if it's not possible to state the facts of the matter, would that mean either (a) that any answer purporting to do so is *false* or (b) that there is simply no *meaningful* distinction to be made between the true and the false in such instances?

These distinctions are tricky enough with alleged facts. But they can also be applied to moral questions. Consider the question, "Is cannibalism wrong?" One can first ask whether this question is about some sort of fact. And if it isn't, does that mean that all possible answers are personal opinions, social conventions, or something else such that "true" and "false" simply have no meaning here? Or, alternatively, if there's no fact of the matter but it seems as though a truth-value (true or false) should be assigned, does that mean all answers are in a sense false (or true)? Of course, even if there is a fact of the matter with regard to this question (and hence it makes sense to say that answers to the question may be either true or false), could anyone ever know what it is?

Realists and cognitivists

Those who think there are facts of the form "such and such is morally right or wrong" are called *moral realists*. If, in addition, they think that such facts can be known, they are called *cognitivists*. Those who deny there is any fact of the matter about which acts are morally right or wrong are called *non-realists* or *anti-realists*. Some non-realists think that their position entails that all moral judgments are therefore meaningless. But others disagree. They think that although there are no moral facts one can *know*, moral judgments are still meaningful, albeit neither true nor false. In other words, the language of morals is meaningful, but it doesn't produce conclusions properly called "knowledge." Such people are known as *non-cognitivists*.

In many ways, cognitivism is the most immediately attractive of the positions. If there are such things as moral facts, and one can know them, then people stand some chance of building a rigorous ethics on a secure foundation. Moral values would be as real as atoms or doughnuts and, if we could know them, they would be as indisputable and authoritative as basic facts about the physical world around us.

The problem is that it is hard to see how there could be such things as moral facts. Facts generally concern things we can see, measure, or observe, directly or indirectly. But the idea that we could see, measure, or observe moral principles seems to be absurd. It is true that there are also facts about how people feel and what they think, but these are facts only about the people themselves, not about the general nature of reality. So even though there are facts about what people feel or believe to be right or wrong, that doesn't give moral values the kind of *objectivity* moral realism demands. Moreover, how could one ever know these facts in the way cognitivism claims? It is hard even to imagine how this would be possible without positing some kind of moral sense or intuition that could detect these facts.

Non-realists and non-cognitivists

That doesn't mean that the alternatives to realism are any more attractive, however. Those non-realists, like A. J. Ayer (1910–89), who claim that moral judgments are not true or false but literally meaningless seem to rob us of one of the most important features of human life. Can we imagine living without any moral values at all?

Most non-cognitivists, on the other hand, don't want to go that far. While they argue, like Ayer et al., that moral claims are not about facts that can be known, they nevertheless maintain that moral claims are far from meaningless. Moral sentimentalists, such as Adam Smith (1723–90) and David Hume (1711–76), argue that moral judgments spring from natural benevolent impulses, such as sympathy and affection, which are rooted in emotional reactions to others and their conduct. People say it's wrong to hurt people needlessly, for example, because they can sympathetically feel the pain that results and because that sort of action offends their moral sensibilities. In a sense, therefore, one *feels* that needless harm is something to be avoided. Reason's role is to help us order these feelings, figure out the causes and effects relevant to the situation, and respond effectively. Reasoning, from this point of view, does not *discover* objective moral truths.

Realists will object, however, that this way of thinking leaves morality without any proper basis at all. If, ultimately, everything just rests on feeling, then how can people argue with those whose feelings are malevolent or perverse, not to mention those who lack moral feeling altogether?

The dilemma is therefore stark. Cognitivists believe that morality is grounded in facts that just don't seem to be there, while non-cognitivists believe morality is grounded in sentiments that don't seem to provide it with anything like an adequate basis. Moral theorists are therefore left in the same position as many shoppers: It seems that what we need isn't available and what is available isn't good enough.

See also

1.13 Intuition, 2.9 Naturalism, 5.14 Skepticism

Reading

*J. L. Mackie, *Ethics: Inventing Right and Wrong* (Harmondsworth, Middlesex: Pelican Books, 1977)

David Owen Brink, *Moral Realism and the Foundation of Ethics* (Cambridge: Cambridge University Press, 1989)
*Geoffrey Sayre-McCord, *Essays on Moral Realism* (Ithaca, NY: Cornell University Press, 1989)

3.7 Commission/omission

Bjorn hates Hans and wishes he were dead. Hans has no idea Bjorn thinks this way, otherwise he wouldn't be so foolish as to take his car into Bjorn's garage to get it serviced. Bjorn fully intends to take advantage of this situation by cutting the brake fluid cable on Hans's car, knowing that there are some treacherous downhill bends on the route away from the garage. But when he goes to make the cut he finds that the cables are already broken. They have just worn through. Bjorn obviously doesn't bother to fix them and Hans does indeed crash and die. Has Bjorn got away with murder, or is it more accurate to say he has got a way with it?

The difference between what people do (*commission*) and what they fail to do (*omission*) seems clear enough. But there are two ways in which the distinction swiftly becomes muddied. The first concerns its moral significance: It might be more accurate to say that Bjorn let Hans die rather than say that he killed him, but given that Bjorn's intentions and abilities to affect the outcome were the same in either scenario, does that make him any less guilty?

The second questions whether or not the distinction holds up, anyway. People often do one thing by doing another. So, for example, I turn on the lights by flicking the switch. But can we sometimes do one thing by *not* doing another? There do seem to be plenty of *prima facie* examples of just this. We deceive people by not revealing things that we know they don't know, that they should know, and that we could easily tell them. We break the law by not paying our taxes. We prevent people from doing things by not giving the permission they need. And so on.

So although it's clear enough that Bjorn simply didn't fix the brake lines rather than actually cut them, this doesn't mean it's obvious he didn't commit murder. Can't one commit murder by not warning someone of an imminent danger just as well as by actually putting that danger in his or her way?

Killing and letting die

This issue has profound implications for medical ethics. How is allowing someone to die when medical treatment is likely to keep that individual alive (which is standard procedure in most hospitals) different from actually administering (even with the patient's consent) a sufficient amount of a deadly drug to kill her (which, at least outside the Netherlands, is commonly illegal)? The former is sometimes called *passive euthanasia*, the latter *active euthanasia*. In both cases the patient dies, but in the latter case the physician actively takes part in the killing, while in the former the physician simply, as they say, lets nature take its course. Does this make a moral difference? Whether it does or not, it seems clear to most people that normally the fact that something is the result of an omission rather than a commission does not in itself mean that no one can be held responsible for it. The disputes concern whether this affects the seriousness of any wrongdoing, and why it is still a wrongdoing.

The culpability of omission

One might argue that people can be morally culpable for their omissions on two grounds. The first is that of *intention*. If what's crucial for moral judgment is the intention of the agent, then what matters is not whether something is brought about by commission or omission, but that it was *intended to happen by someone who could have acted to bring about a different consequence*. Thus, in the case of Bjorn, the fact that he intended to kill Hans and could have repaired the brake line makes him just as culpable as if he had cut it himself.

This line of argument seems very strong. Yet, people still intuitively feel that there's something worse about actually cutting the line than just not fixing it. Perhaps our intuitions are just plain wrong here. But it's also possible they're rooted in an insight into human nature. Perhaps it takes more malevolent effort to act to cause harm, and merely letting harm happen is more a sign of weakness than wickedness. That's why, even though many do not think omissions are exempt from moral censure, they can be less serious than acts.

A second reason to hold us to account for omissions is that morality is for many about the consequences of what we do *and* don't do. Consequences are all, so we are not let off the hook just because some consequences are the result of what we fail to do.

The problem with this line of argument, though, is that it may make us responsible for too much. All sorts of bad things are happening which I could prevent, but I don't. Merely by living a comfortable western life-style and not dedicating my life or income to relieving suffering means bad things are happening that I could have prevented. Perhaps this does make me culpable. Ted Honderich has, in fact, argued that the enormity of western omissions in remedying the suffering of other parts of the world is large enough to justify poorer nations launching attacks against the west (*Terrorism for Humanity*, 2003). On the other hand, there are arguably duties one has to one's self, and an excessive devotion to the needs of others must imply failing in those duties.

No matter how the line is drawn, however, it does seem definite that morality is concerned not only with commissions but with omissions, too. Many things about the case of Bjorn and Hans may be unclear, but that Bjorn is morally culpable for the death of Hans is surely indisputable.

See also

1.2 Agency, 3.14 Intentions/consequences, 5.13 The separateness of persons

Reading

Frances Myrna Kamm, "Harming, Not Aiding, and Positive Rights," *Philosophy and Public Affairs* 15(1) (Winter 1986): 3–32
R. G. Frey and Christopher Wellman, *Blackwell Companion to Applied Ethics* (Oxford: Blackwell, 2003)
Bonnie Steinbock and Alastair Norcross, eds., *Killing and Letting Die*, 2nd edition (New York: Fordham University Press, 2004)

3.8 Consent

In the summer of 1973, a propane gas tank exploded at a small house in Texas, severely injuring a young athlete and military veteran, Donald "Dax" Cowart. Dax was blinded and suffered third-degree burns over more than 65 percent of his body. The heat from the explosion and subsequent fire was so intense that it literally fused a number of his fingers together. Cowart's father died in the blast.

In hospital Dax was forced to undergo – despite repeated objections – agonizing procedures, such as saline baths. When told that without them he would die, Dax clearly indicated that he preferred to do so. A psychiatrist found him mentally competent.

Though he remained severely disfigured and blind, and lost a number of fingers, Dax recovered. Later he married and became an attorney, specializing in patients' rights. Believe it or not, he still maintains that he should have been permitted to die. Why? Because he believes that no one should be forced to undergo medical treatment without his or her consent – even if the treatment will help.

This may seem a strange position, since it permits people to choose to suffer and even die when they might be healed, but it has come to dominate much contemporary ethical discourse, especially in medical ethics. The law has enshrined it in the doctrine known as "informed consent." One might say that informed consent places rights above the good. By this we mean that the requirement of consent recognizes a *right* to refuse even what is *good*. We have the right to choose badly, especially in matters concerned with something as intimate and personal as one's body.

At the heart of this doctrine is the notion of autonomy. Autonomous individuals must be able to determine for themselves the course of their lives and the disposition of their bodies with a minimum of interference – paternalistic, beneficent, or otherwise. To truly consent, one must consent:

1 freely
2 without coercion
3 without compromising stress, emotion, or intoxication
4 with knowledge and understanding of things relevant.

Each of these requirements has its complexities. What exactly is freedom, and to what extent are we really free? What's to count as coercion? When is stress or emotion an inhibiting factor? What knowledge is relevant? It might take days to explain all the possible effects of a medical procedure, and most of us probably wouldn't understand them even then. At the very least, however, informed consent requires that one understand what is likely to happen in the near future upon giving consent, why it is going to happen, what the more distant consequences are likely to be, and what alternatives are possible and available.

Competency

There's something else, however, in addition to the four requirements above. In order to meet all these requirements in a meaningful way one must possess emotional maturity and more than a simplistic grasp of how the world works, as well as a well developed and functioning capacity for reason. Philosophers collect these sorts of ideas under the requirement of competency. Very young children and the mentally impaired can't reasonably be expected to be competent in these ways – even though they may in limited ways be free, have knowledge, etc. In their cases someone must be invested with the power and authority to consent or refuse consent for them, perhaps even against their wishes. Other people can be invested with this power and authority through devices such as power of attorney, parenthood, guardianship, and conservatorship.

Conflicts between the aged, those who care for them, and the state are notoriously difficult on these grounds. Should, for example, an elderly woman who often falls when trying to walk, whose memory is failing, and whose house and clothing have become filthy, be forcibly removed from the home in which she's lived for the past 60 years and be placed against her will in a nursing home?

When teenagers who are considered too young to consent to many other things seek an abortion, things become extremely contentious, indeed. Should minors be required to obtain their parents' consent for an abortion? Should they have to obtain the consent of a judge or other state official? And, of course, there are still other complexities related to consent.

Implied and presumed consent

Must consent be explicitly stated, or can one reasonably infer consent from someone's actions? Does the use of public services, for example, imply that one consents to the authority of the state? The question becomes terribly and sometimes tragically difficult in cases of sexual conduct and misconduct. When precisely is it proper for someone to conclude that someone else has consented to a sexual encounter? Are physical gestures enough? Does one lose the ability to consent after one, three, or eight glasses of wine? This is no small matter. It draws a line separating romance from rape.

For the most part, positive expressions of consent are taken to be necessary for consent to be recognized. But in some cases perhaps it's better to presume that consent is given *unless some negative expression indicates that consent is refused*. For example, if the victim of an automobile accident has been rendered unconscious, we presume that he or she wishes to receive medical care – unless she's given some sort of advanced directive not to be. The US case of Terri Schiavo in 2005 centered on this issue. People are often advised to state their wishes about the sorts of things to which they would and wouldn't consent through instruments like living wills and other advanced directives (see 1.4 Autonomy).

Because of the shortage of organs suitable for transplant, many have argued that everyone should be presumed to have consented to donate their organs when they die – unless they've indicated that they *do not consent*. In places like the UK, however, things currently work the other way around: people are presumed not to have consented to organ donation, unless they've already indicated their consent. Presumed consent for donation certainly would increase the number of organs available to people who desperately need them. But would it presume too much?

See also

1.4 Autonomy, 1.19 Rights, 3.4 Beneficence/non-maleficence

Reading

*Ruth R. Faden, Tom L. Beauchamp, and Nancy M. P. King, eds., *A History and Theory of Informed Consent* (Oxford: Oxford University Press, 1986)

Jessica W. Berg, Paul S. Appelbaum, Lisa S. Parker, Charles W. Lidz, *Informed Consent: Legal Theory and Clinical Practice*, 2nd edition (Oxford: Oxford University Press, 2001)

Alan Wertheimer, *Consent to Sexual Relations* (Cambridge: Cambridge University Press, 2003)

3.9 Facts/values

Women can feed infants through lactation. Ten days from conception, it is still not finally determined whether a fetus will go on to divide into twins. Cocoa bought at market price does not guarantee a living wage to growers.

These are all facts. None are beyond dispute, but all are generally accepted by those who are experts in the given subject areas. Many people, however, believe that facts such as these also have a *normative* content: that is to say, they tell us something about the way things *ought* to be. In somewhat simplified terms, there are those who think that because women can feed infants through lactation, they ought to be the primary caregivers of children; that because the identity of any child or children that would be born from the embryo at 10 days remains undetermined, there would be nothing wrong with aborting it; or that we should buy cocoa at above market price if that guarantees a decent income to growers. In each case a link is being made between facts and values.

Mind the gaps

The nature of this link is, however, deeply problematic. The main problem is that no argument that rests on purely factual premises can generate a conclusion that tells us what we ought to do. There is a gap between a statement like "the 10-day-old fetus is not yet a distinct individual" and "it ought to be permissible to abort such a fetus." Where did this "ought" come from? Not from the premise, since that only describes what *is*, not what *ought to be*.

This is known, rather unimaginatively, as the "is/ought gap." At its most basic, it's a merely logical point about how arguments work. No evaluative conclusions can come from non-evaluative premises, period. So, any jump from talk about facts to talk about values is unjustified. David Hume (1711–76) famously argued this point in his 1740 *A Treatise of Human Nature*, Book III, Part i, §1.

The alleged "fact/value distinction" often goes beyond this logical claim to insist that facts and values belong to entirely separate domains. This idea seems less plausible. For instance, surely we need to know the facts about the nature of the fetus before we can arrive at any moral judgments about how it should be treated? Consider also, for example, how the moral repugnance of racism is tied to the fact that racial superiority is a scientific myth. What then is the link between facts and values if it is not a logical one?

Making the connection: fact and feeling

There are various ways one might try to link facts and values. One is to show that the gap is illusory because apparently factual terms are imbued with evaluative content. The concept of "person," for example, is in part that of a moral category. To be a person is not just to be a physical type but to have certain moral rights. Therefore, the question of whether a fetus is a person or not, although in part a matter of fact, also possesses an ineliminable moral aspect. Similarly, the concept of an "adequate income" is also partly moral, because "adequate" can only be understood in relation to some notion of what a person *ought* to have in order to lead a reasonably full life. Even apparently biological concepts, such as "woman" for example, carry social and evaluative content as well. This critical strategy effectively denies that there is a fact/value distinction and insists that at most there is a blurred boundary between the factual and the evaluative.

Another strategy is to bridge the gap, but not by logic. This seems to be Hume's approach. Hume and other "moral subjectivists" argue that morality itself is not rooted in reason but in feeling or sentiment. Therefore, no moral judgments (no "ought" statements) are exclusively the product or jurisdiction of reason.

Nevertheless, how people feel is informed by what they think; and in this way reason may affect sentiment. So it is, for instance, that people who hold theoretically (albeit wrongly) that certain racial groups are superior to others are likely to feel that there's nothing wrong in treating them as inferiors. Reason also brings to light the facts of various causal systems, knowledge of which may affect moral judgment. Knowing the effects of radiation on the human body, for example, may have an effect on one's judgments concerning the use of nuclear weapons or depleted uranium ordnance. The role of facts is thus to inform our feelings, and doing so sometimes changes them. One simply needs to accept that such changes in moral judgment do not follow logically from the facts themselves.

Critics of this approach argue that it leaves too much down to rationally unjustifiable impulse. What if, for example, a racist learns all the facts about "race" and continues to be prejudiced nonetheless? Because we accept that no values flow inexorably from the facts, how can we criticize him or her for persisting in spite of the facts?

Perhaps moral persuasion and criticism then must involve cultivating certain feelings, sentiments, and sensibilities as well as advancing sound arguments. Thinking about ethics, then, may involve art and literature as well as ethical theory. Richard Rorty (b. 1931), for instance, argues that morality is best discussed through fiction. Perhaps, but however one resolves the difficulty, everyone should accept that there is no simple way of moving from "X is how things are" to "X is how things ought to be."

See also

1.15 Natural law, 2.9 Naturalism

Reading

M. C. Doeser and J. N. Kraay, eds., *Facts and Values: Philosophical Reflections from Western and Non-Western Perspectives* (Dordrecht: Martinus Nijhoff, 1986)

Richard B. Brandt, *Facts, Values, and Morality* (Cambridge: Cambridge University Press, 1996)

Hilary Putnam, *The Collapse of the Fact/Value Dichotomy and Other Essays* (Cambridge, MA: Harvard University Press, 2002)

3.10 The golden mean

The two *Star Wars* trilogies (or the sextet, if you will) portray a classical dualistic view of right and wrong, good and evil. Although (in an apparent nod to the "Tao," of Taoism) "the force" is just one thing with good and dark "sides," morality is essentially portrayed as a series of either/ors.

Although it's common to point out that in real life morality is about shades of gray as well as black and white, the dualistic or binary model still remains the default way of thinking about ethics. Some call this moral dualism *Manicheanism,* after the ancient sect which held that the universe is a place where two opposing deities, one purely good and the other purely evil, struggle against one another. Other philosophical movements, like Pythagoreanism, also advanced dualistic views. Later critics, for example those working in feminist philosophies and deconstruction, have tried to subvert binary models. In any case, whether or not there's a sharp line or a fuzzy border between them and whether or not it would be better to undermine them, the typical binary model presents the dualistic moral alternatives as diametrically opposed. Each virtue, for example, commonly has its opposing vice.

Vice	Virtue
Greed	Generosity
Pride	Humility
Cowardice	Courage

A very different way of conceptualizing right and wrong, however, was developed by Aristotle (384–322 BCE). He thought that virtues should be thought of as the right balance between, on the one hand, a *deficiency* and, on the other hand, an *excess*. Hence, rather than thinking of two terms (a virtue and its corresponding vice) you need to think of three (a virtue, its vice of deficiency, and its vice of excess). For the examples above, that would work out as:

Vice	Virtue	Vice
Greed	Generosity	Wastefulness
Meekness	Humility	Pride
Cowardice	Courage	Rashness

In some cases, the language doesn't make clear which is a vice and which is a virtue. For example, humility can be a vice if it is excessive, and similarly, pride is a virtue as long as it is proportionate. In other cases, the word itself tells us whether the quality is to be prized or pilloried: courage is always good, and cowardice always bad.

Advantages of the schema

This is a remarkably powerful way of schematizing virtues and vices. Indeed, it seems that any virtue or vice can be understood in this way, even if words don't exist for each of the three terms. Take, for example, kindness. It might be thought that this is something you can have too little of, but never too much. But there is a type of excess of kindness that can be patronizing, disempowering, or smothering. You might also think that viciousness is not something you can have too little of. But, if the mean is gentleness, it can also be seen that it is possible to be too gentle, because sometimes you have to be firm and assertive.

This way of thinking takes us some way from the conventional one that sees good and evil as forces in opposition. Because being good is essentially about finding a *balance* or *harmony*, it makes little sense to see it as being opposed by something called "evil." In Nietzsche's terms, it suggests a morality of good and *bad* rather than good and *evil*, where to be bad is to diverge from the optimal path, not to switch sides in an ongoing Manichean struggle.

The model also indicates something central to ancient ethics that's somehow receded to the margins of recent ethical discourses – *limit* (*peras*). Today the idea of being limited is likely to strike people (especially people in highly consumptive and competitive societies) as a bad thing, as synonymous with something like being stunted, thwarted, confined, or held back. But for many ancient Greeks and Romans, limits are essential to both being and being good. To lose one's limits is to lose one's *definition*, the boundaries that define things as what they are and distinguish them from what they're not. The idea of being unlimited, limitless, unbridled, extreme, intense, of "having it all," would have struck many ancients as chaotic, immoderate, excessive, a distortion and corruption of human excellence, and vicious.

Practically speaking, one value of thinking in terms of the mean is that doing so acts as a brake on going too far in what superficially may appear to be the right direction. For example, autonomy is considered to be very important in medical ethics. But if we think of autonomy (self-ruling) as being a good, and heteronomy (being ruled by others) its corresponding vice, it is easy to believe that the more autonomy the better. In a sense, however, one can have too much autonomy, for example in cases where one is left to make decisions about which one doesn't possess the expertise to make sound judgments. Sometimes it's wise to place oneself under the direction of others. In any case, Aristotle's doctrine of the mean reminds us that one can have too much of a good thing.

See also

1.6 Character, 1.11 Harmony, 2.16 Virtue ethics, 3.3 Bad/evil, 4.13 Reflective equilibrium

Reading

Aristotle, *Nicomachean Ethics,* edited by Sarah Broadie (Oxford: Oxford University Press, 2002), Book II, Chapters 6–7
*J. O. Urmson, *Aristotle's Ethics* (Oxford: Blackwell, 1988)
*Sarah Broadie, *Ethics with Aristotle* (Oxford: Oxford University Press, 1991)

3.11 Honor/shame

In the first speech in Francis Ford Coppola's film, *The Godfather*, Amerigo Bonasera tells the mafia boss Don Corleone, "I raised my daughter in the American fashion. I gave her freedom, but – I taught her never to dishonor her family." At once, a major theme of the film is revealed. The central concept of the mob's ethics is not justice, happiness, fairness, or reason, but honor.

Social theorists have distinguished societies based upon honor and shame from others based upon guilt. There's ethical import to this, import that in part explains why there's no word for "compromise" in Arabic.

Honor is something public, in the sense that having it depends upon public recognition. One cannot have honor unless it is publicly recognized and acknowledged. Honor is also public in the sense that it makes a claim to social status, rank, and privilege. Honor makes the claim upon others for respect and trust. To those of lower rank honor commands deference and submission. Throughout *The Godfather* we see this time and again, such as in Michael's indignation that his brother was "slapped around *in public*."

In many societies honor is heritable. One can be born with it. But honor is also something that can be acquired. The ways in which honor can be acquired vary, but invariably honor is acquired through public acts of some sort. Acts that confer honor display virtues like courage, generosity, magnanimity, and mercy. Honor can be acquired through success in competitions where power and skill are exhibited. Honor can also be conferred through public and authoritative rituals such as being knighted or receiving a medal or award. Saluting, bowing, curtsying, and using distinguished titles involve the maintenance of honor.

Honor has been traditionally associated with masculinity, martial virtue and warfare, but it need not be. Acts of extraordinary sacrifice, compassion, and diplomacy also warrant honor. Women's honor has typically through patriarchy been related to their sexual conduct, specifically to their ability to refuse or resist sexual advances from those not entitled or authorized to make them. Hence when Bonasera's daughter refused sex, "she kept her honor." Honor may be individual or collective. So, one can speak of *family honor* or *national honor*.

Not only can honor be acquired; it can also be lost. Loss comes through actions that are publicly perceived (or perceivable) as affronts, insults, or challenges, as well as through conduct that is thought to be dishonorable. When honor is lost, one is *shamed*. To avoid or remove shame, some sort of positive public act of compensation or restoration is required. (Some philosophers have, of course, used the concept of shame in other ways. Kant for example writes about the shame of failing to act autonomously and instead giving in to desire or external pressures.)

It's the public and performative quality of honor and shame that distinguishes it from *guilt* and *pride*. One can privately feel guilty, but one can't have private honor or perhaps private shame (though one can be ashamed of oneself). Conversely, honor and shame don't require the existence of any corresponding subjective state on the part of those who possess them – except perhaps for the recognition of their existence. Of course, an ethic of honor and shame need not exclude guilt. Indeed, one might argue that today the two exist simultaneously. Shame is also commonly defined as referring to the self while guilt refers to the act.

For many people, conduct that yields honor partially defines acts that are considered good or virtuous. Correlatively, conduct that brings dishonor and shame in part defines bad and vicious conduct. Some of the acts that bring or sustain honor cannot be refused. To that extent, the concepts of honor and dishonor establish *duties*. Military service, for example, is not an optional way to gain honor; it is required. The refusal of extra-marital sex is not a way for women to earn higher status; it is a *sine qua non* of honor.

Problems

The concept of honor often troubles ethicists because historically it has been implicated in many bad and violent acts. Commonly, only violent reprisals against those who have brought shame and dishonor to an individual or collective can restore honor. So, dueling or other violent reprisals are required – particularly in the common terms of masculinity – in response to insults.

Women are punished violently (for example by having acid thrown in their faces) for having engaged in illicit sexual conduct – even when having done so unwillingly. Sometimes women who have brought dishonor to their families are killed in a practice known as "honor killing" that is meant both to express shame and to restore family honor.

Nazis, who organized themselves through the concepts of "blood and honor" (e.g. the "Nuremberg Law for the Protection of German Blood and German Honor," 1935) may be understood in part as having unleashed violent reprisals against other parts of Europe for the dishonor and humiliation Germany experienced in the Treaty of Versailles.

Bertram Wyatt-Brown has argued that the concept of honor helped drive the American Confederacy to violent secession because of the shaming and dishonor it experienced from northern abolitionists (*Honor and Violence in the Old South*, 1986). Some explain the intensity Arab nations express toward the Israeli state by the dishonor they have experienced through the occupation of Palestine, the displacement of much of its population, and Israeli military victories.

One might also wonder whether the recognition of honorable people simultaneously requires the establishment of a class defined as shameful or disgraceful. Did the establishment of Southern and Confederate gentlemen require the creation of "niggers" and "slaves," and vice versa? Did the restoration of German honor require the vilifying of Jews? Can "virgins" exist if "whores" do not?

Resolving disputes of honor

If one wishes to resolve a dispute involving issues of honor and shame without challenging those ideas, one must first understand the sorts of conduct and the kinds of duties honor demands. Unless one intends to shame one of the parties, resolution of conflict will be possible only if both parties can save face. This isn't easy.

If one wishes to resolve the dispute by challenging the claims of honor and shame animating the parties, one will have to find a way to undermine, subvert, or dismantle the force of those claims – for example, by arguing that a woman does not dishonor her family in being raped. This isn't easy either, but it may be the only way to escape the violence and oppression so pervasively woven into these concepts.

See also

3.13 Injury, 3.23 Public and private, 4.15 Sex and gender

Reading

Bertram Wyatt-Brown, *Southern Honor: Ethics and Behavior in the Old South* (Oxford: Oxford University Press, 1982)
Bernard Williams, *Shame and Necessity* (Berkeley: University of California Press, 1993)
June Price Tangney and Ronda L. Dearing, *Shame and Guilt* (New York: The Guilford Press, 2002)

3.12 Individual/collective

US coins bear the motto, "*e pluribus unum*": out of many one. The phrase refers to the way one nation (the United States of America) was formed out of a group of already existing political entities (13 British North American colonies). This may be an accurate description of the way the USA was formed, but does it make sense of society generally?

Classical liberal theorists like John Locke (1632–1704), as well as their more contemporary kin such as John Rawls (1921–2002), conceive of society along the lines of what has come to be known as *individualism*. According to this view, society results from the association of individuals; and society is nothing more than the combination of those individual parts. The whole is nothing more than the parts.

Communitarian thought, like that of Charles Taylor (b. 1931), challenges this view in a rather radical way. For communitarians society precedes individuals. That is, individuals don't exist first and then produce society. Instead, individuals appear only out of social contexts. Each of us is born into a family or some other sort of care-giving group, and each becomes an individual in social ways, such as taking on a social role, or taking a position in some social controversy, or engaging in specific social institutions like music, literature, commerce, and philosophy.

Moral judgment itself for communitarians cannot be understood in any abstract, universal, or radically particular way. Rather moral judgment must be understood in terms of the traditions, customs, and communities in which it is concretely situated.

Some take what is in a sense an even stronger position, one associated with *holism*. For collectivists or holists, the whole is both greater than the parts and is even sometimes more important than the parts. So, Jean-Jacques Rousseau (1712–78) argued in *The Social Contract* (1762) that when organized in society, individual wills give rise to something metaphysically different and greater – *the general will* – and it's the general will, not the aggregate of individual wills that expresses the will of the people. Similarly, Karl Marx (1818–83) argued that social classes are more than composites or networks of individuals and that the forces that animate them are more important than individual motives, interests, and desires.

Public goods

From an ethical point of view, what's important is that collectivist and holist theories demand that one consider not only individual goods, rights, and virtues but also *public goods*, the *rights of collectives*, and *civic virtue*. Individual *rights* must be complemented by social and civic *responsibility*. To be truly virtuous one cannot simply serve individual goods; one must be engaged in activities and institutions that care for political and social goods and excellences. Ethical reflection must not only consider the rights of individuals but also the good of the collective whole. An ethically sound life is not sufficiently understood in terms of individual gain and well-being. The well-being or good of the community in which one is situated must be considered as well and perhaps even given precedence.

It's not that individualist theories are silent about civic virtue and social goods, but more holistically-minded critics have often argued that their advocacy doesn't go far enough. Amitai Etzioni (b. 1929) has been extremely influential on this point.

Serving the good of society may arguably mean providing basic health care, education, and a clean environment to everyone. Actually achieving this, however, seems to require the limiting or even violating of individual rights and goods. Providing universal health care may, for example, require individuals to turn over some portion of their individual wealth to the state. It may also mean having fewer options for care and having to face the frustrating delays of rationing or equitable distribution procedures. Here property rights that entitle individuals to dispose of their wealth as they wish conflict with the requirements of social goods.

Immigration control also presents a case where the rights of individuals to travel, work, and live where they wish conflict with what might be understood as the rights of cultures or nations to preserve themselves in the face of immigration. Is France entitled to restrict immigration in order to preserve French culture? Is Israel justified in privileging Jews in its immigration policies and property transfers?

The main problem with concepts of "public good" and "the collective" is that these may appear to be no more than abstractions, unless they are understood more fundamentally in terms of the individuals that comprise them. How, for instance, can we make sense of the idea of serving the "common good" if it doesn't ultimately mean that we are serving the interests of individuals across a wide range of society? Isn't it just contradictory to say that a nation can prosper while individuals in it do not? Moreover, privileging the collective over the individual has a long and terrifying history of justifying the abrogation of individual rights and even mass murder. Can the collective be served without feeding individuals to it?

See also

1.19 Rights, 1.21 Tradition and history, 5.13 The separateness of persons

Reading

Charles Taylor, *Sources of the Self: The Making of Modern Identity* (Cambridge, MA: Harvard University Press, 1989)
Amitai Etzioni, ed., *The Essential Communitarian Reader* (Lanham, MD: Rowman & Littlefield Publishers, 1998)
Michael J. Sandel, *Liberalism and the Limits of Justice*, 2nd edition (Cambridge: Cambridge University Press, 1998)

3.13 Injury

In 1992, in Albuquerque, New Mexico, 70-year-old Stella Liebeck spilt hot coffee on her lap while using a fast-food drive-through. The injury was so severe that it hospitalized her for eight days with third-degree burns requiring skin grafts. She then pursued a tort claim (a claim for legal redress of a damage caused) against the McDonald's Corporation and was awarded $200,000 in compensation.

Liebeck clearly suffered an injury, and the courts decided McDonald's was *legally* culpable for it. But what of the *morality* of injury?

Assessing whether an action is morally permissible or impermissible often involves assessing whether it has or will injure someone. On the face of it the concept of "injury" seems pretty clear, but philosophers, as usual, can quickly dispel this illusion. For instance Aristotle (384–322 BCE) argued, counter-intuitively, that even the dead could be injured, as reputations can be harmed which is an injury only to the person whose reputation it is, even if they are deceased. There are therefore a number of philosophical wrinkles in the concept that make it worth examining.

Diminishing and inhibiting

Perhaps the most common sense of injury is the diminishing or degradation of something that was previously good. So, stabbing someone's previously healthy lung in a way that impairs its function is an injury, as is causing someone who previously enjoyed sound mental health to suffer anxiety attacks, depression, and insomnia. This form of injury comprises mental or physical pain and suffering where none existed before.

But it's not just the diminishing or destruction of an already existing good that counts as injury. Injuries can also thwart or obstruct the realization of potential or possible future goods. So, even if one were to kill a child painlessly and unexpectedly, the child has suffered an injury in so far as the killing has obstructed future goods the child may have (would have?) realized for itself and others.

The case of the child involves simple, raw possibilities, but even those who are much older can suffer this form of injury because humans are, as Martin Heidegger (1889–1976) has argued, beings who engage in projects. Humans don't simply move from one present action to another. Their activities project themselves into the future on the basis of a past history. People don't just read words; they study to earn degrees and become professors, priests, physicians, and social workers. People don't just have sex; they have relationships and build families and kinship networks.

Intent

In evaluating the implications of injury, it's often taken to be important to know whether the injury was caused intentionally. Even though the result is the same, shooting someone accidentally is likely to be something different from shooting someone intentionally. Lack of intent, however, is not by itself a sufficient defense for any resultant injury. This is perhaps most clear in the case of injury that is caused not directly by intended actions, but by negligence. Legally, people define negligence as failing to care for the safety or well-being of someone or something in a prudent and reasonable way. So, a parent whose 5-year-old child drowns in a river may be judged negligent for allowing the child to play there unattended, even though the parent didn't actually push the child's head under.

How far can the concept of negligence be pushed? One curious notion of injury is failing to maximize a good. Does it injure a child not to provide it the absolute best education, nutrition, or healthcare possible? Should it count as an injury to the poor or to poorer nations that the wealthy don't provide them with healthcare, education, and security? In these cases, the ordinary sense of negligence does not seem to apply, but morally speaking we need good reasons to show why it should not.

Injury and redress

The Babylonian Code of Hammurabi and the Torah express the *lex talionis* or "law of retaliation" – the idea that when people injure others, it is just to injure them in some way in return. "And thine eye shall not pity; but life shall go for life, eye for eye, tooth for tooth, hand for hand, foot for foot" (Deuteronomy 19:21). But in Plato's dialogue *Apology* (25a–e) and elsewhere Socrates argues that it's always wrong to harm others, even when they've harmed you, because making other members of one's society worse is likely to make one's own life worse. Moreover, diminishing additional lives hardly makes things better. Those who injure should be thought of as ill and in need of healing and improvement, not harm. Within the Bible, Matthew 5:38–42 seems to countermand Deuteronomy ("whosoever shall smite thee on thy right cheek, turn to him the other also").

Other philosophers have argued that injuring others is sometimes permissible in, for example, war, self-defense, and the punishment of criminals. Niccolo Machiavelli (1496–1527) lays out in typically transparent terms an even harsher logic behind injuring wrongdoers: "If an injury has to be done to a man it should be so severe that his vengeance need not be feared" (*The Prince*, III; 1513).

See also

1.10 Flourishing, 1.17 Pain and pleasure, 3.7 Commission/omission, 3.17 Legal/moral

Reading

Joel Feinberg, *Harm to Others* (Oxford: Oxford University Press, 1984)
Gerald J. Postema, ed., *Philosophy and the Law of Torts* (Cambridge: Cambridge University Press, 2001)
F. M. Kamm, *Intricate Ethics: Rights, Responsibilities, and Permissible Harm* (Oxford: Oxford University Press, 2006)

3.14 Intentions/consequences

Dr Nick and Dr Lecter both administered the same high dose of morphine to their patients, both of whom were terminally ill with the same painful malady. Both patients were equally close to their deaths, and neither had anything administered to them other than the morphine that would have affected their health. The effect of the high dosage on their weak systems was the same – they soon died. In both cases, the doctors knew that death was the likely outcome. Only Dr Nick, however, killed his patient. How is this possible?

The principle of double effect

It's possible if one accepts the principle of *double effect*. This principle has long been important in Catholic theology and is usually traced back to Thomas Aquinas's (1225–74) *Summa Theologica*. The simple idea behind the principle is that actions can have more than one consequence, and not all these consequences are intended. So, for instance, a physician may give a high dose of morphine to a patient with the intention of relieving his pain. But if she does not intend this medicine to kill her patient, the physician is not guilty of murder if it does so. If, however, to kill was her intention, then one would say that the doctor killed the patient (whether or not the killing is justifiable).

Between consequences that are (a) intended and foreseen and (c) unintended and unforeseen, however, lies a middle category: (b) consequences unintended but foreseen. For example, a dentist foresees that a tooth extraction will cause her young patient some pain and distress, pain she foresees but can only ameliorate, not eliminate. People, therefore, don't blame dentists for causing some pain, as they recognize this as the price to pay for the good consequences the dentist intends to bring about – the removal of a tooth and the relief of more pain. The doctrine of double effect maintains that people are sometimes permitted to do things that have or risk bad consequences, even if we can foresee them, just as long as those bad consequences are (a) an unavoidable and (b) an acceptable accompaniment to the good consequences intended.

This allows us to see the difference between Dr Nick and Dr Lecter. Dr Nick intended to kill his patient, and used the high dosage of morphine to achieve this goal. Dr Lecter only wanted to relieve his patient's pain, and he could only do this by administering the potentially lethal dose. Such, however, was the importance of ending the patient's suffering that Dr Lecter calculated this was an acceptable price to pay, an acceptable risk to take. According to the doctrine of double effect, then, only Dr Nick is responsible for killing his patient.

From principle to practice

The principle sometimes seems implausible because people ignore the caveats. The principle does not state, for instance, that it is always permissible to do something with a foreseen bad consequence *just as long as* a good one is intended. In addition, other conditions must be met. These commonly include:

1   There must be no better alternative means for accomplishing the good. Other means of bringing about the good consequence, if there are any, must cause the same or worse harm.
2   The good intended must outweigh the harm. It is not acceptable to do something with a foreseen great harm for the sake of only a small good.
3   The benefit must not be an outcome of the harm, but only of the action itself. So, for example, the intention to reduce suffering by killing isn't acceptable according to the principle. Only if the reduction of pain and the death are both consequences of giving the morphine can the principle apply.

Of course, precisely what these conditions are is the subject of much debate and disagreement, even among those who accept the principle in broad terms. Those who reject the principle out of hand are likely to do so because they believe that, as moral agents, we are responsible for all the consequences of our actions – at least those we can foresee. On this view, both Dr Nick and Dr Lecter know what the consequences of their actions are likely to be, and to decide whether to go ahead they must calculate whether doing so would bring about a better consequence than not doing so. The only intention that might matter (and intentions may not matter at all) is the intention to do whatever has the best overall consequences. Even those who accept the principle of double effect accept that this calculation has to be made. The only difference, it is argued, is that the principle of double effect allows physicians to pretend that they are not actually the agents of the death. Critics argue that it's better if we just face up to our responsibilities more directly.

Warfare also presents an example of the doctrine of double effect in action. Consider two bomber pilots who perform the same act – bombing a target in the course of which innocent civilians are killed. One pilot bombs the target in order to kill the civilians, just for the sadistic pleasure of it. The other pilot bombs the target for the purpose of gaining decisive and proportional military advantage in a just war. It does seem that there's a significant moral difference between the two acts. And, in fact, people often exculpate the pilots of the atomic bombing of Hiroshima and Nagasaki on just these grounds. But because of the magnitude of the suffering of innocents (does it outweigh the good achieved?) and the possibility of alternative means to achieve the same military and political ends (would conditional surrender or invasion have worked better?), the issue remains a controversial one.

See also

3.5 Cause/reason, 3.7 Commission/omission, 3.19 Means/ends

Reading

Thomas Aquinas, *Summa Theologica* [1266–75], edited by the Fathers of the English Dominican Province (Westminster, MD: Christian Classics, 1981), II-II, Question 64, Article 7
Jonathan Glover, *Causing Death and Saving Lives* (Harmondsworth: Penguin, 1977)
★P. A. Woodward, *The Doctrine of Double Effect: Philosophers Debate a Controversial Moral Principle* (South Bend, IN: University of Notre Dame Press, 2001)

3.15 Internalism/externalism

"I know I ought to compost my food waste, but I just don't want to." That sounds a familiar and intelligible enough comment. Don't all people have things they think they ought to do yet don't really want to do? According to some ethical theorists, however, this just isn't possible.

Internalists may be of different sorts. Generally speaking they claim that the moral fact that "I ought to do X" or, anyway, to know, believe, or judge that "I ought to do X" entails that "I am motivated in some way to do X." That doesn't mean I will always act on that motivation. I may, for example, have a stronger motivation to do something else that prevents me from doing the right thing. Nevertheless, for the internalist, no one can sincerely believe that he or she ought to do X without in some way also being motivated to do X. In this way internalists aim to bridge the gap between ideas or reasons and motivation.

Externalists, by contrast, believe that morality is motivationally neutral. The moral fact that "I ought to do X" or my knowing, believing, or judging that "I ought to do X" tells nothing about whether or not I actually want to do X. It's perfectly possible not to want to do what is morally right or even what one thinks is morally right.

Why internalism?

At first blush, externalism usually seems the more intuitively plausible position. After all, people do say, "I know I ought to, but I don't want to." Internalists, however, claim that in such cases people don't literally mean what they say. Consider, for example, the non-composter. When she says, "I know I ought to compost my food waste," perhaps what she really means is: "I know everyone says I ought to compost, but I don't agree," or "I can see the arguments for composting, but I do not judge them to be sound." And this does indeed seem to fit in with what most people in such situations would say if they were to explain what they meant.

For instance, someone might argue, "While I accept that composting is a good thing from an environmental point of view, I don't think that whether I compost or not, in the grand scheme of things, makes much difference. What it will do is irritate me, making life worse for me and my family, and put me off doing other environmentally friendly deeds that are more effective. In short, composting is good, but not so good that I ought to do it irrespective of all its disadvantages." But what that means is that, in fact, she does not think she *ought* to compost after all, only that it would be good if she did.

Now, consider what it would mean for someone really to think that he or she ought to compost. In order for that sentiment to be held sincerely, once more any literal reading must be rejected of statements like: "I know I ought to compost my food waste, but I just don't want to." Stated more clearly, such a person is more likely to say something like, "I believe I ought to compost my food waste, and every time I don't, I feel some kind of impulse to resist just throwing it away. But when I think about keeping a smelly bucket in the kitchen and marching off to the bottom of the garden, I just find that too much. I want to compost, but I want an easier life even more." In this case, the person does *want* to compost after all, she just doesn't want to enough to override her other desires.

Strong internalism

Some internalists would go further. Plato's (427–347 BCE) Socrates argued in *The Apology* that it's impossible to actually do anything that one genuinely knows is wrong. That's because to do wrong is ultimately to harm oneself, and no one would knowingly do that. So, all wrongdoing must in fact be the result of ignorance. This strong internalism is harder to defend and only really makes sense if you accept the premise that it is against our own interests to behave immorally, which is itself highly disputable.

The example of Socrates shows, however, that whether internalism or externalism seems more plausible depends upon one's wider moral commitments. If, for example, one thinks that morality is just what God commands, or is a matter of social convention, it's straightforward to believe that God or society may demand one thing (and therefore you ought to do it) but you want another. Even that, however, may seem unsatisfactory to the internalist. For if you held such a view, wouldn't you really be saying that the wishes of God or society have no moral claim on you at all? Wouldn't you be back in the situation of the person who says they know they ought to do X, but really believes no such thing?

See also

1.7 Conscience, 3.5 Cause/reason, 5.3 Bad faith and self-deception

Reading

*Bernard Williams, "Internal and External Reasons" [1980], in his *Moral Luck: Philosophical Papers 1973–1980* (Cambridge: Cambridge University Press, 1981) 101–13

Derek Parfit, "Reasons and Motivation," *Aristotelian Society Supplementary Volume 71* (1997): 99–130

Elijah Millgram, ed., *Varieties of Practical Reasoning* (Cambridge, MA: MIT Press, 2001)

3.16 Intrinsic/instrumental value

On the outskirts of Greenton there is a small wood that provides the habitat for a lot of rare wildlife. It is here, however, that Walco wants to build its new supermarket. The large majority of Greenton's residents want the development to go ahead. They argue that most people go to the woods very rarely, and although they enjoy them, they would get more use out of the supermarket. Save Our Forest Action (SOFA) does not dispute this, but insists that if the wood is destroyed something of irreplaceable value will be lost. What should the council's planning department decide?

What makes this a difficult issue to resolve is that the two sides see the value of the woods in very different terms. The pro-Walco residents are looking at the *instrumental* value of the wood – meaning that they assess its value in terms of how it can be used and what it can do for them as well as, hopefully, the wider community. The wood is good only because people enjoy going to it. But people will enjoy going to the supermarket more, or will at least get more overall pleasure because they will have a large number of slightly less pleasurable trips there and only the occasional visit to the wood. Therefore, when one looks at the benefits the wood and the supermarket will give to those people who would benefit from them, the supermarket comes out on top.

Interestingly, SOFA does not dispute this, even though it's still opposed to the development. This is because SOFA also sees a second kind of value: *intrinsic* value. That is to say, they do not believe that the wood is valuable only because of what it can do for the residents or anyone else. They also believe that the wood has value in itself, whether or not it serves or affects humans. They may locate this value in one of many areas. The natural beauty of the wood or the mere existence of rare life may, for instance, be seen as valuable in themselves.

The distinction between intrinsic and instrumental value is important in determining moral priorities. People strive for all kinds of things that have instrumental value. The most obvious example is money, which is only valuable because of what one can *do* with it; *in itself* it is of no value at all. The reason people crave money, as well as other things of instrumental value, is presumably because money enables them to obtain things that are intrinsically valuable. Happiness may be one such thing. People don't crave happiness because it is the route to anything else. People want happiness simply for its own sake, because it is good in itself.

Kant (1724–1804) is well known for arguing that people are ends in themselves. One implication of this, according to Kant, is that it's categorically wrong to use them as mere instruments. People should not be enslaved, exploited, or treated merely as means to achieve other ends – even if achieving those ends pleases other people. A lot of people might end up leading happier, more pleasant lives, for example, if we would just use a few unfortunates (against their wills) as human guinea pigs in medical experiments. But even if doing so cured many horrible diseases, according to Kant it would be wrong.

What has intrinsic value?

Assuming, however, that happiness is clearly an intrinsic good and money an instrumental one, that still leaves a lot of goods that are much more difficult to classify. This is perhaps most evident when considering the natural world and the environment. Most people now believe there is a need to "protect the environment." The reasons they give for this often relate to its instrumental value. People will suffer, it is argued, if bio-diversity is reduced, the planet warms up, or rivers are polluted. There doesn't need to be any intrinsic value in nature to want to save it; one just needs to consider humanity's self-interest.

Adherents of what Arne Naess (b. 1912) calls "Deep Ecology," however, think this reasoning doesn't go far enough. When a species goes extinct for reasons of human misconduct (say, a particular flower annihilated by air pollution), that's a bad thing, they claim – whether or not the existence of that species served the interests of humanity. Nature is valuable in itself, and people should protect it for reasons other than self-interest – that is, for its own sake.

The difficulty with this position reflects the difficulties of claiming that anything is intrinsically valuable. It makes sense to think of happiness as being intrinsically valuable because beings that can be happy are beings for whom life can go better or worse from their own points of view (human beings, for example).

When, however, one starts talking about objects that have no point of view, things seem rather different with regard to happiness. It means nothing to those things whether their existence goes better or worse – even if we can make sense of such ideas as "better" and "worse" in this context. Hence it makes no sense at all to speak of those sorts of things as happy or unhappy. If nature is in many of its aspects non-sentient, then does it even make sense to think it better off if "unharmed"? Indeed, what can it mean to harm an inanimate thing?

For there to be value there seems to be a need for sentient beings to do something like *see things as valuable*, either as means to ends or ends in themselves. That is, while some philosophers have maintained that value can somehow be *inherent*, existing in things independently, it seems more plausible to say value can only exist for valuers, or at least in the relationship between the valuer and the thing valued. Are birds and other fauna inhabiting woods sentient valuers in this sense? Are trees? They react to stimuli and can be stressed, but is that enough? Does it make sense to speak of an ecosystem, a species, a habitat, or the natural world as a whole as sentient? Perhaps sentience is too restrictive a criterion, though. Many *biocentric* ethicists have argued that mere life itself has intrinsic value, sentient or not.

Intrinsic value may be thought of as conferred as well as recognized. Perhaps it makes sense to say that for human valuers things like ecosystems (e.g. the Amazon rainforest) and even geological formations (say, like Glen Canyon or Grand Canyon) have value in themselves. That is, humans do the valuing, but they *value them as intrinsically valuable*, despite their lack of instrumental value to humans. In 1998, a deep-sea coral reef was discovered off the northwest coast of Scotland. Called the Darwin Mounds, the reef may be of little or no use to humans. Despite its uselessness, can humans nonetheless value the reef for its own sake, as something intrinsically valuable? Or is the very idea nonsense?

See also

1.12 Interest, 3.1 Absolute/relative, 3.19 Means/ends, 3.21 Moral subjects/moral agents

Reading

Roderick Chisholm, *Ethics and Intrinsic Values*, edited by John R. White (Heidelberg: Universitäts Verlag, 2001)

Michael J. Zimmerman, *The Nature of Intrinsic Value* (Lanham, MD: Rowman & Littlefield, 2001)

*Andrew Light and Holmes Rolston III, *Environmental Ethics* (Malden, MA: Blackwell, 2003)

3.17 **Legal/moral**

After taking legal advice, Gretchen dropped by on her neighbor Al and then proceeded to chop off his right thumb. Al had always annoyed Gretchen but she didn't know what to do about it. Then she came across a long-forgotten law that had never been repealed, which stated that if someone damaged your apple tree you were entitled to remove one of his or her thumbs. Since Al had reversed his car into the tree on her front lawn only last week, this was just the excuse Gretchen needed. She could make him suffer and be in the right to do so.

But surely Gretchen was *not* in the right morally speaking. Just because something is *legal* does not mean it is *moral*. If that were the case, then "immoral law" would be an oxymoron. But people commonly believe that many laws are and have been immoral, for example those laws that legitimated slavery or withheld the vote from women. Likewise, just because something is *illegal*, that does not mean it's *immoral*. Conscientious objectors who deserted or refused to fulfill their legal obligation to serve in the *Wehrmacht* of Nazi Germany were acting morally, not immorally. In short, "moral" is not equivalent to "legal"; neither implies the other.

So, as a matter of fact one can't infer anything about the morality of an action from its legality or vice versa. That much may be clear. But more difficult is the issue of what the relationship between legality and morality *should* be.

Theocracy and natural law

Only advocates of a certain extreme form of theocracy argue that moral and legal codes should be entirely coextensive. Islamic *sharia*, for example, is the moral code by which all Muslims should live. The governments of many predominantly Muslim countries incorporate *sharia* partly but not fully into the laws of the state. Those, such as the Taliban in Afghanistan, who claimed it was the state's duty to enforce *sharia* law more or less in its entirety, are the exception, not the rule. It may be immoral to lie to one's spouse or never give any money to charity, but few think that it is the state's business to legislate against these shortcomings. (Of course, there are also good reasons to hold that civil law shouldn't be based in religious doctrine at all.)

Although few argue that all morality should be enshrined in law, many more argue that all law should be based in or at least consistent with morality. This is the position of the natural law tradition, which argues that basic principles of justice are given by nature, and civil law, although it need not incorporate all natural laws, must be fully consistent with them. Any statute which contravenes natural law is therefore no true or fair law. So it is that British law, for example, recognizes "natural justice" as the basic principles of justice that are universally recognized and self-evident; and if a law is seen to contravene natural justice it may be subject to a process known as judicial review. The American Declaration of Independence (1776) relies on similar reasoning.

Legal positivism

One of the most influential positions on the relation between law and morality in recent times, however, has been legal *positivism*, which argues that the law is a set of rules and institutions implemented and recognized by a society quite separately from morality. More extreme versions of this position maintain that a law's validity is *never* determined by its morality, while less extreme versions allow that a law's validity *may sometimes* be determined by its morality. What all forms of legal positivism have in common is that they would not accept that there is any necessary connection between every law's morality and its legality.

The challenge for legal positivism as well as for any philosophy of law is to show what the relation between the legal and the moral therefore is, since we must surely have some concern for the morality of our legal system. Law seems to establish a separate sphere of obligation and permission, distinct from the moral sphere and with it's own distinct sources of authority. But the two spheres also seem to overlap to some extent. If a law were immoral, then that may not invalidate it, but it would be a reason to attempt to revise that law, or at the very least demand a very good reason why society should not do so. For just as hardly anyone will claim that the totality of morality should be the totality of the law, few are those who would claim that the law has nothing to do with morality at all. The truth seems to lie somewhere in between these two extremes. But the space between them is very large.

See also

1.15 Natural law, 1.19 Rights, 3.23 Public/private

Reading

Jeremy Bentham, *Of Laws in General*, edited by H. L. A. Hart (London: Athlone Press, 1970)

Ronald Dworkin, *Taking Rights Seriously* (Cambridge, MA: Harvard University Press, 1977)

H. L. A. Hart, *The Concept of Law*, 2nd edition (Oxford: Oxford University Press, 1994)

3.18 Liberation/oppression

In France, the wearing of the many forms of *hijab* (modest dress) by Muslim women has been banned from public schools. Critics of these traditional forms of dress (veil, *khimar, chador, burqa*) say that they oppress women by containing them in mobile cages of patriarchy and domesticity, denying them many of the freedoms allowed to men. In reply, it is argued that the ban is itself oppressive, because it denies Muslim women religious freedom as well as the freedom of self-expression. It's even argued that the *hijab* liberates women from the oppressive conceptual systems of western (or at least non-Muslim) beauty, fashion, and sexual exploitation.

That this thorny issue should hinge on notions of oppression and liberation is not surprising, given that the principal political concept of the modern period has been (or was?) liberty. But what do we mean when we invoke the need to liberate people from oppression?

Types of oppression

States can secure and formalize ordered liberty, but they also often deploy instruments of coercion (like the police, military forces, regulatory and tax systems) to deprive people of life, liberty, property, and the means to think in an informed and expansive way. State power is, by turns, one of the most liberating and one of the most destructive and oppressive institutions of the human world.

Oppression can be economic as well as governmental. Economic systems produce and distribute the services and material goods necessary to human life and human flourishing. Those systems also assign labor and the rewards people receive for it. It's important to reflect on whether they do so in a morally sound way. In particular, both (a) the processes of production, distribution, and reward, and (b) the outcomes of those processes must be subjected to moral scrutiny. When poverty is structural (rather than, say, the result of natural disasters), can't one speak of liberation from it?

Recognizing that the participants in economic activity don't command equal amounts of power, philosophers working out of the Marxist tradition criticize many economic relationships as forms of exploitation. Exploitation takes place when those with more power extract more from those with less than they ought to – for example when richly compensated owners and employers use the desperation of laborers to gain their submission to low wages.

Oppression may also be conceptual in the sense that people may come to accept ideas that diminish their liberty. Ideas and beliefs can themselves be tyrannical. Ferreting out this sort of oppression is often a difficult thing since concepts and beliefs become *normalized* and *internalized*. That is, once we are accustomed to them, ideas, beliefs, and practices come to seem normal, natural, and proper – part of who we are, part of the very air we breathe, just the ways things are. So, it came to seem normal and natural that darker-skinned people should be enslaved or relegated to a subordinate social status. It came to seem proper that women not be allowed to vote, or enter contracts, or serve in political office. It came to seem proper that many people earn so little while others possess so much. It came to seem normal and natural to drive in cars and eat beef.

Enlightenment philosophers like Voltaire (1694–1778) and many following them have criticized religious belief as the root of many conceptual (as well as political) forms of oppression. Lynn White (1907–87), for example, has argued that Genesis 1:26 – where God gives humans "dominion" over other creatures – as well as other elements of Abrahamic religion have led to bankrupt environmental ethics in much of the world. Mary Daly (b. 1928) has called attention to the way language (and hence concepts) helps to oppress women (*Beyond God the Father: Toward a Philosophy of Women's Liberation*, 1973). On the other hand, proponents of *liberation theology* like Gustavo Gutierrez (b. 1928) have argued that religion can function as an instrument of liberation (*Teologia de la liberación*, 1971).

Real life

Racism as it has affected Africans presents a particularly toxic confluence of all these forms of oppression. The power of the state has been used to confine and limit "black Africans," both in Africa and abroad. Economic deprivations and power imbalances have led to exploitation and poverty. Religion has been used to justify (as well as to oppose) racial subordination. And theories of mental inferiority and criminal tendency have been normalized and internalized by oppressor and oppressed alike.

It's this issue of how and whether oppression can be internalized which provides the greatest difficulties. Take the example of the *hijab*. The fact that many women choose to wear these forms of dress does not necessarily counter the case against them. It can be argued that women who claim to have made such choices freely aren't being fully honest, either with others or themselves. They may be affected by forms of coercion and influence about which they are ignorant or in denial. They may have unfortunately internalized values and ideas designed to oppress them. Their "choices" are therefore not truly free but conditioned. Can anyone who chooses to be a slave really be thought to have made a free choice?

This form of criticism is both extremely trenchant and extremely risky.

When internalized or blindly accepted by the oppressed, oppression can become especially tenacious. Not only does oppression become invisible; it becomes enforced and sustained by the victims of oppression themselves. The jailed become their own jailers. The possibility of this happening becomes a difficult problem for democratic theory since it implies that the wishes and choices of people may be distorted in favor of a less free society. The trouble is, however, once we start claiming that, unlike ourselves, others are mistaken in thinking they act freely, we place ourselves at risk not only of arrogance, hypocrisy, and imperialism but also of denying others the full humanity we attribute to ourselves.

See also

4.15 Sex and gender, 5.6 False consciousness, 5.11 Power

Reading

Frantz Fanon, *The Wretched of the Earth,* with a preface by Jean-Paul Sartre [1961] (New York: Grove Press, 1963)
Peter Singer, *Animal Liberation* [1975], 2nd edition (New York: New York Review of Books, 1990)
Christina Hendricks and Kelly Oliver, eds., *Language and Liberation: Feminism, Philosophy, and Language* (Albany: State University of New York Press, 1999)

3.19 Means/ends

Even in the black and white moral universe of the Hollywood epic, gray areas emerge. Consider the worries of Randal in the 1994 slacker movie *Clerks*. He's uneasy about the episode in *Star Wars* when the rebels (the good guys) destroy the second Death Star. Why? "I'll bet there were independent contractors working on that thing: plumbers, aluminum siders, roofers," he explains. "All those innocent contractors hired to do a job were killed – casualties of a war they had nothing to do with."

You could argue that these contractors were not innocent, that they knew the evil nature of their employer. But even if we allow their innocence, can't we just say that the end justifies the means? The Death Star was capable of destroying entire planets; and its owner, the Empire, intended to use it to wreak terror on the universe. If the only way to stop it being built was to kill a couple of thousand innocent contractors, so be it. Better them than whole planets of innocents. You can't make an omelette without breaking a few eggs.

Although the extreme power of the Death Star makes the example seem somewhat unreal, the same problem arises with the "collateral damage" of wars closer to home. Anyone who goes to war knows that innocent civilians will be killed. Are there any ends – regime change, repelling an invader, bringing a halt to genocide – that would justify using these means?

Theoretical implications

Consequentialist moral theories are the most open to means/ends trade-offs. Consequentialists maintain that actions or rules are right or wrong depending on whether they result in good or bad consequences. But one has to take into account all the consequences, or at least the direct ones. So, on this view, it is quite easy to see how you could justify an action that results in the deaths of many innocents if it saved the lives of many more.

Deontological moral theories, by contrast, are less tolerant of means/ends calculations. Deontologists argue that actions are right and wrong in themselves, and that if a wrong action has a good consequence, that doesn't make the action right or justifiable. So, killing innocent people is always wrong, even if many more live as a result.

While consequentialism and deontological ethics can in part be defined by their attitudes to means/ends calculations, that's not the case for other kinds of moral theory, such as virtue ethics. There's nothing in the theoretical grounding of virtue ethics that entails a general rule or position on the relation between means and ends.

Problems

It is precisely their clarity on the issue, however, that creates problems for both consequentialists and deontologists.

The problem for deontological ethics is that it seems absurd never to allow unsavory means to desirable ends. Surely, for example, if faced with the prospect of something so evil and unstoppable as the Death Star, one can't afford to be squeamish about killing some innocents to stop it. There is a risk here of "moral self-indulgence": refusing to do anything that may compromise our own moral purity – or vanity – at the expense of real suffering or even death to others. The challenge for the deontologist is therefore to show that her position does not entirely prohibit doing what is usually bad for a much higher good; or to come up with a very good reason why this is never allowed.

The problem for the consequentialist is just as stark. For if the overall consequences are all that count, all sorts of injustice seem to be tolerable. Just as long as the positive pay-off is good enough, one can do anything to the innocent – kill, rob, or even torture them. Yet, surely some basic human rights, or at least principles that demand we treat others decently, ought to be honored. In order to prevent sliding down a slippery slope leading to a place where anything goes, it seems there ought to be some principles that can't be trumped by calculations purely concerned with consequences. The consequentialist calculus seems indifferent to the dignity and value of the individual life. The challenge for the consequentialist is therefore to show that his position does not allow doing anything for a much higher good; or to come up with a very good reason why it does.

John Dewey (1859–1952) and other pragmatists have registered the criticism that there is something artificial and misleading about distinguishing the ends and means in a thoroughgoing way. In making a moral judgment about a course of action, one judges the means *together* with the ends. While the importance of the ends must surely be considered in deciding which means are acceptable, how can it make moral sense to consider either in isolation from the other? Severing means and ends incautiously risks oversimplifying the world.

See also

Reading

Bernard Williams, "Utilitarianism and Moral Self-Indulgence," in his *Moral Luck: Philosophical Papers 1973–1980* (Cambridge: Cambridge University Press, 1981)

Henry S. Richardson, *Practical Reasoning about Final Ends* (Cambridge: Cambridge University Press, 1994)

Ted Honderich, *On Political Means and Social Ends* (Edinburgh: Edinburgh University Press, 2005)

3.20 Metaethics/normative ethics

Ari and Jan both believe that arranged marriages are wrong, while Hilary and Billy believe they are fine. Yet, on this issue (and others) in a very important respect Ari and Jan also disagree, as do Hilary and Billy. How can this be possible?

The solution to this conundrum lies in the distinction between metaethics and normative ethics. *Normative ethics* is about making judgments about what particular things are right or wrong – for example, arranged marriage. Hence Ari and Jan make the same normative judgment, as do Hilary and Billy. But this is only part of what moral thinking is about. In addition, there is also *metaethics*, which is concerned with the very nature of ethics and with its most basic concepts – for example, "right" and "wrong," "good" and "bad." The term derives from the Greek term, *meta*, which means above, beyond, or stretching across.

In this example, while Ari and Jan agree on a point of normative ethics, they disagree about the metaethics. Ari believes that moral judgments are about objective facts, while Jan believes they are merely expressions of personal preference or feeling. On this score, Hilary agrees with Ari, and Billy agrees with Jan. Hence no one in this foursome completely agrees with anyone else, as the table below illustrates.

		Metaethical position	
		Moral judgments are about objective facts	Moral judgments express subjective preferences
Normative position	Arranged marriages are morally wrong	Ari	Jan
	Arranged marriages are morally acceptable	Hilary	Billy

So, people can *agree* about metaethics but make different particular normative moral judgments; or make the same normative judgments but disagree about the metaethics.

Metaethical positions

Among the most popular metaethical positions are:

- *Moral non-realism* or *anti-realism*: There are no such things as moral facts.
- *Non-cognitivism*: There are no moral truths that can be known, and moral statements are neither true nor false.
- *Cognitivism*: Moral truths can be known, and moral statements are either true or false.
- *Subjectivism*: Moral judgments are fundamentally based on the subjective responses of moral agents, such as approval or disapproval; and moral terms like "good" and "bad" can be understood only by reference to those subjective responses.

Normative positions

Some of the more popular normative moral positions are:

- *Utilitarianism*: A consequentialist ethic that specifies good and bad consequences in terms of their utility or value.
- *Kantian ethics*: A deontological ethic that takes it as our fundamental duty – following what Immanuel Kant (1724–1804) calls the "categorical imperative" – to act only on that maxim or rule that you could will as universal law: to never treat others as mere means to ends but always as ends in themselves.
- *Particular religious ethics*: codes of moral conduct specified by religion that detail which actions are right or wrong, morally permissible or prohibited.

A clear distinction?

Metaethical positions say something about what *kind of things* moral judgments are and how their terms are meaningful, while the normative positions tell us *what actions or kinds of actions* are right or wrong.

However, although these two different levels of moral reasoning may seem clear enough, they cannot be entirely separated. For example, given that Ari and Jan hold such radically different metaethical views, their apparent agreement about the issue of arranged marriage is not as clear as it might superficially appear. When Ari says it's "wrong," he thinks it's absolutely, objectively wrong. But when Jan says she thinks it's "wrong," she is by her own admission merely expressing her own feelings. Now, Jan's feelings may be quite strong, but it wouldn't be surprising if her metaethical stance ultimately yields a difference in their normative claims. Ari may, for example, be less tolerant than Jan of the "wrongness" of arranged marriages, since Jan has to accept that others disagree with her and that there is finally no objective reason she can offer as to why her opinion is preferable. For her, at some point argument simply reaches its end. (Of course, at that point she might resort to force, instead of tolerance.) That means the moral attitude that's expressed by the statement "arranged marriages are wrong" can only be fully understood if one also takes into account the metaethical views of the person who states it. Metaethics colors normative ethics.

See also

2.4 Deontological ethics, 2.6 Divine command, 3.1 Absolute/relative, 3.6 Cognitivism/non-cognitivism, 3.16 Intrinsic/instrumental value

Reading

A. J. Ayer, *Language, Truth, and Logic* (New York: Dover Publications, 1946)
*Peter Singer, ed., *A Companion to Ethics* (Oxford: Blackwell, 1993)
*James Fieser, *Metaethics, Normative Ethics, and Applied Ethics: Contemporary and Historical Readings* (Florence, KY: Wadsworth Publishing, 1999)

3.21 Moral subjects/moral agents

Benjamin Franklin (1706–90) was a vegetarian for many years. But on his first voyage from Boston, his ship became becalmed. The ship's sailors caught some cod and started cooking it.

> I had formerly been a great Lover of Fish, [recalled Franklin in his autobiography] & when this came hot out of the Frying Pan, it smelt admirably

well. I balanc'd some time between Principle & inclination: till I recol-
lected, that when the Fish were opened, I saw smaller Fish taken out of
their Stomachs:—
   Then, thought I, if you eat one another, I don't see why we mayn't eat
you. So I din'd upon Cod very heartily.

Whether this is a good reason to abandon vegetarianism or not, the story
nicely illustrates the distinction between moral subjects and agents, as well
as the importance of that distinction. A *moral agent* is one who has moral
responsibility, who can act morally or immorally and who can be judged
to have acted well or badly on moral grounds. An automaton, for example,
is not a moral agent, even if it's programmed to do good or evil things,
because it has no control over what it does and so cannot be held in any way
responsible.

   A *moral subject*, in contrast, is something *for whom things can go well or
badly* and that therefore whose interests a moral agent has responsibility
to take into account. In other words, moral subjects have a right to *moral
standing* such that other moral beings ought to take due consideration of
them when deliberating about alternative courses of action. Perhaps the
clearest example of this is a baby. Babies are not yet moral agents. They
don't know what they're doing; they have no comprehension of right and
wrong. So if, for example, a baby should hurl something at a cat and kill the
unfortunate creature, it would be absurd to hold the child morally responsible for its conduct. Babies are, however, almost always considered to be
moral subjects. If you intentionally hurled something at a baby and killing
it, you would be held morally responsible.

   It's important to recognize that moral subjects are the only things whose
welfare or *welfare interests* we have to consider. Continuing the hurling theme,
if someone throws a stone at a vase and breaks it, as a moral agent the stone
thrower would be responsible for the damage. But this does not mean the
vase is a moral subject. That's because the stone thrower's actions don't
affect how well things go for the vase, since the vase has no point of view
from which things can go well or badly. Breaking the vase is morally wrong
only if it affects the welfare of moral subjects, such as its owners and the
owners of all other breakable objects.

Are only agents subjects?

When he was a vegetarian, Benjamin Franklin thought that it was his responsibility, as a moral agent, not to kill non-human animals, because they were
moral subjects. What then caused him to change his mind about fish? He

noticed that the fish themselves did not worry at all about killing other fish. They don't see each other or themselves as moral subjects. They don't take due consideration of welfare interests. And that's because they're not moral agents and aren't even capable of recognizing moral subjects.

Now, Franklin doesn't explain his reasoning in any detail, so it is possible to misinterpret him. But in formal terms, what Franklin seems to have thought is that, since fish are not moral agents, he need not treat them as moral subjects. They don't care about what they kill, so he shouldn't care if he kills them.

This suggests a general principle that only moral agents can be moral subjects. In other words, as moral agents, people need take into account the welfare interests of other things or creatures only if (a) they too are moral agents or (b) the welfare of other moral agents depends on them.

This contrasts with the view developed by Jeremy Bentham (1749–1832), among others, which holds that something can be a moral subject even if it's not a moral agent. "The question is not," he wrote, "Can they reason?, nor Can they talk? but, Can they suffer?"

Linking the concepts of moral subject and agent very tightly creates difficulties when it comes to liminal beings like newborn babies and the severely mentally disabled. As these are not moral agents, does that mean one should not treat them as moral subjects? Some have argued that people should treat them as subjects because they are *of a kind* of being (*homo sapiens*) whose members are, *as a whole* or *typically*, moral subjects. But that argument seems weak, because species membership does not seem to be a moral category.

It is possible to see both concepts as varying in degree. After all, even human beings are not entirely autonomous, responsible agents: our decisions and preferences are moulded by genes, upbringing, and culture. So, perhaps fish, not being moral agents, are less fully moral subjects, but moral subjects nonetheless. The worry here, however, is that this solution is even more slippery than the fish.

See also

1.2 Agency, 1.12 Interest, 4.16 Speciesism

Reading

Peter Singer, *Animal Liberation*, 2nd edition (London: Jonathan Cape, 1990)

Michael Slote, *Morals from Motives* (Oxford: Oxford University Press, 2001)
Tom Regan, *Animal Rights and Human Wrongs* (Lanham, MD: Rowman &
   Littlefield Publishers, 2003)

3.22 Prudence

In 1991, US President George H. W. Bush argued that ordering the US
army on to Baghdad after expelling the Iraqi forces from Kuwait wasn't, in
his own words, "prudent." His son, George W. Bush, came to a rather different conclusion at the time of the second Gulf War. Is this because the
two men subscribe to different moral and political theories? Is it because
circumstances have changed? Or is it because one Bush is simply more
"prudent" than the other?

In modern parlance, "prudence" is often used to mean "caution" or
"carefulness." But in philosophy, prudence retains something of its ancient
usage, most fully articulated by Aristotle (384–322 BCE). Aristotle observed
that some people are extremely knowledgeable with regard to matters of
theory but somehow extremely inept when it comes to the business of
actual life. Aristotle explained this peculiar phenomenon by distinguishing the kind of intellectual ability it takes to deal with theory from the
kind it takes to deal with practice. The former he called *sophia* (theoretical
wisdom); the latter he called *phronesis* or prudence (practical wisdom, via
the Latin, *prudentia*).

This distinction helps explain why successful professors of ethics sometimes fail dismally in their own moral lives. More generally, the concept is
useful for calling attention to an important element of ethical reasoning –
namely, the application of general moral theory to particular real situations.
Ethical reasoning about conduct might be formalized this way:

1   Live according to moral principle X.
2   Y is the way to live according to X in this situation.
3   Therefore, do Y.

That seems easy enough, but actually deploying "practical syllogisms"
like this or otherwise engaging in practical reasoning is fraught with
difficulties.

General rules, particular situations

It's hard enough to determine the best moral principle. That's the work of moral theorists using prudence to determine, as Aristotle says, "what promotes living well in general" (*Nicomachean Ethics* 1140a25–30, 1140b4–6). But more than that, moral life also requires intelligently figuring out in particular situations just how to realize the ideals of the theory and have *good judgment (gnomē)*.

Aristotle and those following him call the process of figuring out how to do this *deliberation*. One might say, then, that prudence is sound reasoning and effective deliberation that leads to morally right practice. (Because this process requires reasoning, non-rational beings can't, properly speaking, act morally.)

While everyone in a courtroom may know the law, figuring out how it applies to a particular situation often requires a lot of thought. Hence after hearing testimony and learning about the facts of the matter, judges and juries must deliberate. If the process of deliberation weren't required to accomplish it, figuring out how justice is served in a legal case would be as simple as a mathematical formula. One could do it with a table or a computer.

Prudence seems different from theoretical reasoning in so far as prudence requires experience in life in addition to the ability to reason well using general principles, laws, and concepts. Perhaps prudence also requires things like sensitivity to the variations of relevant factors, understanding how things work and how causal sequences play out in the world, and of course the skill to bring all these together.

All this makes it clear why the question of whether it was "prudent" to march on Baghdad is a much subtler and important one than may at first appear.

See also

1.7 Conscience, 4.9 Justice and lawfulness, 5.12 Radical particularity

Readings

Aristotle, *Nicomachean Ethics*, edited by Sarah Broadie (Oxford: Oxford University Press, 2002), Book VI, Chapters 7–8

*Thomas Aquinas, *Summa Theologica* [1266–75], edited by the Fathers of the English Dominican Province (Westminster, MD: Christian Classics, 1981), II-II, Questions 47–55

Robert Hariman, ed., *Prudence: Classical Virtue, Postmodern Practice* (University Park: Pennsylvania State University Press, 2003)

3.23 Public/private

Godfrey lives a blameless life. He is a good citizen who is kind to others, never prejudiced and always fair. Most days, however, he will retreat to the locked, windowless attic room in the house he lives in alone and work on his password-protected computer perfecting his pet project: a hyper-realistic video game which is based around the killing and torture of animals, Jews, and children, a game which also features scenes of violent pornography. Does that mean Godfrey is not a good man after all, but a morally deviant monster? Or is what he gets up to behind closed doors entirely his own business and not something we should morally judge?

In the morality of the Abrahamic faiths, the privacy of one's actions makes no difference. God is the source of morality, and nothing is hidden from him: "For a man's ways are in full view of the Lord, and He examines all his paths" (Proverbs 5:21). The rise of secularism and liberalism in the west, however, has seen a concomitant separation of the public and private spheres. John Stuart Mill (1806–73), for instance, argued in his highly influential text, *On Liberty* (1859), that "Over himself, over his own body and mind, the individual is sovereign." Others have no right to judge someone for the things she does, just as long as those things affect her and her alone.

These two positions, however, are entirely compatible. All Mill is saying is that society, in the form of its government and legal institutions, has no business in the private affairs of individuals. But that doesn't mean it's impossible for a person to do immoral things in private. All it means is that private immorality is solely the concern of the individual (and perhaps God). So, for instance, we might think that Godfrey is behaving very badly in his attic and yet also agree it's not for us to chastise him about it. Only if he starts trying to put his sordid game in the public domain does his private immorality become public business, or perhaps if he becomes *likely* to affect others through his immoral conduct.

Is strictly private immorality possible?

Nevertheless, the very possibility of purely private immorality has become less intuitively plausible to many. "If it's not harming anyone, what's wrong with it?" And, anyway, isn't morality necessarily about relationships, about the treatment of moral subjects by others and therefore essentially not something that applies to solitary conduct?

Even if, however, one does take the strictly consequentialist line that it makes no sense to say something is wrong if there is no harm caused, and even if morality is essentially about relationships, there are still at least three reasons to be concerned about the actions of someone like Godfrey.

The first is what economists like to call opportunity costs. Every time we do something, we're not doing something else. So, you might say that there's a cost to the time Godfrey invests in his video game – namely, the good things that he's not doing but could be.

The second reason is that harm to oneself should be taken seriously. If it is morally wrong to harm people, then it is morally wrong to harm oneself. There may be reasons for arguing that the state or others should allow you to harm yourself if you so wish, but that does not mean what you are doing isn't causing harm and is morally sound. One relates to oneself. In the case of Godfrey, what harm is he doing to himself? We might say his project is morally corrosive, that it's fostering vicious habits and attitudes – for example, anti-Semitism, the objectification of women, indifference to suffering, and so forth.

In terms of the story about Godfrey, that may seem implausible, since his behavior toward others in public remains impeccable. But this only leads to the third reason for concern about Godfrey. This story (a fiction, after all) just isn't plausible. What one does in private, at least with regard to some behaviors, is likely to affect how one behaves in public.

If we can detect no signs of misogyny or racism in Godfrey, it's likely only because he is covering up his prejudices well. While perhaps possible, it's improbable that someone who indulges in his kind of private pleasures would switch off the aberrant desires and judgments that engender them as soon as he steps outside his front door. On this view, the reason we should be concerned with private as well as public morality is simply that we do not lead neatly divided lives: the public spills over to the private and vice versa.

Again, and it's important to see this, the fact that our selves can't be cleanly divided between public and private doesn't justify legal sanctions against private behavior. Liberty interests may arguably trump moral concerns here. But it does justify possible moral judgment, though of a milder form than judgments about public behavior.

One counterargument is that, far from encouraging anti-social behaviors, private indulgence can provide a release for people with immoral desires – a kind of *catharsis* that actually prevents public wrongdoing. This has been one argument in favor of pornography: better that people fantasize in private than act out their fantasies in public. Perhaps empirical data should be key to resolving this dispute. Whether private fantasy encourages people to act out their antisocial desires or simply provides a release from them is something well-devised psychological experimentation should be able to determine. Perhaps this is one area where moral philosophers could use the assistance of other professionals.

But, of course, our presumption should be against judging any private conduct. It's a powerful cautionary note to remember that the private conduct of homosexuals, inter-racial couples, Jews, Protestants, Catholics, Muslims, and others would in the past have appeared much like Godfrey's conduct – perverse and immoral. How sure must we be about the pernicious public effects of private conduct before we make moral judgments about it – or, if we make a judgment, before we intervene to alter it?

Matters of conscience

Of course, sometimes the tension runs in the other direction. What, if any, are the duties a good person owes to a bad public – for example, an immoral community, nation, or employer?

For conscientious objectors and tax resisters, this can become a rather acute question. On the one hand, arguably all citizens of a polity bear a duty to uphold the public laws, even laws with which one disagrees. One can't simply ignore the speed limit on the local motorway because one disagrees with it. On the other hand, when the state engages in what one privately regards as seriously immoral conduct, like an unjust war or persecution, then isn't it the case that it's not only permissible for individuals to break public law and oppose community codes of conduct, but obligatory for them to do so?

People operating the Underground Railroad that helped slaves of the American South escape to free states or Canada were breaking the law and opposing custom. So were blacks who violated segregation laws and customs by sitting at "whites only" lunch counters. Just how strong and certain must one's personal moral judgment about the immorality of a public institution become before one defies public obligations? Who's to make the judgment?

These are difficult questions, and they're likely to continue to vex both governments and private individuals for quite some time.

See also

1.6 Character, 1.10 Flourishing, 1.19 Rights, 3.17 Legal/moral

Reading

*Donald G. Jones, ed., *Private and Public Ethics: Tensions Between Conscience and Institutional Responsibility* (New York: The Mellen Press, 1978)

Raymond Geuss, *Public Goods, Private Goods* (Princeton, NJ: Princeton University Press, 2003)

*Christopher Wellman and John Simmons, *Is There a Duty to Obey the Law?* (Cambridge: Cambridge University Press, 2005)

3.24 Stoic cosmopolitanism

Individuals are citizens of particular polities. The rights and obligations to which they may make claim (and which may make claims upon them) extend, some say, only from the positive civil law (*jus civilis*) of those political domains. Similarly, those whom we might call ethical *parochialists* hold that moral values, principles, and duties are inextricably rooted in and extend no farther than the local governments, cultures, ethnic, and identity communities to which people belong. But why shouldn't we extend moral consideration beyond the boundaries of those communities? And doesn't it seem absurd that someone should acquire moral standing just because he or she has migrated across an arbitrary political boundary, or any other community boundary for that matter?

Cosmopolis

Ancient Stoics would agree and, in contrast to parochialists, advanced the doctrine of a universal natural law (*jus naturalis*) that binds all people to its duties and to each other – even perhaps to other species. For the Stoics our obligations aren't limited to the boundaries of our local communities. We share in a common nature, a common rationality, and a shared basis for moral conversation and dispute. Every other person in the world is to be recognized as a neighbor, and our local arrangements can be criticized from a standpoint that extends well beyond them.

Diogenes of Sinope, the Cynic (fourth century BCE), "when he was asked where he came from, he replied, 'I am a citizen of the world'" (Diogenes Laertius, *Lives of Eminent Philosophers*, VI: 63). Similarly, the Stoics described the entire universe as a single society, one to which every rational being belongs and through which all are fellow citizens. People who apprehend the natural law and act accordingly live not only as citizens of their individual polities but also as citizens of the universal community, the Cosmopolis.

Nussbaum and shared multiculturalism

Martha Nussbaum (b. 1947) has been influential in arguing that an updated, less metaphysical form of Stoic cosmopolitanism offers people today a useful moral framework in which to deliberate. Chief among her claims is that Stoic cosmopolitanism makes possible the sustenance of local political and moral distinctions without their devolving into separatist, isolated, and parochial communities that remain inscrutable and hostile to one another. Cosmopolitanism demands that we cultivate and respect obligations to one another and that we seek out shared ways to converse and reason with one another. In this way, it provides a counterweight both to Hobbesian (or "realist") doctrines that construe political-ethical issues solely in terms of national and personal interest and to relativistic conceptions that divide us and offer no common ground.

Early modern political documents like the French Revolution's Declaration of the Rights of Man and of the Citizen (1789) and Thomas Jefferson's Declaration of Independence (1776), which proclaim universal human rights, are animated by similar project. One of the most recent examples of this gesture is the Universal Declaration of Human Rights adopted by the United Nations in 1948.

Perhaps the International Criminal Court (ICC) may be considered as an instance of cosmopolitanism, but like the notion of universal human rights, perhaps here certain dangers lurk. Can such a court really be expected to be impartial, prosecuting cases against the mighty as well as the relatively weak, or will it be a mask for the extension of arbitrary, even imperialistic power? Judges are appointed to the court arguably at a distance from popular election, and they don't face the same processes of approval and recall to which domestic judges are subject. Moreover, many of the member nations of the UN are profoundly undemocratic and have little respect in their own practice for human rights. Why should they have a voice – even a veto – in the determination of international justice?

The Chinese are among those who have argued that many conceptions of universal rights are actually parochial ideas that the west imposes (often with ulterior motives) on others. This claim raises important questions. Is a non-parochial set of rights even possible? Can people really be cosmopolitan, citizens of the world?

See also

1.15 Natural law, 2.13 Rationalism, 2.14 Relativism

Readings

Cicero, *On Moral Ends*, edited by Julia Annas (Cambridge: Cambridge University Press, 2001)

Immanuel Kant, *Perpetual Peace and Other Essays* [1795], translated by Ted Humphrey (Indianapolis, IN: Hackett Publishing, 1983)

Martha Nussbaum, "Patriotism and Cosmopolitanism" [1996] in her *For Love of Country?* (Boston, MA: Beacon Press, 2002)

Part IV

Assessment, Judgment, and Critique

4.1 Alienation

Has the Internet brought people closer together or driven them apart? Instant messaging and e-mail offer immediate communication across vast distances. But those with their eyes glued to computer screens all day and night have less contact with the flesh and blood people around them. The barrage of e-mail absorbs our time; the multiplying maze of websites buries us under a mountain of often worthless information. Online sex substitutes for the real thing. Electronic pets make organic ones redundant. Virtual games take the place of sport.

These downsides of the connected world are often summed up with the claim that technology is alienating. Contemporary life is held to be frenetic, isolating, and competitive. Humans have arranged things so that they must compete with one another for jobs, for medical care, for the goods, services, and comforts of life. People interact with others principally through the cash nexus, through commercial interaction by which others attend to us (and we to them) for money. Family becomes an instrument of consumption and exchange. And of course the relationship between owners and workers (not to mention races and religions) is one of ongoing struggle. This way of life has alienated us from something fundamental to what Karl Marx called our *species being*, something thinkers as diverse as Aristotle and evolutionary biologists have observed – our sociability, our cooperative, communal needs.

Forms of alienation

But alienation need not only be from others. One can also be alienated from one's true self. To be thus alienated is to be estranged, to be at a distance from oneself, to be somehow not where it's natural to be, where one fits or is at home, where one can truly be oneself.

What is one likely to do after a hard day at the factory or office where neither our minds nor our bodies are fully our own? What is likely to interest people after fighting traffic and public transport congestion, after shopping, cooking, and tending to their dependents? Not difficult intellectual or artistic pursuits. One is more likely to seek something pain numbing, something simple or carnal, something like alcohol, television, or sex. But a life like this alienates us from our intellectual capacities and the essential satisfactions they afford.

Marxists in particular also talk about alienation from one's creation. In modern capitalist production systems workers principally do what they're told. They follow management plans formulated by others and produce goods designed by others for others. But people need more, say critics, than this alienating way of life. Humans are not so much *homo sapiens* as *homo faber*. They are makers, beings that realize themselves through their personal, free, self-initiated, self-directed creativity.

Some critics also complain about the way contemporary artificial lives have distanced people from the natural world. Our well-lit and comfortable cities may offer lots of entertainment, shopping, and work; but they seal people off from plants and other animals as well as from the beauty, quiet, and even struggle people need to make their lives complete and happy. Others point to the way our ideas about sex roles, gendered labor, and (hetero)sexual identity alienate individuals from the much greater diversity that's possible in human life.

To criticize a practice or theory as alienating is therefore not directly to question the validity of its arguments or the truth of its premises. Rather, it is to claim that it takes us from what our true nature should be and leaves us disconnected from the things that really matter in life.

See also

1.4 Autonomy, 1.16 Need, 4.2 Authenticity

Reading

Karl Marx, "Alienated Labor" in his *Economic and Philosophical Manuscripts of 1844* (Amherst, NY: Prometheus Books, 1988)
Martin Heidegger, "The Question Concerning Technology" [1954], in David Farrell Krell, ed., *Martin Heidegger: Basic Writings*, revised and expanded edition (New York: Harper Collins, 1993)
Bertell Ollman, *Alienation: Marx's Conception of Man in a Capitalist Society*, 2nd edition (Cambridge: Cambridge University Press, 1976)

4.2 Authenticity

The idea of "keeping it real" is a very seductive one in popular culture. The cool never admit a liking for pop, which is seen as manufactured and inauthentic – for example, consider the Monkees, the Backstreet Boys or the Spice Girls, whose music, costumes, and even performers are selected by a music industry with the overriding objective of profit. Authentic music is sought in folk, local, ethnic, and avant-garde music, new hybrids like alt. country, and indie rock. In a culture where artifice is everywhere, a premium is placed on the real, authentic thing.

Sometimes it seems as though everything one thinks, feels, desires, believes, and does has been prescribed by someone else. Parents, peers, advertising, religious authorities, intellectuals, government officials, celebrities, and countless others seem to brandish imperatives and formulas about how one is supposed to be. But to some philosophers, living according to the prescriptions of others (especially when doing so isn't consciously recognized) is a repudiation of human freedom and of one's true self. It is, therefore, *inauthentic* and something to be refused.

Authenticity and existentialism

The use of "authenticity" as a critical term is associated primarily with existentialist philosophers like Jean-Paul Sartre (1905–80) and Simone de Beauvoir (1908–86). Sartre's and Beauvoir's conception, however, was drawn from the work of phenomenologist Martin Heidegger (1889–1976), especially *Being and Time* (1927).

Existentialists proclaimed, "existence precedes essence." By this they meant, contrary to the views of most of the philosophers before them, that there is no human nature or intrinsic essence. First, humans exist. They find themselves simply abandoned, thrown into a meaningless and ultimately crushing universe. Then, through their own free choices and creative activity, human beings create themselves, their values, and the meanings of the world.

Facing human reality as it is and accepting responsibility for what they are and believe is, however, difficult for people. Most live in what Sartre called *mauvaise foi* (bad faith), pretending that what they are has been determined by forces beyond themselves (*Being and Nothingness*, 1944). People would rather believe they are social "constructs," products of the dialectical march of history, the creations of consumer mass culture, the necessary effects of chains of natural causes, the results of natural selection, or the creations of some deity. And in many ways the social order has been structured to mask or inhibit realizing this. Simone de Beauvoir argued powerfully that the sadistic and patriarchal order of contemporary society thwarted the authenticity of women, rendering them as *The Second Sex* – the title of her 1949 book.

Doctrines and beliefs that mask human freedom and responsibility are not simply false, according to existentialists, but in the very assertion of them, people on some level know them to be false. They are, therefore, more than false; they're bad faith. Even if moral imperatives were somehow presented to people by God or nature, it would still be up to us whether or not to accept them: Moses was free to give the Ten Commandments back.

Living authentically, then, means not living in bad faith. It means acknowledging and respecting human freedom and taking responsibility for who and what one is. People become authentic, according to many existentialists, by first lucidly facing the reality of their own deaths and the meaninglessness of existence. They then must resolutely in good faith choose what to be, that is, choose their ownmost way of being.

Choosing authentically

On April 14, 1975, 21-year-old Karen Ann Quinlan collapsed and then slipped into a persistent vegetative state. After a period of legal struggle her family faced the decision of whether or not to remove her from the life-support devices that were sustaining her. Quinlan's family did remove the life-support equipment only to discover that Karen was able to breathe on her own. She continued to live in a persistent vegetative state until her death in 1985.

The choice the family had to make was extremely difficult. In situations like theirs (indeed, in nearly any situation) our society presents people with a lot of inauthentic options. To make such a choice authentically means first accepting the difficulty head-on and not pretending that there's a simple answer ready-made for us by others. While others may advise us, it would be inauthentic simply to defer to authorities – like, for example, the authorities of religion, medicine, popular culture, academia, or even the state. Authenticity means not shifting responsibility. One has to take the burden upon oneself entirely; make the decision freely, acknowledging one's finitude, on the basis only of one's ownmost and resolute choice of being. No one else can choose for you.

No doubt this is difficult. But is it even really possible? Critics argue that the idea of authenticity imagines falsely that we are entirely free, self-determining agents, when really we are constrained by custom, tradition, human nature, social pressure, and external authority. We may like the idea of being authentic, but can we ever truly be so?

See also

1.2 Agency, 1.4 Autonomy, 3.2 Act/rule

Reading

*Robert C. Solomon, ed., *Existentialism* (New York: Random House, 1974)
Charles Taylor, *The Ethics of Authenticity* (Cambridge, MA: Harvard University Press, 1992)
*Corey Anton, *Selfhood and Authenticity* (Albany: State University of New York Press, 2001)

4.3 Consistency

When Jean-Jacques Rousseau (1712–78) wrote, "I should rather be a man of paradoxes than a man of prejudices," he was expressing a widely held idea that moral goodness is not primarily a matter of rigorous logic but rather human feeling. Being consistent, therefore, may be the highest demand of logic, but not of ethics. Perhaps compassion, for example, is a greater moral virtue that absolute consistency. More pointedly, why should one think the rational demands of consistency have any moral claim on people at all? So what if people behave in ways that are rationally inconsistent? Doing so may offend lovers of reason, such as philosophers. But is a crime against reason an offense against morality, too? Perhaps Ralph Waldo Emerson (1803–82) was right, at least about ethics, when he said, "A foolish consistency is the hobgoblin of little minds" ("Self Reliance," 1841).

However, the idea that consistency is at the very least a constraint on ethical behavior has a fine pedigree, in common sense as well as in theoretical philosophy. When someone acts in ways inconsistent with his or her moral declarations, it's not just logicians who protest: such people are generally known as hypocrites. To advocate vegetarianism while tucking into a bacon sandwich; to protest against capitalism while living off one's stock dividends; or to preach monogamy while conducting a secret affair; saying that these are mere logical inconsistencies seems to fly in the face of what ordinary people expect from morality.

The demand of consistency

If we accept, then, *contra* Rousseau, that consistency has a role to play in ethics, what is that role? The first point to note is that for moral inconsistency to be truly logical inconsistency, moral rules must apply to all moral agents. Moral agents must all stand before the bar of moral judgment in the same way, without exception. If not, then many examples of moral hypocrisy may not, strictly speaking, be logically inconsistent. For example, consider these pairs of injunctions:

1 Monogamy is a moral imperative.
2 But not for me.

1 Other people should not eat meat.
2 But I can.

There is no logical inconsistency between each proposition, because the first applies to other people, and the second only to me. Logical contradictions only emerge when people cannot make exceptions to moral rules. So, for example, to say "monogamy is a moral imperative" is just to say that it is an imperative for all. And "other people should not eat meat" is an ill-formed moral rule, since no moral principle can apply only to "other people" without very good reason. Indeed, one might say that it's a hallmark of moral principles that they apply *universally*, or at least must universally apply to those who advocate them.

Most ethical theorists accept these demands of consistency. There are, however, some – if you'll pardon the expression – exceptions. *Particularists* would reject consistency constraints (or at least what normally appear to be consistency constraints) on the grounds that it's simply not possible to generate moral rules that are general enough to apply to the complex, diverse, and even unique situations typical of moral life; and without rules that apply to more than one case, inconsistency is impossible. *Emotivists* don't believe that moral declarations are statements that can even be true or false; they're simply not the kind of thing that can produce logical contradiction or contrariety.

Consistency as a foundation and a test

If there are some who reject the consistency constraint, others argue that consistency is not just a constraint on morality, but that it grounds what morality is at its very root. Most importantly, Immanuel Kant's (1724–1804) "categorical imperative" placed consistency at the center of ethics: "Act only on that maxim through which you can at the same time will that it should become a universal law" (*Groundwork of the Metaphysics of Morals*, 1785). What this means is that consistency is crucial to any test for whether or not a principle of conduct is morally sound.

For Kant, a principle or "maxim" of conduct is moral only if it's logically possible for everyone to engage in that conduct. For instance, lying cannot be universal, since it's possible to lie only to people who assume they're being told the truth – but if everyone always lied no one would make that assumption. Similarly, theft can't become universally accepted since one can only steal from those who object to having things taken from them – but if everyone agrees to everyone taking from anyone whatever one wishes, whenever one wishes it, no one can object. Objecting would quickly lead to logical inconsistency, because then one would be both in favor of and against the same thing being permissible. For Kant, this sort of inconsistency is typical of immoral behavior – immoral people logically require others to be bound by principles from which they exempt themselves. Moreover, for Kant if conduct is grounded in a maxim that requires consistency, it's morally sound.

Consistently wrong

Consistency by itself, however, is not enough to guarantee moral acceptability. Although it may be a necessary condition for conduct being moral, it seems implausible to argue that it is a sufficient one. The problem is that many morally repugnant value systems may also be perfectly consistent. It's consistent, for example, to advocate a system that grants different rights to men and women, or even one ethnic group over another. To show that these moral systems are wrong, one needs to appeal to more than inconsistency.

One needs to show that there's no justification for discriminating against certain members of the population, for establishing a hierarchy of rights and privileges.

Even if the discrimination can be shown to rest upon an inconsistency, it's difficult to make the case that every single moral dispute arises because the disputants have erred through an inconsistency. Difficult, but perhaps not impossible. Plenty still follow in Kant's footsteps and see consistency as the key to ethics.

See also

2.10 Particularism, 2.13 Rationalism, 4.18 Universalizability

Reading

*Robert Paul Wolff, *The Autonomy of Reason: A Commentary on Kant's Groundwork of the Metaphysics of Morals* (New York: Harper Collins, 1974)
Alasdair MacIntyre, *Whose Justice? Which Rationality?* (South Bend, IN: University of Notre Dame Press, 1988)
Elijah Milgram, *Ethics Done Right: Practical Reasoning as a Foundation for Moral Theory* (Cambridge: Cambridge University Press, 2005)

4.4 Counterexamples

Fertility treatments have enabled women to become mothers at ever older ages. But in cases such as that of the 66-year-old Romanian Adriana Iliescu, who gave birth to a baby girl in January 2005, not everyone is ready to congratulate the mother. The Catholic journalist, Cristina Odone, wrote: "It is unnatural to give birth beyond a certain age." Richard Kennedy, the mother's obstetrician, declared: "Pregnancy for a woman of that age is a potentially hazardous adventure . . . Any doctor who advises women otherwise would be unprofessional and wrong." Another pundit, Amanda Platell, lamented the fact that the child would have "an old woman in a nursing home" for a mother.

One powerful way of rebutting all these criticisms is with counterexamples. First, against Odone's complaint that the birth was unnatural, one can point out the many unnatural things of which people thoroughly approve, such as virtually all of modern medicine and material comforts.

These counterexamples show that the fact that the births were unnatural is not enough to show that they were wrong.

Against Kennedy's complaint that the pregnancy was dangerous, one might point to examples of people who tried to have children when they were not fully fit, perhaps doing so even during times of war or other peril. If critics aren't prepared to say that those people were wrong, then they shouldn't claim that the mere danger of the pregnancy is a reason to condemn it. Indeed, one might say it's a reason to see the mother as brave.

Against Platell, one might point out that many people become parents who are not ideally positioned in life. But unless critics are prepared to maintain that the disabled, imprisoned, poor, depressed, or unintelligent are wrong to have children, they shouldn't condemn Ms Iliescu simply because she couldn't be the ideal parent to her child.

The form of arguments from counterexample

Of course, none of these responses ends the debate. But each one is a striking demonstration of the power of counterexamples. The way an argument from a counterexample works is as follows:

1 It is claimed that p (e.g. that x is wrong).
2 In counterexample a, p is not true (x is not wrong).
3 p cannot be both true and not true (x cannot be wrong and not wrong).
4 So either the claim that p is false or the counterexample a is false.
5 Counterexample a is not false.
6 Therefore p is false (and x is not wrong)

Clearly, then, for such an argument to work, the counterexample must be well chosen so that it is itself true (5) and that it shows that p is not true (2). If these two conditions are met, the argument from counterexample can be decisive. Equally clearly, to rebut an argument from counterexample, one needs to show that either of these conditions does not obtain.

Rejecting counterexamples

For example, Kennedy's objection might be upheld on the grounds that the counterexamples fail to show that the proposition he advances (it's wrong to advise a dangerous pregnancy) is false, since it can be argued that it is indeed wrong to advise anyone to try for children if she's not fully fit or not living in a safe place. In this case, the counterexample may serve to focus our attention on what exactly is being claimed: Kennedy did not argue that the mother was wrong to have the child, merely that a doctor would be wrong to advise her to try for one.

One could also argue against the objection to Platell by claiming that critics *should* hold that disabled, poor, depressed, or unintelligent people are wrong to have children. The counterexample only demonstrates what most people think, not what ought to be the case. But, of course, for that reply to work, Platell would have to bite the bullet and agree with that harsh judgment of some people's fitness to be parents, and provide grounds for doing so.

This is why counterexamples can be very powerful. They can shift the onus of the argument so that someone is forced to defend his or her position in the face of the counterexample, or else be forced to accept what may be an unpalatable corollary that the counterexample makes plain.

See also

4.3 Consistency, 4.13 Reflective equilibrium, 4.17 Thought experiments

Reading

*Elias E. Savellos, *Reasoning in the Courts: The Elements* (Belmont, CA: Wadsworth Publishing, 2000)
*Julie van Camp, *Ethical Issues in the Courts: A Companion to Philosophical Ethics* (Belmont, CA: Wadsworth Publishing, 2000)
*Patrick J. Hurley, *A Concise Introduction to Logic*, 9th edition (Belmont, CA: Wadsworth Publishing, 2005)

4.5 Fairness

Children often complain, when denied something by their parents, that "It's not fair." Indeed, "fairness" is a common and enduring ethical concept. It's also, however, fairly vague.

Fairness seems to require consideration of two elements:

1 The idea of *distribution*, the way in which something is meted out; and
2 The *comparison* of some class of recipients and what they receive through that distribution with some other class.

Of course the extent to which life can be made fair is limited to the extent we have no control over the way some things are distributed (for example illness and intelligence – though note the way things we do control, like pollution and education, affect these). To say, moreover, that fairness is achieved when the distribution is made appropriate to the comparison between the recipients sounds hopelessly tautological: fairness becomes a fair distribution.

Aristotle in his *Nicomachean Ethics* offers a principle that is perhaps a more illuminating explanation of what fairness is. It's often paraphrased as: "treat equals equally and unequals unequally" (Books II.6 and V.3). Applied to fairness, one might say then that fairness requires that equals receive equally what is distributed and unequals receive unequally (in a way proper to their equality); doing this in both cases comprises treating people *equitably*. (Of course, figuring out who are equals and who are unequals has engaged enormous political and ethical struggle.)

For instance, if all citizens are equal, then all citizens should receive equal rights and equal treatment before the law. But since children are unequals in comparison with adults, rights and privileges should be distributed in an unequal way between them – but an unequal way that's still equitable, that's proper to their inequality. Adults, for example, possess the right to vote, to make contracts, and sit on juries, while children do not (the converse would be unfair). On the other hand, children have the right to be fed and supported by caregivers, while normal, healthy adults do not (and doing this the other way around would be unfair).

Another hotly contested controversy in contemporary ethical conversation is whether it is fair to deny homosexuals access to the institutions of marriage. In most countries, for the most part homosexual couples are denied the rights, privileges, and protections distributed to heterosexual couples through marriage; that is, the distribution is unequal.

Proponents of gay and lesbian marriage argue that the existing distribution is unfair, since both sorts of pairings involve competent, consenting, adult citizens who share the same vulnerabilities and produce the same goods as straight couples. Opponents of homosexual marriage argue that homosexual and heterosexual unions are in some sense unequal, and so it's not appropriate to grant the same rights of marriage to both.

Justice as fairness

John Rawls (1921–2002) has famously articulated in his *A Theory of Justice* (1971) and related articles, a way of defining justice through a specific conception of fairness. "Fairness is distributing things according to principles to which rational and competent people would agree if they were wholly free of personal interest."

To help clarify this concept Rawls developed the idea of a "veil of ignorance," a device that prevents people from knowing anything personal about themselves. So, under the veil of ignorance, one is prevented from knowing one's sex, class, race, religion, physical or intellectual capacity, family history, etc. Rawls has argued that this imaginary device illuminates what it means to select principles that do not privilege any group over another. Principles selected in this way will be "fair" to all (at least if people deliberate in the way Rawls thinks they would under the veil).

One of the principles Rawls thinks would be selected under the veil of ignorance has been called the *maximin* principle of distribution. According to Rawls, equality of distribution is the presumption of fairness. The only departures from equality that would be fair would be those distributions that also raise the standard of the least well off. The fairest unequal distribution, then, would be the one that maximizes the position of the minimum, the worst off. So, if a perfectly equitable distribution resulted in a standard of living index of, say, 100, then any acceptable redistribution producing inequality will be acceptable only if it leaves the worst off at a standard of 101 or more. Any redistribution that leaves the worst off at 100 or below is unacceptable. An unequal distribution that only raised the minimum to 140 would be worse than an unequal distribution that raised the minimum to 150, no matter how much it increased the standing of the wealthiest.

See also

1.19 Rights, 2.2 Contractarianism, 4.3 Consistency

Reading

Matthew Clayton and Andrew Williams, eds., *Social Justice* (Malden, MA: Blackwell, 2004)

*John Rawls, *Justice as Fairness: A Restatement*, edited by Erin Kelly (Cambridge, MA: The Belknap Press, 2001)

Amartya Sen, *Inequality Reexamined* (Cambridge, MA: Harvard University Press, 1992)

4.6 Fallacies

> This committee must recognize that Prof. Frankenstein's proposed research on human stem cells is immoral. We know from past experience that when scientists are allowed to experiment with human life, dire consequences usually follow. We know Frankenstein is a very disagreeable character. And we also know that this research is opposed by the vast majority of the public. So, we have a choice: do we allow the professor to take us down a dangerous road, or do we make a stand for what is right and deny his application?

In moral discourse, as in all others, bad reasoning is legion. And this imagined paragraph is full of it. Therefore, to argue well in ethics, one needs to be able to spot these errors of logic and avoid making them oneself. To do this it helps to be familiar with common fallacies.

Formal fallacies

An argument that doesn't work is described as fallacious. But fallacies come in various forms. Formal fallacies are those where the error lies in the structure of the argument. In these fallacies, one can often see why the argument is fallacious without even paying attention to what it is about. Consider this example:

1   If you kill innocent people for the mere fun of it, you are a bad person.
2   You are a bad person.
3   Therefore, you kill innocent people for the mere fun of it.

This fallacy is called, "affirming the consequent," and any argument that has its structure must be fallacious. The structure can be represented like this:

1   If p, then q
2   q
3   Therefore, p

The conclusion just doesn't follow from the premises. One can see this clearly in a counterexample that uses the structure to draw a clearly false conclusion from true premises:

1   If it's a cat (p), then it's a mammal (q).
2   This dog is a mammal (q).
3   Therefore, this dog is a cat (p).

Informal fallacies

Informal fallacies, in contrast, are fallacious in virtue of their actual content. For example, in the speech above, several reasons are presented for the conclusion that the proposed research is wrong. One is that "it is opposed by the vast majority of the public." So, the argument hinges on the premise that "If something is opposed by the public, it is wrong." If we accept that premise, the argument does follow logically:

1   If something is opposed by a majority of the public, it's wrong.
2   Stem cell research is opposed by a majority of the public.
3   Therefore, stem cell research is wrong.

This is a valid structure (called *modus ponens*), therefore there's no formal fallacy. But there's an informal one, because the first premise is false (and false in a commonly misleading way). If a majority of the public believed that the Sun orbited the Earth or that witches existed, that wouldn't make it true. Because this fallacious way of reasoning is so common, it has its own name: *argumentum ad populum*.

Four more fallacies

The short speech above actually contains examples of at least four other fallacies. An *argumentum ad hominem* attacks the person holding a position rather than the position itself: the fact that Prof. Frankenstein has "a very disagreeable character" is irrelevant to the morality of his research.

"Do we allow the professor to take us down a dangerous road, or do we make a stand for what is right and deny his application?" presents a *false dichotomy* and also *begs the question*. It presents a false dichotomy (or false alternatives) by offering just two exclusive choices whereas in fact there are other options – such as allowing the professor to conduct his research with certain conditions attached. It begs the question because it assumes what is supposed to be still up for debate: that it would be wrong to allow the research to go ahead.

Still there's more: The speech also commits the *fallacy of accident*, in that it argues from what is (allegedly) *usually* the case (that when scientists are allowed to experiment with human life, dire consequences follow) to the conclusion that this *particular* case is wrong. But what's "usual" rather than "universal" is by its very nature subject to exceptions. So, it can't be assumed that any particular result will follow from what is usual; it might in the given case be an exception.

There are simply too many varieties of fallacy to be listed in a book dedicated specifically to ethics. Although it's more than possible to spot examples of fallacious arguments without formally studying the classic varieties, it's certainly useful to familiarize yourself with their most common forms. After all, the reason why they're so common is that they're very effective: people don't seem to be naturally very good at spotting them, and many people even seem to find them convincing. To study fallacies is therefore to help immunize oneself against the rhetorical power of bad but persuasive arguments. It's a precaution that's well worth the time.

See also

4.3 Consistency, 4.4 Counterexamples, 5.3 Bad faith and self-deception

Reading

John Shand, *Arguing Well* (London: Routledge, 2000)
Nigel Warburton, *Thinking from A to Z*, 2nd edition (London: Routledge, 2000)
*Julian Baggini and Peter S. Fosl, *The Philosopher's Toolkit: A Compendium of Philosophical Concepts and Methods* (Oxford: Blackwell, 2003)

4.7 Impartiality and objectivity

Chapter nine of Jung Chang's *Wild Swans* (1992) is called "Living with an incorruptible man." The man in question was Chang's father, Wang Yu, a regional governor in Mao's China. He strictly adhered to the communist party's line that it was wrong to give any privileges to family members. He went so far as to reprimand a colleague who sent for an official car to take his wife home from hospital after giving birth, saving her a half-hour walk. Wang Yu insisted that an official car should not be used unless the official himself was in it, and he was out of town at the time.

Whatever one thinks of the value system that Wang Yu was following, isn't it nevertheless admirable that he applied it so objectively? Isn't objectivity to be desired in ethics? Yet, most people's initial reaction to the story is that his response was heartless, not morally upright.

The meanings of objectivity

The story brings into question just what moral "objectivity" means. In its strictest sense, morality is objective if it exists or can be defined independently of human conventions, desires, beliefs, or anything else subjective. This is objectivity with regard to the nature of ethical principles themselves.

There is, however, another sense of "objective" that concerns the way morality is applied – irrespective of whether moral principles are themselves truly objective. Compare this sense to the way a teacher might impose rules on a classroom. Clearly, these rules are merely artificial social constructs that have no objective existence outside of the culture and context in which they have been created. But nevertheless, the teacher can apply these rules objectively, if she treats everybody the same and neither grants favors nor withdraws privileges arbitrarily.

This kind of objectivity is often called "impartiality," and there are clearly many occasions when it's the appropriate way to follow moral maxims. As Jung Chang's story suggests, however, to be completely impartial and never privilege those with whom one has a special relationship seems inhuman. So, must objectivity always entail complete impartiality?

Objective but partial

Not necessarily. To see why, we need to distinguish rules themselves, their application, and their justification. As it turns out, it's possible for moral rules to permit partiality and still be objective (in the sense of being applied or justified impartially). In short, things break down this way:

- *Impartiality of rules.* Moral rules do not allow us to treat those close to us any differently, and we must follow these rules objectively.
- *Impartiality of application.* Moral rules do allow us to treat those close to us differently in certain ways, and we must follow these rules objectively.
- *Impartiality in the justification of rules.* Moral rules may allow for, or even require, partiality in many contexts but these rules may themselves be justified from a completely impartial perspective, by a normative position such as utilitarianism.

The second possibility shows how it is possible to imagine a moral system that itself allows people to show more concern and care for immediate family and close friends. The requirement to apply moral rules objectively therefore would involve the need not to bend the rules in inappropriate ways for those close to us and to allow others to also favor their own in the same way. The rules may permit a variety of conduct, but each rule must be upheld as strictly and consistently as the other.

Conversely, when it comes to moral obligations, there may be significant differences, too. For example, with regard to emergencies like saving people from a sinking ship, it can be argued that one has special, additional obligations to help members of one's family and other intimates, obligations that don't require one to help strangers in the same ways.

Impartial ethical systems

Several moral systems do seem to require impartiality of rules, not just application. Jeremy Bentham's (1749–1832) utilitarianism, for example, requires that "each is to count for one, and no one for more than one." Followed strictly, that would seem to require that in ethics no special treatment should be given to friends and family, as that would require them to count for more than others.

Christian ethics, if it's to follow the teachings of the Gospels, would also seem to require a weakening of family ties. This seems to be the message of several passages, including: "Then his mother and his brothers came to him, but they could not reach him for the crowd. And he was told, 'Your mother and your brothers are standing outside, desiring to see you.' But he said to them, 'My mother and my brothers are those who hear the word of God and do it'" (Luke 8:19–21).

That moral rules need to be applied impartially seems to be a requirement of consistency. That moral rules themselves must not allow for any kind of partiality is a much stronger claim, and one that is much more controversial.

See also

3.6 Cognitivism/non-cognitivism, 4.3 Consistency, 5.13 The separateness of persons

Reading

Brian Barry, *Justice as Impartiality* (Oxford: Oxford University Press, 1995)
Brad Hooker, *Ideal Code, Real World: A Rule-Consequentialist Theory of Morality* (Oxford: Oxford University Press, 2000)
Michael Moore, *Objectivity in Ethics and Law* (Burlington, VT: Ashgate, 2004)

4.8 The "is/ought gap"

According to the World Health Organization, the acute health effects of cannabis or marijuana use include impairment of cognitive development and psychomotor performance. The chronic effects on health of smoking it include: the selective and sometimes permanent impairment of cognitive functioning; the development of cannabis dependence; the exacerbation of schizophrenia; the epithelial injury of the trachea and major bronchi; lung inflammation; diminished pulmonary defenses against infection; and impairment in fetal development leading to a reduction in birth weight. This shows that cannabis use is morally wrong.

Each sentence in the preceding paragraph, apart from the last one, contains only matters of fact. The paragraph ends, however, with something else, namely the value judgment that "smoking cannabis is morally wrong." But is it possible to get from the former statements about what *is* the case to the latter claim about what *ought* to be the case? The difficulty of bridging the is/ought gap has been a major issue in moral philosophy, and one that's still not entirely resolved.

Hume's problem

The modern discussion of the issue began with Hume, who remarked in his 1740 *A Treatise of Human Nature*:

> In every system of morality, which I have hitherto met with, I have always remark'd, that the author proceeds for some time in the ordinary way of reasoning, and establishes the being of a God, or makes observations concerning human affairs; when of a sudden I am surpriz'd to find, that instead of the usual copulations of propositions, *is*, and *is not*, I meet with no proposition that is not connected with an *ought*, or an *ought not*. This change is imperceptible; but is, however, of the last consequence. (Book III, Part i, §1)

At its most basic level this is a simple point of logic. An argument can no more proceed from premises that only contain "is" statements to a conclusion that expresses an "ought" than it can from premises that only mention fish to conclusions about prime ministers. Conclusions have to be established by their premises, and this is impossible if the premises make no mention of what is in the conclusion.

This is why the opening paragraph about cannabis is not a sound argument. Although there's a long list of the harms cannabis use causes, it's just a list of facts. It says nothing about what ought to be the case, only what is.

So, to conclude from these facts that smoking cannabis is wrong is to say more than the facts establish.

What one would need to bridge this gap is an evaluative premise such as, "It is wrong to consume products that have many and wide-ranging negative effects on the consumer's health." It needs to be noted, however, that no such premise could itself be established by facts alone, for the same reason as the original conclusion did not follow from facts alone: no ought can ever be derived from a mere is.

The "fact/value distinction"

The "is/ought gap" is often taken to be synonymous with the "fact/value distinction." There are, however, two importantly different ideas that lay claim to these labels.

1 No evaluative conclusion can be deduced from purely factual premises.
2 Facts have no evaluative content: facts are value-free.

The second is a stronger thesis than the first. For example, it's consistent with (1) to argue that factual premises may not be *purely* factual: some facts, in contradiction to (2), do have evaluative content. By this account, therefore, facts and values do not belong to two mutually exclusive realms, and although (1) holds for *purely* factual premises, that doesn't mean facts and values can never be mixed in other arguments.

If we had our way, we'd be able to tell you that the "is/ought gap," as described by Hume, amounts to nothing more than (1); and that the so-called "fact/value distinction," which has exercised so many contemporary philosophers, refers to the different and stronger claim expressed in (2). The fact of the matter, however, is that the actual usage of these terms among philosophers is more ambiguous and controversial. We therefore counsel caution and attentiveness to the various ways that the "is/ought gap" and the "fact/value distinction" may be defined.

See also

1.15 Natural law, 2.9 Naturalism, 3.5 Cause/reason, 3.6 Cognitivism/non-cognitivism, 3.9 Facts/values

Reading

*David Hume, *An Enquiry Concerning the Principles of Morals* [1751]:*A Critical Edition* (Oxford: Clarendon Press, 1999)
Hilary Putnam, *The Collapse of the Fact/Value Dichotomy and Other Essays* (Cambridge, MA: Harvard University Press, 2002)
Peter Railton, *Facts, Values, and Norms* (Cambridge: Cambridge University Press, 2003)

4.9 Justice and lawfulness

Justice is one of those strange things which is most noticed when it is not there. People may be for justice, but they are more against injustice. To say that something is unjust is therefore a common and powerful way of raising a moral objection. Justice, however, means various things. Most cynically, in Plato's (427–347 BCE) *Republic*, the character Thrasymachus argues that "justice is the advantage of the stronger" (Book II). In other words, what ideas, laws, and practices go by the name of "just" are simply those that the powerful have invented to secure, expand, and administer their power. French post-structuralist Michel Foucault (1926–84) argues to a similar conclusion (*Discipline and Punish*, 1975).

Platonic justice: everything in its place

Plato's *Republic* develops one of the most famous but also, perhaps, one of the most unusual concepts of justice to which people appeal. There Plato describes justice not only as a political ideal but also as a virtue of the soul.

Justice, in Plato's portrayal (or at least the portrayal presented by the character of Socrates in his story), is the condition where the parts of city or soul and their activities have been unified into a harmonious, rationally governed, and perfected whole. Each citizen and each class of people has been placed in the social order in the way that *best suits their natures.*

Those best at producing and serving are placed in positions of production and service (or servitude!); those best at war are placed in the role of warriors or "guardians"; those best at thinking and ruling are placed in the role of "philosopher kings and queens." It's an attractive view. After all, what's wrong with a society ruled by the most competent leaders, in which everyone does what he or she is best suited to do in the most harmonious and perfect way possible?

For many, however, Plato's republic looks like the model of an unjust society: everyone must do what he or she is told to do, and power is wielded only by an elite. As critics like Karl Popper (1902–94) and Michael Oakeshott (1901–90) have argued, Plato's justice looks like the justice of totalitarian regimes such as Pol Pot's Cambodia.

Justice, rights, and law

From different philosophical positions, justice maintains different relationships with law.

- *Legal positivists* hold that there's no necessary or intrinsic connection between law and morality, that the two are essentially separate and distinct. Justice accordingly for the positivist is either (a) an amoral term that means simply "what the law stipulates" or (b) something to which one might appeal in criticizing laws but that is itself independent of lawfulness.
- *Natural law theorists*, by contrast, maintain that there's an intimate connection between law and morality. They do this by making a distinction between the positive *civil law* and a *natural law* that transcends the laws of any actual society and grounds what might be called *natural justice*. On this view, civil laws should conform to or at least be consistent with the *natural law*. When they do so, they're just; when they don't they're unjust. This conception offers grounds for criticizing existing law.
- *Common law traditionalists* hold that justice flows from the history, traditions, and customs of a culture. In much the same way, ancient Roman lawmakers looked to the unwritten *mores maiorum* (law of tradition) and Confucian rulers tried to discern justice through *Li* (law, propriety, tradition, ritual, courtesy).
- *Rights conceptions of justice*, like natural law theories, also offer a fulcrum upon which to leverage critiques of positive law. When laws or policies violate fundamental rights, they are unjust; when they honor, secure, or even extend fundamental rights, they are just. Fundamental rights functioning in this way may be grounded in a constitution that supersedes particular civil laws, in the common law or precedents of case law, or something beyond the political order like nature or God.

Distributive justice

A further form of justice is distributive – that is, concerning the way various goods and services, principally economic goods and services, are distributed.

Some argue that a certain outcome or "end state" (as Robert Nozick called it in *Anarchy, State, and Utopia* (1974)) may be unjust even if no laws or procedures were violated in reaching it. Unless goods, services, protections, and well-being generally are distributed in a certain way, or within a specific range of possibilities, or in a way that includes the proper classes of people (and perhaps other living things), critics of this sort argue that the social order is unjust. For example, some philosophers argue that a society is just when people receive what they "deserve" or "merit" – whether it be benefits, rewards, or punishments. Others maintain that at least a minimal requirement of a just distribution is that people receive what they "need" (see 1.14 and 1.16). Others defend a purely *formal* or *procedural* conception of justice, arguing that if the proper procedures are followed, if due process is honored, then whatever the outcome, justice has been served.

Distributive critics, then, are likely to maintain that the whole may be unjust even if the parts are not. But is this possible? Cicero (106–43 BCE) famously remarked in *De Legibus* [*On the Laws*] that "the good of the people is the greatest law" (Book 3, Chapter 3, §8). Does this mean the people as a whole or individually?

Justice and punishment

Courts exist to see that "justice is done." Justice is served when punishment of the proper sort is meted out to the proper recipients, in the proper manner and proportion, by the proper authorities, for the proper reasons.

There are five main justifications for punishment:

1 *Retribution* (inflicting some punishment or harm upon those who have acted wrongly in return or reprisal for that wrong);
2 *restoration* of whatever goods were damaged or destroyed by the crime;
3 *deterrence* to future wrongdoing;
4 *reform* of the criminal; and
5 *protection* of the public.

Whether a criminal justice system is just or not depends on the extent to which these justifications of punishment are reasonable, and how far the system actually achieves the goals they demand.

See also

2.2 Contractarianism, 4.5 Fairness, 4.14 Restoration

Reading

H. L. A. Hart, *The Concept of Law* [1961], 2nd edition (Oxford: Oxford University Press, 1997)
*Ronald Dworkin, *Law's Empire* (Cambridge, MA: The Belknap Press, 1986)
David Miller, *Principles of Social Justice* (Cambridge, MA: Harvard University Press, 1999)

4.10 Just war theory

Try to imagine a situation utterly devoid of ethical principle and practice. It's likely to resemble war. It's no wonder that Thomas Hobbes (1588–1679) described the life of human beings outside the bounds of law and morality as a "war of all against all" (*De Cive*, 1651). Since the stakes are so high – survival – aren't people warranted in disregarding any moral prohibition during war? War seems decidedly amoral.

But, on the other hand, war is a supremely social phenomenon. It requires social organization, legitimation, financing, industry, etc. Like other things normally thought to lie within the scope of morality, war produces serious effects upon others and upon the world. And isn't it better to perish morally than live immorally? Indeed, in many cases, morality arguably demands sacrifice. Because of its social quality, the gravity of its effects, and the demands of morality even in the face of death, perhaps war is a phenomenon eminently suited to moral stricture, after all.

Just war theory

Although societies around the globe have commonly established rules related to war, most philosophers credit Augustine (354–430) with formally defining just war theory. The general features of the theory divide between two issues: (1) the question of whether to engage in war in the first place (*jus ad bellum*) and (2) the manner in which the war is conducted (*jus in bello*). A number of the most prominent principles philosophers have developed for reflecting on these issues include:

1   *Legitimate and competent authority.* This criterion usually entails a formal declaration by a legitimate and competent government with a proper procedure for declaring war. Some hold that only democratic governments

are competent authorities; formal approval of military action by the United Nations is also often thought to be required.

2 *Just cause.* Most commonly a just cause is taken to be self-defense in the face of an "imminent threat" or a "clear and present danger." Recently, however, in the wake of events in Rwanda and Bosnia-Herzegovina, thinkers like Samantha Power (b. 1970) (*A Problem from Hell*, 2003) have argued with increasing intensity for military interventions justified by humanitarian purposes. When both sides have suffered harms, one side is warranted in going to war only when the number of those among its population who have suffered significantly exceeds those on the other side who have suffered, and when more harm may be expected in the future.

3 *Last resort.* By this standard, war may be waged only after all peaceful, non-violent, and non-bellicose means have been exhausted.

4 *Right intention.* This criterion may involve assessing the subjective states of those involved, and it is for that reason sometimes difficult to employ. Nevertheless, the criterion requires that while the intention of the war need not match the cause, at least the intent must be a good one. Wars fought for just causes (e.g. self-defense) but with bad intentions (e.g. plunder or revenge) remain, by this standard, unjust wars.

5 *Right ends of objectives.* Usually the aim of just war is to restore or establish peace and sometimes order. War should not be waged for the purpose of inflicting suffering or torment or retribution. Right ends should also include some definite, effective procedure for identifying and calling an end to hostilities, for example a declaration of surrender.

6 *Success.* Just war theorists hold that there should be a reasonable expectation that the military action will succeed in achieving its ends. Wars fought in vain are not justifiable.

7 *Right means.* Wars may be fought only with appropriate weapons. Commonly, those that inflict disproportionate harm upon non-combatants or the innocent or inflict excessive suffering are regarded as objectionable. For example, weapons like nuclear bombs, land mines, chemical weapons, biological agents, and depleted uranium have been cited as immoral.

8 *Proportionality.* Essentially, this criterion requires that the force deployed should somehow be related to the nature of the wrong to which the war responds. Invading another country for a copyright violation would, for example, be a disproportionate response.

9 *Minimal casualties/minimum force.* Many just war theorists hold that as few people should be harmed as possible, that the minimum force should be used to achieve the war aims and no more. Environmental damage and the impact of the war on non-human populations should

also be minimized. War should not be waged, according to this requirement, in a gratuitous, cruel, or excessive manner.

10 *Right treatment of prisoners and occupied territories.* This standard of ethics
requires some recognized and effective procedure for surrender (like
flying a white flag). Once captive, prisoners are entitled to: identifica-
tion and tracking; release if civilian; adequate food and water; safe and
hygienic housing; access to international humanitarian agencies like the
Red Cross and Red Crescent. Prisoners should not be tortured, forced
to labor, used in experimentation, humiliated, used in propaganda, or
put on public display. Occupied territory should not be annexed, plundered, or colonized; the civilian population should not be punished and
should be left undisturbed and able to conduct the normal affairs of life,
so far as possible.

11 *Other exclusions.* Commonly, military actions should avoid or minimally
affect sacred sites, objects of great cultural and historic value, cemeter-
ies, the press, and humanitarian services.

Conscientious objection

One of the persistent questions regarding the ethics of war is that of con-
scription: is it morally permissible to compel people to fight in wars? Some
have held that the same requirements that obligate people to pay taxes obligate them to fight in just wars their nation wages. Does the seriousness of
the actions required in war make that analogy a weak one? Should states
respect the deeply held religious beliefs and dictates of conscience some
hold with regard to engaging in war?

See also

1.19 Rights, 4.9 Justice and lawfulness, 5.2 Amoralism

Reading

Augustine of Hippo, *The City of God against the Pagans* [410 CE], edited by
R. W. Dyson (Cambridge: Cambridge University Press, 1998); Book XV,
Chapter 4; Book XIX, Chapters 7, 12–14, 17

*Michael Walzer, *Just and Unjust Wars: A Moral Argument with Historical
Illustrations*, 3rd edition (New York: Basic Books, 2000)

Brian Orend, "Justice after War," *Ethics and International Affairs* 16(1)
(April, 2002): 43–57

4.11 Paternalism

There are many things that are potentially bad for people: taking crack cocaine, climbing mountains, eating too much saturated fat, driving without a seatbelt, boxing, not exercising, excessive buying on credit. People are nonetheless perfectly entitled to engage in most of these things, if they so wish, while only some have been made illegal. But is the distinction between those that are permitted and those that are banned rational? If not, should more be banned or permitted?

These days, morality is often thought of as concerning rules and prohibitions that govern conduct in order to prevent people from engaging in the wrong *kind of acts*. But certainly for the ancient Greeks, ethics was concerned more broadly with how to be the right *kind of person*, which included how to make one's life go as well as possible.

It's fairly easy to identify many of both (a) good and bad acts and (b) good and bad types of people. But having done so, what happens next? Should individuals decide whether to do the right thing and become the right kinds of people by themselves, or should the state intervene to help them along by, for example, stopping people from doing things that harm them? In other words, does the state have the moral responsibility to interfere in people's lives for their own good?

When a state or authority does intervene in this way, it's said to act "paternalistically." And there are several reasons for arguing that paternalism is a bad thing. Criticisms generally take two forms: the principled and the pragmatic.

Principled objections to paternalism

Principled criticisms typically focus on the autonomy of individuals – their capacity for self-governance. Human beings, the critics claim, possess the capacity to make free choices for themselves, and it's their right to exercise this faculty unhindered – well or badly. It's not simply their right, it's of the utmost importance that they be autonomous, because autonomy makes possible human beings' greatest dignity, fulfillment, and happiness.

Freedom, of course, must have limits, but only when free choices interfere with or harm others. As John Stuart Mill (1806–73) put it in what's come to be known as his "Harm Principle" (*On Liberty*, Chapter 1, 1859): "the only purpose for which power can be rightfully exercised over any member of a civilized community, against his will, is to prevent harm to others. His own good, either physical or moral, is not sufficient warrant." On this account, paternalism undermines human liberty.

The main weakness of principled arguments is that they arguably overstate the extent to which humans are autonomous. The image of the free, independent, self-reliant, rational human being, fully in control of his or her decision-making powers, is an attractive one. But in many ways, it's a fantasy. People are the results of their genetic and other physical endowments interacting with their environments. They're subject to the influences and manipulation of advertisers, parents, friends, films, national heroes, religious authorities, and so on – not to mention the effects of caffeine, serotonin, dopamine, various pheromones, testosterone, and estrogen. And, of course, power imbalances among people have profound effects upon what they are and are not able to do. Adults may not be children. But just as children's lack of autonomy makes it reasonable to act paternalistically toward them, it's also reasonable to act paternalistically toward adults, albeit in a more limited way, if we believe they have less than complete autonomy. Even more radically, free will may itself be an illusion.

Moreover, defenders of state paternalism may respond to principled critiques with a principled response that their duty to provide certain goods (like public health) simply overrides individuals' interests in liberty.

Pragmatic objections to paternalism

Pragmatic arguments get around these difficulties by arguing that, whether they are ultimately autonomous or not, treating people as if they were not is harmful to society and to individuals.

People need to *feel* as though they're responsible for their own lives and be encouraged to take responsibility. If they do not, they become passive, dependent, less responsible, more susceptible to malign outside influences, less productive, and less fulfilled.

Furthermore, it can be argued that paternalism doesn't work. Drug prohibition, for example, has a poor record at reducing consumption. It is hard, however, to argue that paternalism can *never* work. Most experts would agree that the compulsory wearing of seat belts has reduced road deaths.

A question of culture

Different cultures take different default attitudes to paternalism. The United States lays claim to a relatively strong anti-paternalist streak, whereas in Europe citizens are much more comfortable with the state acting to support them and protect them from their own bad choices. In both, however, very few people have such a pure commitment to individual liberty that they would abolish *all* regulations that can be seen as paternalistic. Hence the fact that a measure can be described as paternalist is not automatically a reason to reject it. It is, however, an invitation to question the intervention and ask whether it is necessary and justified.

See also

1.4 Autonomy, 3.17 Legal/moral, 3.23 Public and private

Reading

*John Stuart Mill, *The Basic Writings of John Stuart Mill: On Liberty, The Subjection of Women, and Utilitarianism* (New York: The Modern Library, 2002)

Robert Nozick, *Anarchy, State, and Utopia* (New York: Basic Books, 1974)

Guy Standing, *Beyond the New Paternalism: Basic Security as Equality* (New York: W. W. Norton & Co., 2002)

4.12 Proportionality

People are likely to object to decapitation as a punishment for parking violations. A lawsuit seeking one billion dollars in damages for a small dent in someone's car is likely to elicit incredulity as well as outrage.

But how much is enough? Justice requires not only the distribution of benefits and punishments, it requires that the distribution be made in a fitting or *proportional* way. Part of the task of ethical deliberation, then is to figure out what's fitting and what's not.

Punishment of criminals

Among the most important principles of retributive justice is *proportionality*. Milanese philosopher Cesare Bonesana, the Marchese Beccaria (1738–94), argued that punishments ought to be *consistently* applied (similar wrongs should receive similar punishments). But more than this, he maintained that the punishment should fit the crime both in *degree* and in *kind*.

Severe punishments should only be administered for serious crimes. Petty crimes should only receive mild punishments. And the punishment should somehow reflect the nature of the crime. For example, punishment should not be, in the words of the Eighth Amendment to the US Constitution, "cruel and unusual." But what punishments are cruel? What punishments properly do fit various crimes?

Beccaria argued against capital punishment, but isn't death a proportionate punishment for death? Mahatma Gandhi once said that "an eye for an eye leaves the whole world blind," and in the same spirit, people often say that "two wrongs don't make a right." Jesus is said to have told his followers to "Love your enemies" (Luke 6:27–36) and also that "whosoever shall smite thee on thy right cheek, turn to him the other also." (Matthew 5:39).

Many have come to believe that the requirements of morals, justice, and even civilization require some sort of humane response to wrongs. What should such a response be? The forfeiture of property and the deprivation of liberty have emerged as the preferred options. They may be more humane, but are they proportionate?

The principle of proportionality may appear in many ethical deliberations. For example, are the efforts and resources expended on a patient proportional to his or her need, especially in light of competing needs? Is the harm done to laboratory or food animals proportional to the gains in scientific knowledge and nutrition obtained, or is it excessive?

Proportional responses?

In the wake of September 11, 2001 the United States government rounded up and deported hundreds of people for minor visa violations. Many were expelled secretly, without due process, and without even the opportunity to contact friends and family. Some of the deportees had lived in the United States for years, worked, paid taxes, raised children, and forged bonds of family and community. The visa violations were in many cases real, but critics argued deportation was a disproportionate punishment to that violation.

In addition to its use in punishment, the concept of proportionality is important in evaluating the justice of war. It would be wrong for one nation to launch a nuclear attack against another for the violation of territorial fishing waters or in response to a disagreement on tariff policy. The use of military force should somehow be proportional to the wrongs that warranted its use in the first place. The 1949 Geneva Convention formalizes this principle, prohibiting force that is "excessive in relation to the concrete and direct military advantage anticipated."

On the morning of August 6, 1945, a small aircraft named after the pilot's mother (*Enola Gay*) released from its belly an atomic bomb (called

"Little Boy") over the Japanese city of Hiroshima. As a result of the detonation, over 66,000 people were killed with another 69,000 injured, most of them civilians. Three days later, an atomic blast killed 39,000 and injured 25,000 in Nagasaki. By 1950 perhaps another 250,000 would die from radiation-related illnesses. Five months before Hiroshima, on the night of March 9–10, firebombs dropped on Tokyo intentionally incinerated 100,000 living humans beings.

The morality of these attacks has been hotly contested. Did the high stakes of World War II warrant violence of this magnitude? Is it proper to kill (foreign) civilians in such numbers in order to spare (one's own) soldiers? Did securing a US victory before the Soviets could sweep down and take more of Japan than just the Kiril Islands justify the bombings? Proportionality is clear in theory, but often difficult to measure in practice.

See also

4.3 Consistency, 4.9 Justice and lawfulness, 4.10 Just war theory

Reading

Cesare Beccaria, "*On Crimes and Punishments*" *and Other Writings* [1764], edited by Richard Bellamy (Cambridge: Cambridge University Press, 1995)
*Christopher Kaczor, ed., *Proportionalism: For and Against* (Milwaukee, WI: Marquette University Press, 2002)
Jesper Ryberg, *The Ethics of Proportionate Punishment* (Dordrecht: Springer, 2004)

4.13 Reflective equilibrium

In a country that enshrines freedom of speech in its constitution, a play is performed which gives great offense to a sizeable minority of the population. There are calls for it to be banned, while others rush to defend the playwright's freedom of expression. This initiates a "national debate" about the limits of free speech in an open society. How could this debate be resolved?

One way would be to go back to the most basic moral principles that govern society and work out their implications with regard to this specific case. This is a broadly *foundationalist* approach. The foundationalist view is that morality rests on one or more *basic principles*; and once we discover these, all particular moral judgments will find their justification in them.

It's an appealing view, perhaps the most intuitively plausible. But the problem is that cases such as the one of the controversial play often do not arise out of a failure to apply general moral principles, but rather from disagreements about what those principles are – difficulties that are made evident by the new hard case. Moreover, basic principles may not be as durable or as complete as their original formulators had hoped.

One might find, for example, that the principle of free speech enshrined in the Constitution does not seem to take account of historical developments since its ratification – developments that now make it morally important to address the kind of deep offense the play provoked. Perhaps the principle fails in this way because it was formulated at a time when there was more moral consensus and thus less of a need to worry about what, say, people of differing religious beliefs might think; or perhaps moral regard for the treatment of minorities has changed since then. Sometimes general principles may fail simply because they're too general to speak to the peculiarities of the given case.

When foundations fail

An alternative to foundationalism is the method of *reflective equilibrium*, associated in particular with Nelson Goodman (1906–98) and John Rawls. The starting point of this process is the recognition that people hold many values, ranging from the more general (free speech is a right) to the more specific (it's wrong to incite hatred on the grounds of race). Moral disputes emerge when people find that these values no longer fit comfortably together.

There are tensions where one value seems to demand one thing and another value something quite to the contrary. To sort this out, one cannot just go back to the more general values and principles and "read off" or deduce their implications for the disputed case; for it may well be that the general principles are themselves in need of revision in the light of this new circumstance (see 2.12 Pragmatism). Rather, disputants must reflect upon a whole range of values (established and novel) and engage in a process of modifying them until, through deliberation, they can return to a position where values, interests, and principles all once again *balance* or *harmonize* with each other in a way that satisfies the demands of the operant principles and values – e.g. fairness, justice, and duty (see 1.11 Harmony).

This method does not presume that morality rests on one or more foundational principles. Rather, it takes a more holistic approach, seeing moral values as being held together in a flexible web of mutual interdependence, not supported from below. Moral values need to *cohere* – with each other, with known facts about the world, and with our basic moral attitudes. They assume greater and lesser weight, accommodate losses and additions, and become reconfigured in new constellations as the physical, social, and moral universes change.

Coherent but wrong?

Thinking about ethics in terms of reflective equilibrium has the virtue of cohering with facts about how people actually do in practice resolve moral disagreements. Critics, however, say that if this is the best moral reasoning can do, then ethics is much diminished. For such a method, if applied at a societal level, seems to privilege consensus over moral truth. Isn't it possible for people to revise their values so that they achieve equilibrium with each other, but do so in such a way that society is taken further from "true morality" (whatever that is)? A coherent and balanced perversion is still perverse.

Other critics point out that if applied at the individual level, reflective equilibrium seems to rest too much on people's pre-reflective hunches or intuitions about what's right and good. Their views cohere only when they fit prior convictions. But why should we suppose these convictions are the right ones? Isn't another word for prior conviction, "prejudice"?

What unites these two criticisms is that reflective equilibrium, because it rests on the needs of coherence, leaves morality with no secure foundation. Of course, proponents of the view accept this, saying that such is human finitude, the human condition. Moreover, say defenders, there's nothing that could provide the sort of security foundationalists fantasize about, anyway. Nevertheless, the doubt remains: without firm roots that can be rigorously justified, can such a free-floating ethics possess the authority needed of morality?

See also

2.5 Discourse ethics, 2.13 Rationalism, 4.3 Consistency

Reading

Nelson Goodman, *Fact, Fiction, and Forecast* (Cambridge, MA: Harvard University Press, 1955)

John Rawls, *A Theory of Justice* [1971], revised edition (Cambridge, MA: The Belknap Press, 1999)

*Thomas Pogge, *John Rawls: An Introduction* (Oxford: Oxford University Press, 2005)

4.14 Restoration

Lately many have argued that it's time to put things right with regard to the wrongs of the European and American slave trade through some sort of reparations. Payments, for example, could be made to the descendants of slaves. This raises all sorts of difficulties, however. Can remediation be made across generations? Should the descendants of wrong-doers be responsible to the descendants of those wronged? How far does responsibility extend?

Most fundamental is the question of whether anything can compensate people for a wrong of such magnitude. Can justice be served by compensating victims? Or must all attempts at compensation trivialize the wrong?

Justice is concerned with lawfulness, harmony, unity, distribution, and reciprocity. Many philosophers, however, have also advanced the idea that it's concerned with repairing the damage done by some wrongdoing. Repairing things, morally speaking, also goes by the name of *remedial* or *restorative justice*. In other words, to achieve a just state of affairs in the wake of some wrong, things must somehow be restored to the way they were before the wrongdoing – at least as much as it's reasonably possible to do so.

The idea of seeking compensation for damages in civil suits and tort law depends upon this. In most cases, compensation directed to remediation (as opposed to punishment) comprises transfers of money and property to the wronged parties from those who have wronged them – or, anyway, from those authorized to act on behalf of those who wronged them. Can more be done?

Ways to restoration

Some forms of punishment have included apologies, public and private, in part because demonstrations of regret and admissions of guilt are thought to be in some sense restorative.

Others have prescribed voluntary public service as a remedial measure. Since many wrongs not only harm individuals but also undermine the public good (by undermining lawfulness or security), it seems fitting that some sort of restitution be made to the common good as well as to individuals.

Nineteenth-century Quakers advocated re-structuring prisons as "penitentiaries," places where wrongdoers can reflect upon their wrongs. This in a sense aims to restore criminals to the status of responsible citizens.

Some have argued that some restoration can be made through punishment. Proponents of this view, like William Ian Miller, say that humans naturally and properly experience a kind of satisfaction in the knowledge that those who have wronged them have suffered or at least been punished.

Judges, accordingly, have at times prescribed shaming (stocks and public humiliation) and suffering through hard labor not simply in retribution, but as a form of restorative justice. Even Thomas Aquinas (1225–74) (or at least those who compiled the last part of the *Summa Theologica*) maintained that the blessed in heaven will observe and will rejoice in the punishments of the damned (*ST*, Supplement, IIIa, Question 94, Articles 1–3; cf. Isaiah 56:24; Psalms 57:11).

The phenomenon of the scapegoat even suggests that it may not entirely matter to people whether or not it's the guilty who pay. It's as if people gain in satisfaction so long as someone is punished, anyone. More recently, people in favor of capital punishment have spoken about the psychological need among victims for the closure it serves.

Limits of restoration

Even if restoration is one noble goal of the penal system, it seems unable to account for all punishment. For instance, it seems far-fetched to say that the satisfaction the public gets from seeing criminals punished is in anyway restorative. Even if it can be viewed in this way, it is far from clear that punishments, especially severe punishments, should be conceived as a form of therapy.

If someone is murdered or dies as the result of medical malpractice, it just seems impossible to restore things. The dead can't be returned to life or replaced. And if someone has become so vicious as to engage in serious crime, is it reasonable to think that his or her moral character can be restored? Can departments of "corrections" really correct?

Andrei Chikatilo, also known as the "Shelter Belt Killer" was convicted in 1992 of murdering 52 people, most of them children. He mutilated the genitalia of many of the children; in some cases he gouged out their eyes while they were alive and conscious. What possible restorative justice can be achieved in such cases?

The Russian authorities put Chikatilo to death with a bullet behind his right ear, but this didn't bring a single child back or erase the suffering his victims endured. Nor would torturing him have done so. As Ivan Karamazov complains in Fyodor Dostoevsky's (1821–88) famous novel, "What good would it do to send the monsters to hell *after* they have finished inflicting their suffering on children? How can their being in hell *put things right?*" (*The Brothers Karamazov*, 1880).

See also

1.16 Need, 3.13 Injury, 4.9 Justice and lawfulness

Readings

*Heather Strang and John Braithwaite, eds., *Restorative Justice: Philosophy to Practice* (Burlington, VT: Ashgate Publishing, 2000)
*Matthew Clayton and Andrew Williams, eds., *Social Justice* (Malden, MA: Blackwell, 2004)
Howard Zehr and Barb Toews, eds., *Critical Issues in Restorative Justice* (St Louis, MO: Criminal Justice Press, 2004)

4.15 Sex and gender

An old saying declares that, "Boys will be boys." On the surface it seems like a simple tautology, a statement of identity. As everyone knows, however, there's a lot more to it than that. This little remark shelters a mountain of ideas about sex and gender, and it takes a lot of hard intellectual work to uncover and untangle them. One might say that the point of a great deal of feminist ethical inquiry and criticism has been to do just that.

One of the first things the adage depends upon is the distinction between sex and gender. *Sex*, one might say, is biological. It's those physical dimensions of certain organisms that distinguish them as female or male. So, sperm are male while ova are female; organisms with XX chromosome pairs are female, while organisms with XY chromosomes are male.

Gender, on the other hand, is cultural. It's the ideas, attitudes, beliefs, fashions, manners, rituals, and roles assigned to each gender as "feminine" and "masculine." So, wearing red lipstick, skirts, pearl earrings, long hair, and lacy blouses, as well as engaging in activities like childcare, housekeeping, and nursing are thought of as feminine; while wearing trousers, dark earth colors, work boots, no make-up, and short hair, as well as engaging in rough language, heavy labor, warfare, hunting, are thought of as masculine.

Ideas about sex and gender are often thought to be limiting and defining. Sex and gender not only define fashion and manners; they define gender roles in families, employment, and social life generally. These definitions are often violently enforced. One hundred Saudi men were imprisoned and flogged in 2005 for "behaving like women" at a party. In October 1998, Matthew Shepard was beaten to death in Laramie, Wyoming, for being homosexual.

Sex and gender as critique

Awareness of these subtleties can lead to many ways of criticizing theories and practices by bringing to the surface assumptions contained within them about sex and gender and arguing that they're false or undesirable. Most obviously, critics often try to show that some practice or some way of conceiving things contains an implicit conception of gender that subordinates or limits women (usually) and privileges men. This project has been pursued in a wide variety of ways – focusing on class, hierarchy, the environment, religion, and language, for example.

There is, however, a major disagreement among those who pursue these lines of critique. Is eradicating unfair gender bias the pursuit of a deep equality or are there differences between the sexes that need to be honored? Feminists are accordingly often divided between "equal rights" and "difference" feminists.

One of the most interesting issues to arise from difference feminism is the question of whether or not women possess distinctive forms of moral deliberation and judgment. Carol Gilligan (b. 1936) has famously argued in her 1982 book, *In a Different Voice*, that girls and women develop a way of thinking about ethical issues that's different from (and perhaps superior to) men's.

Women, says Gilligan, use rules and principles (or what Gilligan calls "justice") less than men, and instead consider the particularities of human relationships (what she calls "care") in their deliberations. Perhaps men can adopt this form of thinking, too; and some argue that they should. Critics, however, maintain that this does not present a rich new field of moral thinking, but simply rehashes old stereotypes.

More than two?

One complicating factor is that many have come to see the binary distinction between the sexes as contingent, overly simplistic, culturally determined, and fluid. Some people are, for example, *intersexed* (what once was called hermaphroditic), having some of the physical characteristics of both sexes. Other people have the outward physical characteristics of one sex but the chromosomal features of another. Others maintain that their psychic life and their physical bodies belong to different sexes. Some cultures identify more than two genders, identifying a mixed or third gender in addition to male and female, commonly called now *berdache* or "two-spirited."

Still others become transsexual and transgendered, taking on some of the sexual and gendered characteristics associated with one sex/gender (perhaps a beard, larger muscles, and masculine clothing) but still retaining some of the features associated with the other (vaginal and uterine structures, interests in cooking and childrearing). Perhaps what we select to define sex is in part a cultural matter, too. Perhaps the world doesn't fit into the binary conceptual boxes of male and female as easily as many assume.

See also

1.5 Care, 4.5 Fairness, 4.9 Justice and lawfulness

Reading

Carol Gilligan, *In a Different Voice* [1982], new edition (Cambridge, MA: Harvard University Press, 1993)
*Philip E. Devine and Celia Wolf-Devine, *Sex and Gender: A Spectrum of Views* (Belmont, CA: Wadsworth, 2002)
Judith Butler, *Undoing Gender* (New York: Routledge, 2004)

4.16 Speciesism

The UK's Race Relations Act (1976) prohibits discrimination against people on the grounds of race. Most people can easily see the moral case for this legislation and similar laws enacted throughout the world. Justice demands that people be treated differently only if there's a compelling reason to do so. In people's personal lives, those reasons can simply be that they prefer some people to others, or are related to those others in special ways. But in the civic sphere, personal prejudices should not get in the way. The fact that some have different ethnic and racial backgrounds is not a morally significant reason to treat them better or worse than other people.

There are, perhaps, exceptions to this general rule. Correcting historical injustices may, for example, present cases where it's morally justifiable to treat people differently by conferring benefits upon one group (the historically oppressed) denied to another group (the historically oppressive or the beneficiaries of historical oppression). Of course, here the effort is aimed at balancing the scales – at rectifying the effects that prior differences in treatment have produced. Moreover, the difference in treatment is not justified on the basis of purported intrinsic differences (e.g. racial differences) but on the basis of historical injustices committed by different groupings of power. In that sense, the differences in treatment characteristic of, say, affirmative action programs are not strictly speaking race-based; rather they are power-based. American slave owners enjoyed certain benefits on the basis of race; the descendents of the slaves they owned enjoy benefits based not, strictly speaking, on race but on membership of a historically oppressed group.

Species prejudice

The idea that differences in treatment may be either just or unjust invites the question: are there any persisting ways in which people today discriminate against others in morally unjustifiable ways? It's widely acknowledged that sometimes people discriminate without cause on grounds of sex, sexuality, religion, and age. But, hypothetically at least, people can also unfairly discriminate on grounds of species.

Consider the fictional case of the father of Mr Spock from *Star Trek*, who is a Vulcan. It would surely be wrong to deny him his right to life simply because he does not belong to the species *homo sapiens*. He still possesses the morally relevant characteristics associated with beings in enjoying a recognized right to life – such as human-like intelligence, a sense of self, sentience, the capacity for moral action, and the capacity to suffer.

If these reasons are sufficient to justify recognizing a right to life for Vulcans, it makes sense to talk of "speciesism": the unjustified discrimination against a creature purely on the grounds of species membership. But are people guilty of speciesism (a term first coined by Richard D. Ryder) in the real world?

People who tend to dismiss the idea of speciesism out of hand tend to miss the point of the idea. It is, of course, justifiable to give different species different rights and privileges in different contexts. It would be absurd, for example, to give cats the vote or allow simians to run for president. (Insert your own obvious joke here.) It's only speciesism if the discrimination is *purely* on the grounds of species membership – where members of the species in question have the morally relevant characteristics that should guarantee them rights, but those rights are denied them anyway. Cats aren't prohibited from voting because they are cats *per se*, but because they don't have the capacity to vote, to participate meaningfully in the institution.

Many animal rights campaigners claim that immoral speciesism does exist. One of the strongest reasons for claiming this is that the members of many non-human species do have one very important morally relevant capacity. As Jeremy Bentham (1749–1832) put it: "The question is not, Can they reason? nor Can they talk? but, Can they suffer?" The argument is that if a creature can feel pain, then moral agents, beings that can grasp and act upon moral principles, are obligated not to cause it unnecessary pain. To refuse to respect this right purely on the grounds of species membership would therefore be an example of speciesism.

Denying speciesism

The idea of speciesism is very powerful, because the reasoning behind the use of the term is precisely the same as that behind terms such as sexism and racism. One of the best ways to resist the idea of speciesism is to argue that, unlike cases of racism and sexism, the members of other species face discrimination for good reason. Non-human animals, for example, aren't treated differently simply because they belong to another class of things. Rather, they're treated differently because it's characteristic of the members of these other classes that they possess certain morally relevant properties.

The differences cited to justify species discrimination tend to be explained in terms of cognitive and practical abilities: animals, even higher primates, lack the kind of mental and historical sophistication that humans posses. Without the ability to formulate and execute long-term projects, to take part in historical movements and institutions, to develop complex theoretical and social institutions, to acquire a full sense of self, and so forth, it makes no sense to talk about a being having rights. In response, it's pointed out that very young children, the senile, and the severely mentally handicapped also lack these faculties, yet they're acknowledged to have more rights than even the fittest members of other highly intelligent animal species, such as gorillas and dolphins.

However these disputes are resolved, speciesism does seem to be a perfectly coherent concept. The outcome of debates around speciesism, therefore, will depend largely upon whether those who wish to defend human privilege can explain what it is that makes humans as a species so special.

See also

1.17 Pain and pleasure, 1.19 Rights, 3.21 Moral subjects/moral agents

Reading

Jeremy Bentham, *Introduction to the Principles of Morals and Legislation* (Oxford: Oxford University Press, 1996), Chapter 17
*Peter Singer, *Animal Liberation*, 2nd edition (London: Jonathan Cape, 1990)
Richard D. Ryder, *Animal Revolution: Changing Attitudes Towards Speciesism* (Oxford: Berg, 2000)

4.17 Thought experiments

A runaway train is hurtling toward a junction. If it's allowed to follow its current course, it will hurtle into a group of 20 workers laboring in a tunnel in a place that makes it impossible to warn them in time. But if you pull a lever, you can divert the train onto a different track, a track that will send it into another tunnel. In this other tunnel, however, four different people are working. So, do you *fail to stop* the probable deaths of up to 20 men, or *act to bring about* the probable deaths of four?

This scenario, devised by Philippa Foot (b. 1920), is a famous example of the use of thought experiments in moral philosophy. A thought experiment is an imaginary scenario that's used to help concentrate the mind on certain key factors in moral reasoning. The basic principles of thought experiments are the same as those for actual scientific experiments: isolate the variables to be tested; see how individually altering these factors affects the result; then draw general conclusions about the significance of these variables. In contrast with scientific experiments, of course, the significance of thought experiments in moral philosophy will be moral rather than physical.

In the runaway train example, the scenario is designed to focus our attention on the distinction between "omission" and "commission" as well as their moral significance. Whoever controls the lever can, to a large extent, determine what happens next. If she does not act, more lives are put at risk than if she does. In terms of the probable outcomes, therefore, it is clear that acting is much more likely to lead to fewer deaths than not acting. If, however, the lever is switched, the person is *actively* bringing about the deaths of the people in the less populated tunnel, whereas if she does nothing she is *passively* allowing a greater number of people to die. The advantage of this story is that it presents a clean, clear example of a moral dilemma that allows us to isolate and focus upon a single, very specific question – whether or not there's an important difference between those things people actively bring about and those they simply allow to happen.

Limits on thought experiments

Thought experiment such as these have been very useful aids to moral reasoning. But they do have their limits. Most obviously, in contrast to scientific experiments, moral judgment rather than natural law determines what the results are. One cannot simply run the experiment and allow it to generate a moral judgment. As such, thought experiments cannot "prove anything" in the way that experiments in the natural sciences do. At best, they can make the issues clearer and facilitate moral reasoning.

A more subtle concern, though, is that the experiments may not really be well enough devised to isolate the variables as intended. For example, the runaway train experiment is supposed to help us reach a general conclusion about the moral significance of the acts of omission/commission distinction. But, of course, the experiment itself addresses only a specific case where that issue is relevant. The experiment may not yield a conclusion that's applicable to other kinds of cases.

For instance, let's assume hypothetically that the train experiment leads to this result: an omission that permits death is just as bad as an act that causes it. But consider the case of euthanasia. The results of the experiment seem to suggest this: if it is right to not intervene to prevent death when that's what the patient wants, then it should also be right to intervene and actually kill the patient when that's what the patient wants. But in the runaway train scenario, someone will certainly die very soon in either case; whereas in the euthanasia example, since the course of all disease is uncertain, not acting may lead to a substantially longer life for the patient. This may be an important difference, so one shouldn't be too hasty to reach general conclusions from the very particular example of the train.

Similarly, some complain that because thought experiments are artificial they are pointless. Better to stick to examples drawn from the real world.

And among real world examples, it's better to stick to issues that commonly arise rather than obsess over extremely rare or unique examples. It's more important to get the problems real people really and commonly face straightened out than it is to worry about things that will never or will only rarely occur. Indeed, the nature of moral theory might be such that problematic and even irresolvable cases will arise (both real and imaginary cases). That doesn't mean that moral theory is worthless. A tool that works for the most part still has value. After all, seat belts sometimes fail, too.

For these and similar reasons, thought experiments need to be handled with caution. Make sure they isolate the proper variables. Remember that they can't prove a result by themselves. Be careful about drawing general conclusions from what remain particular, hypothetical cases. And remember that the real world is often a different and much more complex place than the laboratory of the mind.

See also

3.22 Prudence, 4.3 Consistency, 4.4 Counterexamples

Reading

Philippa Foot, "The Problem of Abortion and the Doctrine of Double Effect," [1967] in her *Virtues and Vices* (Oxford: Oxford University Press, 2002)
*Roy Sorenson, *Thought Experiments* (Oxford: Oxford University Press, 1992)
*Martin Cohen, *Wittgenstein's Beetle and Other Classic Thought Experiments* (Oxford: Blackwell, 2004)

4.18 Universalizability

A mother discovers that her son is illegally copying DVDs and confronts him about it, telling him she thinks it's not just against the law but morally wrong. "I'm not hurting anyone," he protests. "Maybe not," replies his mother, "but what if everybody did it?" The son looks at her, perplexed. "But not everybody does it."

The mother is appealing to a principle that in one form or another is common to many ethical systems: the principle of universalizability. This principle states that, for something to be morally permissible in a certain circumstance, it must be permissible for anyone to do the same in relevantly similar circumstances. So, if it were right for you to cheat on your taxes, it would be right for everyone else in similar financial circumstances to cheat on theirs. Similarly, it is only acceptable for the son to pirate DVDs if it is acceptable for everyone else to do the same.

Probably the most important attempt to frame morality in such a fashion was made by Immanuel Kant (1724–1804) in his *Groundwork of the Metaphysics of Morals* (1785). One way to get into Kant's argument is to see that there is something self-contradictory in demanding one rule for others and another for oneself. Say, for example, that someone thinks others should always pay their taxes but that he or she shouldn't. From a rational point of view, this is just inconsistent. If others should pay their taxes, and one is a person just like others, what reason could there be to make an exception of oneself? Consistency is required if you are to be rational here; what applies to one applies to all.

Now, think about what else follows if one accepts that rationality requires consistency. One then can only select those moral rules that *can* be followed consistently by others. For instance, the rule "evade taxes" could not be followed by everyone in any society where the need for some taxation is required. The rule would totally undermine the basis of fair taxation, and as such it is not a rule that one could rationally choose. In fact, the only rational and consistent rule possible in this instance seems to be that everyone should pay his or her taxes. This line of reasoning led Kant to formulate the general principle: "Act only on that maxim through which you can at the same time will that it should become a universal law."

According to this line of argument, then, rationality demands consistency, and the only consistent moral rules are those that could be chosen as universal laws (which in the jargon means they must be *universalizable*). Such laws demand of all moral beings that they act in ways all can recognize as moral – or so many moralists wish. So it is that rationality provides the basis of morality.

Critique

Many, however, wouldn't go all the way with Kant. While the majority of ethical theorists would accept that consistency is a *constraint* on moral thinking, far fewer think that it can actually form the *basis* of moral thinking. One reason for this is that consistent immoral rules seem possible, too. A racist might think that the principle "always give preference to those who look most similar to you" is a perfectly universalizable moral principle. Or, consider this one: "establish the dominion of the Aryan race over all others." Everyone could act according to these maxims without any contradiction, but they seem to be profoundly immoral positions to take.

Another difficulty comes in explaining how we could ever get from pure rationality to reasons or motives for acting at all. Consider these three very different maxims that obey Kant's imperative: never hit an innocent baby; always drive on the left in Great Britain; when in Wales, eat an apple and smile every day. The first is clearly a moral injunction, the second, though sensible, does not seem to be moral at all. Driving on the right is equally moral, just as long as everyone does it. The last is not only irrelevant to ethics, but pointless. Why would anyone will that as a universal law? That's a question Kant's theory doesn't answer. And it suggests the theory's weakness: morality has to start with certain impulses that are not themselves generated by rationality. Moral goals, such as happiness and the welfare of others, are rooted not in reason but something else, perhaps feeling or a moral authority.

How universal?

Moreover, the principle itself isn't even as straightforward as it might seem. Obviously, circumstances have to be taken into account. It may not be possible to will that everyone follow the maxim "drive at 70 mph" at all times, but it is perfectly acceptable to propose that as a rule for driving on clear freeways. Even something like stealing, although usually condemned, can be willed as a universal law in circumstances where it's the only option available to save a life or prevent starvation.

Consider again the example of the son copying DVDs. He could argue that he is not saying that everyone should copy DVDs, but that it is perfectly possible to will that people like him do so. If people who would not otherwise buy DVDs copy them, then the economies of DVD production and distribution are not harmed. Indeed, it can be argued that a limited illegal distribution actually helps, because it encourages some who see the movies to go and buy them. When he gets older and has more disposable income, given the habits his DVD interest is producing, he will become one of those who do buy. Until then, he is doing no wrong by pirating.

Is the son right? The trouble for the son's position is that there's a moral difference between (a) paying proper attention to differing circumstances and (b) making unjustifiable ad hoc, self-interested exceptions to rules. But can Kantian theory discriminate between the two? Both maneuvers can be compatible with the general requirement of universalizability; and if this is so, can't one render nearly *any* action or maxim permissible by Kant's criterion simply by limiting it to the circumstances at hand? In other words, can't people always say: "This can be willed to be a universal law of nature for all people like me in circumstances like this"?

See also

2.13 Rationalism, 4.3 Consistency, 5.12 Radical particularity

Reading

*Lewis White Beck, *A Commentary on Kant's Critique of Practical Reason* (Chicago: University of Chicago Press, 1960)

Barbara Herman, *The Practice of Moral Judgment* (Cambridge, MA: Harvard University Press, 1993)

Paul Guyer, ed., *Kant's Groundwork of the Metaphysics of Morals: Critical Essays* (Lanham, MD: Rowman & Littlefield, 1998)

Part V

The Limits of Ethics

5.1 *Akrasia*

Oscar Wilde's character Lord Darlington famously remarks in *Lady Wind-ermere's Fan* (1892) that, "I can resist anything except temptation." He is, alas, not alone in this. Most of us have at some time done something that we've known to be wrong but found ourselves unable to resist doing. Aris-totle (384–322 BCE) called this failing *akrasia* (lack of self-mastery or moral "incontinence"; *Nicomachean Ethics*, VII 1–10), otherwise known as moral "weakness" (*astheneia*), or "weakness of the will."

This phenomenon has puzzled philosophers for centuries. Why do we do what we know or believe we should not? There are various explanations.

According to the Socrates of Plato (427–347 BCE), all wrongdoing is the result of ignorance. People act badly simply because they are ignorant about what's truly good or right – in that situation or generally. On this view *akrasia* is impossible, since if we truly knew what was right we'd never choose not to do it. Apparent examples of *akrasia* are therefore not what they seem: people never do what they truly know is wrong. If someone has an affair, for example, and says "I know it is wrong" the adulterer is being disingenuous. He or she may know it involves deceit or hurt, but on balance somehow the adulterer thinks going ahead is still justifiable.

Augustine (354–430), on the other hand, saw wrongdoing as a charac-teristic of human sinfulness. People clearly know the good but choose the bad, anyway; sometimes they even do what's bad because it's bad, as a form of rebellion.

According to Aristotle, people, through the immediate urgings of passion, act without thinking, or at least without thinking clearly. If they had thought about the issue more carefully and deliberately, they might well have acted differently; but the need came over them with sudden forcefulness. Desire and anger are the common culprits in this sort of impetuous act, a sort of act that might be described as "akratic impetuosity."

Aristotle also talks of "akratic weakness." Here immediacy isn't the issue. People take the time to think things through and come to the right decision about how to act. But sometimes they simply can't bring themselves to act that way because they are overwhelmed by sustained passions, especially desire or anger, perhaps also fear.

What's at stake

Which account we take to be true (Plato, Aristotle, or Augustine) affects how we evaluate the extent to which people can be expected to realize moral rectitude. Just because something is the ethically right thing to do, is it reasonable to expect people to be able to do it? How much should the presence of strong emotion mitigate one's judgment about an ethical lapse or a morally wrong action?

Consider, for example, the distinction drawn between someone coolly, in a premeditated and carefully planned way, murdering someone; and cases where someone kills another in a fit of rage triggered by some traumatic event, such as the sudden discovery that the victim had murdered the killer's child. Many think of the cases as different because of what one understands about the power and nature of passion and the reasonable limits of human moral restraint.

Acting well, doing what's right, becoming and remaining virtuous are difficult things for human beings. How much slack should they be given? When, if ever, might the force of passion be thought of as so strong as to render an action non-voluntary? How generous and forgiving should one be in moral judgment?

See also

1.2 Agency, 3.22 Prudence, 5.5 Fallenness

Reading

Norman O. Dahl, *Practical Reason, Aristotle, and Weakness of the Will* (Minneapolis: University of Minnesota Press, 1984)

Alfred R. Mele, *Irrationality: An Essay on* Akrasia, *Self-Deception, and Self-Control* (Oxford: Oxford University Press, 1987)

T. D. J. Chappell, *Aristotle and Augustine on Freedom: Two Theories of Freedom, Voluntary Action and* Akrasia (New York: St Martin's Press, 1995)

5.2 Amoralism

An old saying tells people that "All's fair in love and war." Although few sincerely believe it, many do accept that sometimes the categories of the moral and immoral have no place. In such situations, we are left with the amoral: that which is neither good nor bad but which stands outside morality.

The activities of businesses and corporations, for instance, are sometimes held to be about one thing and one thing only: profit. Whether one is kind, honest, generous, and trustworthy is irrelevant to the conduct of commercial affairs – unless being that way helps maximize profit. This view can be presented as a critique of capitalism, as stark realism, or perhaps even as a defense of capitalism (by arguing that amoral conduct in the market actually produces the best outcomes for everyone, as if, as Adam Smith (1723–90) maintained, the market were guided by a beneficent "invisible hand").

In war, too, amoralists argue, there is only one objective: victory. Anything that contributes to victory is permissible – lying, killing, stealing, destroying property, etc. In fact, like the context of commerce, obeying moral rules will probably inhibit one from realizing the goal of war.

Politics, too, has been described as an amoral context. Machiavelli (1469–1527) famously described how the successful leader must be prepared to present the appearance of moral rectitude but in reality be prepared to engage in the most ruthless vice in order to obtain and secure power. Many who maintain that national politics should be governed by moral principle nevertheless argue that international politics, like war, is entirely amoral. Those holding these views sometimes prefer to be called political "realists" rather than amoralists.

Drawing the line

If it's accepted that some human activities fall outside moral consideration, where do we draw the line that separates the moral from the amoral?

One way of doing this is to appeal to divine principle and argue that there are some activities that divine commands neither require nor prohibit. Perhaps tugging gently on one's earlobe is neither moral nor immoral – although tugging on it in order to send a signal to someone across the room to steal something would be.

Another way of sectioning off the moral from the amoral is to use the harm and happiness principles. Those acts that lead to or at least are likely to lead to some sort of harm, especially serious harm, are to be regarded as immoral; while those that contribute to happiness or are likely to contribute to happiness are to be regarded as moral. Activities, however, that contribute neither to harm nor to happiness or are likely not to do so are amoral. It's not likely, in most contexts, that a few tugs on one's ear will contribute to people's happiness or unhappiness in any way. So, that action is perfectly amoral – unless one argues that the opportunity cost of tugging on one's ear rather than doing something else is an immoral waste of resources.

More radical is the claim that there's no line to be drawn, anyway, since morality is an illusion, and the world is in fact entirely amoral. Even if we don't go quite this far, many see actual moral codes as in some sense a sham or a deceit or an instrument by which the strong manipulate the weak. Joseph Conrad's *Heart of Darkness* (1902) and André Gide's *The Immoralist* (1902), for example, are both fictional narratives about Europeans who see the moral systems that had seemed so solid crumble before their eyes. It seems an affliction suffered by many. Even recent continental philosophers like Gilles Deleuze (1925–95) and Jacques Derrida (1930–2004) have held that subverting the objectionable dimensions of what goes by the name of ethics and morality is to stand in a posture of permanent critique against it.

The trouble is that even those most cynical about established moralities seem not to be fully fledged amoralists, since their righteous indignation itself requires that they hold some values. Calls to rebellion, freedom, and critique may entail subverting existing moral orders, but they seem also to imply moralities themselves.

See also

3.3 Bad/evil, 5.9 Nihilism, 5.11 Power

Reading

Niccolo Machiavelli, *The Prince* [1513], edited by Russell Price (Cambridge: Cambridge University Press, 1988)

Marquis de Sade, *Justine, Philosophy in the Bedroom, and Other Essays* (New York: Grove Press, 1990)

Robert E. Frederick, *A Companion to Business Ethics* (Oxford: Blackwell, 1999)

5.3 Bad faith and self-deception

Poor old Barbra Streisand and Donna Summer. In "No More Tears" they sang that they always dreamed they'd find the perfect lover, but he turned out to be just like every other man. Still, it wasn't their fault it all went so wrong. "I had no choice from the start," they sang, "I've gotta listen to my heart."

At the risk of being pedantic, however, surely we do all have the power to choose whether or not to get involved with a lover, and how far we take the relationship? The trouble is that we would rather kid ourselves that we are not in control. That way, we avoid responsibility for the consequences of our actions. But given how common this sort of rationalization is, doesn't it threaten our capacity to make moral choices?

Self-deception

The very concept of "self-deception" is a curious one, for it requires that one is both the liar (who knows the truth) and the victim of the lie (from whom the truth has been hidden). But how is this even possible?

Perhaps the self isn't a unitary whole but is actually somehow fractured into discrete parts. One of the most popular ways of explaining self-deception this way is to divide the self between the conscious and the unconscious. Sigmund Freud (1856–1939) is perhaps most famous for this gesture. But the same general idea recurs in various forms throughout the history of ideas.

For Immanuel Kant (1724–1804), the self one is able to observe is only an empirical, superficial self, behind which deeper selves lie. One might say, in fact, that modern questions about self-deception and an unconscious begin with Descartes's (1596–1650) worry, in *Meditations on First Philosophy*, about whether or not he is possessed by a demon and whether he may be the source of his own possibly false ideas about the world and God.

Søren Kierkegaard (1815–55) criticized the modern, scientific, rationalistic age and what passes for Christianity in it in terms of self-deception. The modern world lulls people into a self-deceptive state in which they pretend they're leading meaningful lives predicated on faith and reason, when really they are steeped in a deep despair or malaise.

It's characteristic of this despair, for Kierkegaard, that people are unconscious of it, refusing to admit it to themselves. They therefore live in an inauthentic state, failing to become authentic, passionate selves. Instead each merely exists as what Kierkegaardian Walker Percy described in *The Moviegoer* (1960) as an "Anyone living Anywhere" – not as a true individual but as a neutral, indefinite "one." As Kierkegaard wrote in *The Sickness unto Death*, "the specific character of despair is this: it is unaware of being despair."

Bad faith

A specific form of self-deception has been called, "bad faith" (*mauvaise foi*), a term of criticism developed by existentialist thinkers like Jean-Paul Sartre (*Being and Nothingness*, 1944) and Simone de Beauvoir (*Ethics of Ambiguity*, 1947). It means a number of things – none of them good.

In the first place, bad faith is an effort to avoid the anxiety and responsibility humans must bear because they are free. To avoid freedom and its responsibility, people say in bad faith that they are merely the products of society, the results of their upbringing, the unchangeable effects of natural causes. In doing so they deny their capacities to choose as subjects and stress their status as *objects*. But, according to the existentialists, all this is said in bad faith, because on some level it is immediately evident to people that they are free consciousnesses.

Second, as strange as this sounds, bad faith is manifest when people try to pretend that they *are* something, that they have an *essence*. But people have no fixed essence which defines their being. At every instant we must choose to be something (a "husband," a "waiter," a "woman," a "homosexual," "French," "American," "black," or "white," an "evolved animal"). But this choice can't be fixed, solidified, or made permanent; as soon as the choice is made it's transcended into a new moment where a new free choice must be made. Nevertheless, one's present identities ("I am a leftist Lithuanian professor") are claimed as if they were real and enduring.

People also engage in a third form of bad faith when they deny others the same freedom they would have for themselves. The problem with doing so isn't simply logical, one of consistency. It also stems from our knowing that everyone else is also a free consciousness and that practically speaking each person's freedom depends on the freedom of others. The urgent effort to prove, for example, that black Africans weren't equal to European whites betrays the fact that the slaveholders knew that blacks were enslaved humans like themselves, not sub-human animals. Those who oppress others, who characterize them as "cockroaches" (as the Hutu militia characterized their Tutsi victims) and "vermin" (as Nazis characterized Jews), typically do so in bad faith.

For some, the widespread prevalence of self-deception in humans makes them skeptical of the human capacity to make authentic, moral choices. We must doubt not only the sincerity of others, but also that of our own moral reasoning. Might we not be kidding ourselves when we argue for moral values as if they were authentically our own? For the existentialists, however, there are grounds for optimism. We can be truly free and avoid bad faith. If we do not share this optimism, then we have to accept that moral discourse will always be infected with self- deception.

See also

2.13 Rationalism, 4.2 Authenticity, 5.6 False consciousness

Reading

*Herbert Finagrette, *Self Deception* [1969], *with a New Chapter* (Berkeley: University of California Press, 2000)

John Douglas Mullen, *Kierkegaard's Philosophy: Self-Deception and Cowardice in the Present Age* (Lanham, MD: University Presses of America, 1995)

Ronald E. Santoni, *Bad Faith, Good Faith, and Authenticity in Sartre's Early Philosophy* (Philadelphia, PA: Temple University Press, 1995)

5.4 Casuistry and rationalization

Xiao is a manager for a large multinational mining company. He takes ethics very seriously which is why he is concerned about his latest project. It requires him to pay a bribe, forcibly evict indigenous people from their land, employ children, and destroy an important, bio-diverse habitat. He reasons, however, that bribes are just the local way of doing things, as is the practice of employing children, who actually make an important con-tribution to stretched household budgets. The evicted people will get compensation, and it is not as though western countries don't have com-pulsory purchase orders. As for the environmental damage, the company has pledged to create a new sanctuary near the site. Anyway, if he refuses, the company will simply get someone else to do it. Xiao is uncomfortable, but his conscience is appeased.

Are the justifications for Xiao's actions adequate, or are they merely con-venient ways for him to excuse what's really morally abhorrent behavior? It's impossible to tell from such a brief description, but the suspicion is cer-tainly that a more impartial examination of the relevant rights and wrongs may come to a different conclusion as to the morality of his actions.

This kind of danger is ever-present in the real world of practical ethics, particularly in business ethics. It would be too cynical to suggest that the authors of corporate ethics policies are always simply trying to provide a respectable veneer for their employers' callous self-interest. But whether the relevant conduct is commercial or personal, it's easy to end up looking for moral justifications for what one really wants to do, even if one's desire to be good is sincere. By contrast, it's hard to assess the morality of an action in which one has an interest fairly, dispassionately, and objectively. There are always arguments to be found for and against any given action, and since ethics is not like mathematics, it's easy to give more weight to the reasons that suit than to those that don't.

Casuistry

Finding justifications for what one wants to do anyway is sometimes described as "casuistry." But in fact this is a little misleading, since genuine casuistry is a sincere attempt to arrive at solutions to moral dilemmas on a case-by-case basis, by appeal to paradigm cases and precedents, rather than to a particular moral framework. This makes it particularly useful for solving real-world debates, since it does not assume a consensus of moral theory among those attempting to resolve the dilemma. Among other instances, casuistry has a rather noble history in English common law, and it in part grounds the common legal practice to day of citing precedent cases to justify rulings. All casuistry requires is that everyone agrees what the right thing to do is in certain given circumstances, which people holding different theoretical commitments often do. This is why, although it is not usually described in this way, a lot of work in applied bioethics today takes the form of casuistry.

Because, however, casuistic thinking leaves a lot of room for interpretation and is not about applying a set of clear moral principles, it's open to abuse, which is why it got a bad name. Catholic Blaise Pascal (1623–62), in his *Provincial Letters* (1656–7) for example, lambasted the Church for misusing casuistry to rationalize the sinful behavior of the powerful and privileged; and, of course, a host of Protestant reformers shared his view, reserving special criticism for Jesuit abuses of the casuist method. Where there is a need for subtlety and interpretation there is also room for self-serving evasiveness and rationalization.

Correcting bias

But how can one employ casuistry properly and make sure that its reasoning isn't distorted by desire or interest? First and foremost, one simply has to accept that everyone is prone to such distortions, even those (perhaps especially those) who are utterly confident in their ability to make impartial assessments.

One must, therefore, in the second place, make a careful, conscious effort to correct biases – including biases that may seem imperceptible or of which one seems free. This takes real self-knowledge, vigilance, and care. A useful technique is to ask oneself honestly what solution one really wants to be justified and then make an extra effort to see opposing arguments in their strongest light. This kind of self-monitoring can compensate for the natural, but regrettable, inclination to follow the arguments, not where they lead (as Socrates advised in Plato's *Phaedo*), but where we want them to go.

Understanding some of the mechanisms of self-deception, avoidance, and denial – as well as some of the typical things that people deny, avoid, or deceive themselves about – can help pull back the cloaks behind which immoral motives commonly hide themselves. Still, another effective technique is to discuss one's choice and the justifications for and against it with someone who is both disinterested and competent in moral reasoning. A disinterested ear is often the best protection against a clever desire.

See also

1.12 Interest, 4.7 Impartiality and objectivity, 5.3 Bad faith and self-deception, 5.6 False consciousness

Reading

*Kenneth E. Kirk, *Conscience and Its Problems: An Introduction to Casuistry* [1927] (Louisville, KY: Westminster John Knox Press, 1999)
*Albert R. Jonsen and Stephen Toulmin, *The Abuse of Casuistry: A History of Moral Reasoning* (Berkeley: University of California Press, 1988)
Richard B. Miller, *Casuistry and Modern Ethics: A Poetics of Practical Reasoning* (Chicago: University of Chicago Press, 1996)

5.5 Fallenness

How are we to make sense of events like the Rwandan genocide, petty cruelties, and perhaps even environmental degradation? Typically we look for the causes in poor socialization, ignorance, history, or political dynamics. These travesties are not inevitable but could all be avoided if we could order our societies and ourselves better.

But there is an older, now less fashionable, way of interpreting phenomena like these. Human beings are inclined to evil because they are *fallen*. Sinfulness is a part of our nature, and to counter it we require not simply moral and intellectual virtue, but theological virtue and divine assistance as well. In short, a purely secular ethics which fails to take into account our fallen natures and the gap between us and the divine is woefully inadequate.

Fallenness and sin

The Abrahamic religious traditions share broadly speaking an endorsement of the account of Genesis 2–3, where Adam and Eve eat the fruit taken from the tree of knowledge of good and evil – the very knowledge investigated by moral philosophy! God had forbidden them to eat this fruit, so in punishment for their transgression He casts them out of Eden.

This transgression or sin and subsequent punishment is called the "Fall." Its punishments have been thought to include, variously interpreted, the pain of childbirth, the requirement to labor for sustenance, mortality, the subordination of women to men, the weakening of the will, the perversion of desire, and the darkening of the intellect.

These last three in particular suggest limits to what one may expect of people, ethically speaking. Because the will has been weakened, humanity lacks the rectitude to adhere to moral principle in the face of adversity or temptation. Because of the perversion of desire, the lust for earthly pleasures (*concupiscence*), people can't be expected to be consistently or naturally inclined to desire the good. On the contrary, they can be expected to want what's in fact bad for them and for others, what's evil. Because the intellect has been darkened, despite having eaten the fruit of the tree of moral knowledge, people can be expected to be commonly ignorant about right and wrong and to possess limited capacities to figure it out on their own. Many Christians hold the additional belief that all people are born with original sin (the moral stain we inherit as descendents of Adam), and so all humans are inherently subject to weakness and sin.

Because of fallenness, then, despite their vigorous and even desperate efforts to improve things on their own, people can be expected frequently to fail to be good. War, crime, and vice of every sort are inevitable. Sins of the intellect and sins of the emotions will be pervasive.

Dealing with or denial of?

One might say that modernity has been in part the effort to overcome through reason and technology the consequences of the Fall. Medicine and the health sciences work to reverse and limit pain and even mortality. Machines reduce the need for labor. Modern science and philosophy raise claims to having acquired knowledge, while modern ethics and political theory struggle to achieve practical wisdom. René Descartes lays out much of this in his *Discourse on Method* (1637). But those who find the account of fallenness compelling are likely to think that there's vanity in the modern project, that humanity can only overcome the Fall through divine assistance. For Christians this assistance is typically articulated through concepts such as: grace, salvation, redemption, and the sacrifice of the Messiah or Christ.

Martin Heidegger, in *Being and Time* (1927) developed a different though also ethically relevant conception of "fallenness" (*Verfallenheit, das Verfallen*). Following Søren Kierkegaard's diagnosis of modern society's pathologies, Heidegger describes how in average everyday life individuals fall prey to idle busy-talk, habit, as well as practical, commercial, and technical projects in ways that alienate them from their authentic and "ownmost" ways of being (as well as from being, *Sein*, itself).

People who fall into this state of average everydayness can understand themselves only as the impersonal *they* understands them, in the way that what Heidegger calls *das Man* conceives things. Individuals become average "they-selves," *one* (as the neutral grammatical pronoun). To break out of this fallenness and averageness and resolutely achieve authenticity is, one might say, the ethical purpose of Heideggerian phenomenology (despite his claim that there is nothing moral or political about it). Doing so requires, among other things (as it does for many existentialists), coming to terms with human mortality, as well as the way we are vulnerable to falling.

Of course, if you do not accept Abrahamic theology, all this talk of fallenness might just sound like old-fashioned guff. But even without religious beliefs, the idea that human beings are by nature inclined toward wrongdoing must be seriously considered. If accepted, it has major repercussions for what we think to be possible ethically.

See also

2.16 Virtue ethics, 3.3 Bad/evil, 4.2 Authenticity, 5.1 *Akrasia*, 5.3 Bad faith and self-deception

Reading

*Wayne G. Boulton, Thomas D. Kennedy, and Allen Verhey, eds., *From Christ to the World: Introductory Readings in Christian Ethics* (Grand Rapids, MI: W. B. Eerdmans, 1994)
*Tatha Wiley, *Original Sin: Origins, Developments, Contemporary Meanings* (Mahwah, NJ: Paulist Press, 2002)

5.6   False consciousness

If you've ever heard someone say that they deserve what they have because they've earned it, you've encountered an example of what some social critics call *false consciousness*.

But what on earth could be false about something that in many cases seems so obviously true? It's perhaps not false that people who say they've earned what they've got have worked very hard for it and perhaps exercised remarkable intelligence, creativity, and sacrifice. There is, however, no divine or natural law about what sort of return or reward someone is to receive for hard work, intelligence, creativity, sacrifice, or anything else. It's only the peculiar social arrangements of our society (as well as, in many cases, a fair measure of good fortune) that have distributed to any particular individual the precise amount he or she claims to have earned. Other social arrangements might have distributed far less or far more.

So, we might define "false consciousness" briefly as a set of beliefs people hold, usually called *ideologies*, that obscure from them the real social-political-economic relationships that govern their lives and the true nature of the social-political-economic order in which they live. In an 1893 correspondence with Karl Marx (1818–83), Friedrich Engels (1820–95) remarked that:

> Ideology is a process accomplished by the so-called thinker consciously, it is true, but with a false consciousness. The real motive forces impelling him remain unknown to him; otherwise it simply would not be an ideological process. Hence he imagines false or seeming motive forces.

It's a single brief and fleeting remark. Marx himself never used the phrase. Nevertheless, Marx did lay the groundwork for much of what later thinkers made of the idea. Principally, Marxian theories of false consciousness rely on Marx's description in *Das Kapital* (1867) and elsewhere of the way that capitalism distorts the self-understanding of the proletariat about its real situation.

Among the principal forms of false consciousness is the understanding people acquire about themselves through what Marx and others have called the fetishism of commodities. "Fetishism" is a process whereby people project value upon things and then pretend or convince themselves that it's there intrinsically. So, people come to believe that diamonds or BMWs have great intrinsic value, when in fact they are shiny pebbles and machines whose value comes only from the social world in which they're situated. A BMW is likely to have little or no value to a nomadic herdsman in the Himalayas. A diamond or a stock certificate would have had no value to an ancient Spartan.

Updating the idea

Later critics like Guy Debord (1931–94) and Jean Baudrillard (b. 1929) have described the way in which devices like the media and advertising convince people that they're defined and have value to the extent they buy or own certain things and imitate the images that pervade their lives. In Debord's terms, "spectacle" replaces human social relations. In Baudrillard's formulation, we become images of images, imitations of imitations, *simulacra* not of real things but rather of other *simulacra*. People even begin to prefer imitations or cyber-realities to reality itself. For example, people prefer Disney Europe to Europe, resorts to beaches, malls to neighborhoods, Internet relationships to flesh and blood, video games to sport. The wars people know are not real wars but the spectacular images they see on TV.

Frankfurt School critics like Theodor Adorno (1903–69) describe how even the simplest dimensions of our lives – even things like lipstick and pop music – hide oppressions at the very time they advance them.

Even the predominant liberal political beliefs with which people understand and justify the social relations they do observe are, according to many critics, instruments of false consciousness. Talk of "free" markets blinds people to the coercion and manipulation that are endemic to them. Talk of "freedom of speech" obscures how speech only actually matters politically if one has access to the media. Talk of "property rights" masks how the ideology of private property makes it possible for vast concentrations of it to deprive others of their holdings and degrade the natural world with impunity.

The limit on ethical deliberation implied here, then, is that people steeped in false consciousness cannot be expected to reach sound ethical conclusions when their understanding of themselves and their world is deeply distorted in a way that prevents them from understanding many of the ethically salient features of the realities they face.

Of course, the critique only makes sense if you accept that the various beliefs comprising "false consciousness" are indeed false. They may not be. Moreover, the accusation of false consciousness might sometimes be turned on its accusers. Is it false consciousness to *deny* that the value of goods is determined by markets, for example? At its worst, saying that something is an example of false consciousness can thus degenerate into mere name-calling: you don't accept what I see as the truth, therefore you must be the victim of false consciousness. Those who wish to level the charge of "false consciousness," therefore, will do well not only to describe the content of the false consciousness they've identified but also present an *error theory* which accounts for the mechanism or reasons why reasonable people see things so wrongly. Otherwise it will be difficult to get around the presumption of clear-sightedness.

See also

1.16 Need, 2.3 Culture critique, 3.18 Liberation/oppression, 5.15 Standpoint

Reading

Guy Debord, *The Society of the Spectacle* [1967] (New York: Zone Books, 1995)
*Christopher L. Pines, *Ideology and False Consciousness: Marx and His Progenitors* (Albany: State University of New York Press, 1993)
Michael Rosen, *On Voluntary Servitude: False Consciousness and the Theory of Ideology* (Cambridge, MA: Harvard University Press, 1996)

5.7 Free will and determinism

In law and in everyday morality, people make allowances for mitigating circumstances. A wife who murders her husband may be given a lighter sentence if she can show that he frequently battered her and that she committed her crime under sustained stress. People who can demonstrate diminished responsibility due to mental illness, chronic or acute, will (or at least should) receive more treatment and less punishment. It's also widely accepted that to a certain extent a difficult upbringing can make someone more likely to turn to crime.

What this shows is that people do not believe that free will is all-powerful. Sometimes people's actions are partly determined by what has happened to them, and this makes them less responsible for what they do. But what if free will *normally* makes less of a contribution to our actions than we think, or even plays no role at all? What if, when closely scrutinized, the very concept of free will doesn't make sense? Wouldn't that totally undercut our common sense notions of responsibility and blame?

Ted Honderich (b. 1933) maintains that free will doesn't exist at all and that our ordinary ideas of moral responsibility will have to go. On Honderich's view, moral responsibility only makes sense if one accepts "origination" – the view that the *first* causes of human actions *originate* within human agents themselves, and that these first causes are not themselves caused by anything outside the agents. Honderich argues that there can be no such thing as origination. Human beings are as much part of the natural, material world as anything else, and in this world everything that happens is the effect of past causes. Causes determine their effects necessarily and uniformly. There is, therefore, simply no room for something called free will to step in and change the physical course of events, in the brain or in the ordinary world of human experience J. L. Austin (1911–60) called the world of "medium sized dry goods." It follows, then, that determinism is true, and that most ideas we have about moral responsibility are false.

More radically, does the concept of origination even make sense? If nothing at all causes human decisions of the will, then, as David Hume argued, they're no different from random events (*Enquiry Concerning Human Understanding*, 1748; Section VIII). But it hardly seems palatable to maintain that moral responsibility rests on something random, a matter of pure chance, without any cause.

Compatibilism

Talking about free acts in moral discourses and otherwise may still be acceptable, however, through a strategy known as "compatibilism." This theory accepts that human actions are as much caused by prior events as any other. But it also holds that it makes perfect sense to say that people have free will, just as long as by the words, "free will," one means just that human actions are not the result of external coercion or outside force. So long as the proximate (that is, nearest) causes of an action are in some sense within or part of the person acting, especially if the act flows from the actor's character, the act can meaningfully be described as a "free" act. If one jumps through a window because one chooses to do so, it's done freely (even if that choice was caused). If one is thrown through a window against one's wishes, one's act of defenestration is not a free one. On this account, however, it still seems true to say that people really could not do other than they do, and that, for many, still undercuts what is necessary to attribute moral responsibility.

Harry Frankfurt (b. 1929) has argued, using what have come to be known as "Frankfurt-style" cases ("Alternative Possibilities and Moral Responsibility," 1969), that even if it's true that one can't do otherwise, it still can make sense to describe one's action as free. Suppose, for example, someone possesses a secret device to force you to do X but won't use it unless you try to do something else besides X. If you do in fact choose to do X, says Frankfurt, it's true both that you couldn't do otherwise (that alternatives weren't possible) *and* that you chose freely. But for many, the simple idea even in these cases that people really could not do other than they do undercuts what is necessary to attribute moral responsibility.

Saving free will

The ability to act otherwise than one has is one way to define freedom. Other definitions include ideas like acting independently of the causal order of the natural world, acting on the basis of reason alone, acting independently of desire, acting at any time in opposition to one's current line of action. In any case, using a variety of definitions, many philosophers have tried to save free will, or at least freedom. In the *Critique of Practical Reason* (1788), for example, Kant advanced a "transcendental argument" for the reality of free will: people recognize that they have moral duties, but moral duties can only exist if people have free will. Therefore, since in order for morality to make sense free will must exist, it's reasonable to "postulate" that people have free wills – even though there is and in fact can be no proper *proof* for it and even though some plausible arguments maintain that it doesn't exist.

Thomas Nagel (b. 1937) adopts a position similar to Kant's, arguing that free will seems undeniably not to exist from a third-person point of view on the world – and undeniably to exist from a first-person point of view. Humans thus seem condemned to endure a perpetual "double vision" understanding of the reality of free will.

A weaker argument for free will might be described this way: irrespective of the ultimate truth, people somehow have to act *as though* they have free will. This seems to be psychologically true: no matter what people cling to intellectually, they always seem to feel and act as though they're free. But as a philosophical solution this option seems unsatisfactory, as it seems to imply that everyone must inevitably live under a delusion.

Jean-Paul Sartre maintained, in *Being and Nothingness* (1943), that human freedom is immediately, phenomenologically evident to consciousness. On the one hand, that option seems to be a disappointing cop-out – an attempt to resolve the issue through mere assertion rather than careful argument. If someone simply replies, "Well, I don't see it that way," the debate reaches an impasse. All the Sartrean can respond with is: "Look again." But, on the other hand, perhaps for many serious philosophical issues, at some point one reaches what Ludwig Wittgenstein (1889–1951) called bedrock, where one simply has to make a fundamental philosophical decision, or where ultimately one simply sees it or doesn't. Perhaps Sartre's appeal to what's simply evident is enough to cut the Gordian knot.

Things for those on the other side of the barricades aren't easy either. The challenge for those who reject both origination and Sartrean immediacy is to explain how one can make sense of moral responsibility while simultaneously not ignoring the disquieting implications determinism has for it. It's a tough row to hoe, but an important one. Indeed, this is perhaps one of the most vibrant philosophical debates today.

See also

1.2 Agency, 4.11 Paternalism, 5.3 Bad faith and self-deception, 5.8 Moral luck

Reading

*Daniel C. Dennett, *Elbow Room: The Varieties of Free Will Worth Wanting* (Cambridge, MA: MIT Press, 1984)

Thomas Nagel, *The View from Nowhere* (Oxford: Oxford University Press, 1986)

Ted Honderich, *How Free Are You? The Determinism Problem*, 2nd edition (Oxford: Oxford University Press, 2002)

5.8 Moral luck

Aisha was driving home through London one day when her mobile phone rang. She didn't have a hands-free set, but she answered it anyway. When the conversation finished, she put the phone down and carried on with her life. Had she been caught by the police, she would have faced a large fine and could have lost her license.

At the same time, somewhere else, Sophia was also driving home, and she too answered a mobile phone call manually. But as she was talking, a child ran out into the road in front of her. Distracted, and with only one hand on the steering wheel, she was unable to avoid a collision. The child died as a result. Sophia is now facing a prison sentence of up to 14 years. Had she not been on the phone at the time, she would have avoided killing the child.

What's particularly interesting about this comparison is that the only difference between Sophia and Aisha is luck. Had a child run into the road in front of Aisha, she too would have become a killer. So we have two women, both of whom performed the same acts; but in one case that act led to the death of a child and in the other case it did not – and only luck determined which was which. Is it fair that one woman is punished while the other is not?

Can luck enter into morality?

One's moral standing isn't usually considered to be a matter of luck or fortune. But situations such as this suggest it may play a very important role. The law certainly won't treat the two women equally, even though their characters and behavior may be just the same. Morally speaking, most would also consider Sophia more culpable than Aisha, even though Aisha was driving just as dangerously. The implication seems to be that how good or bad one is depends partly on what the consequences of our actions are, but consequences are in turn determined in part by luck.

Accepting luck as a factor in moral status is certainly a counter-intuitive view, and one with which many today disagree (interestingly, the ancients seem to have taken *fortuna* more seriously). We might justify the resistance to luck by arguing that although the law does – and perhaps has to – distinguish between reckless driving that leads to death and reckless driving that doesn't, morally speaking both women are in truth equally culpable. Perhaps contemporary moral intuitions that distinguish the two are distorted by the knowledge of what consequences actually follow. Perhaps either Aisha should be morally condemned a lot more, or Sophia should be condemned a lot less. Perhaps recognizing that only good fortune prevents most drivers from becoming careless killers should yield more sympathy for the killers. Indeed, how many of us can honestly claim to drive with due care and attention at all times?

To deny that moral luck exists at all, however, one needs to deny that actions become better or worse depending on what their consequences are, since what actually happens is almost always beyond anyone's full control. But this option also seems counter-intuitive: surely it does matter what actually happens. To judge people purely on the basis of their intentions or on the nature of the act itself seems to diminish the importance of what actually happens.

Constitutive luck

There is another kind of moral luck, known as *constitutive luck*. How good or bad one is depends a great deal on one's personality or character. But character is formed through both nature and nurture, and by the time one becomes mature enough to be considered a morally responsible adult, these character traits are more or less set. So, for example, a kind person hasn't fully chosen to be kind: that's how she grew up. Certainly many cruel and nasty people were themselves mistreated as children; that abuse almost certainly affected the way their personalities developed. Since people don't choose their genes, or their parents, or their culture of origin, or a lot of the other factors that affect moral development, there therefore seems to be another important element of luck in morality.

Martha Nussbaum has argued in *The Fragility of Goodness* (1986) that for the ancient Greeks not only does a good life depend upon constitutive luck, it also depends upon good luck in the sense of avoiding increased danger. The very attempt to be good, says Nussbaum, makes one vulnerable to many bad things that don't threaten the vicious. For example, the attempt to fulfill their duties led Hector, Agamemnon, Antigone, and Oedipus each to tragic ends. Perhaps Socrates might be thought of this way as well.

Given that the role of luck or fortune in life seems indubitable, but the idea of moral luck oxymoronic, isn't the best solution to say that where luck enters in, morality cannot be found? Yet, that too is a controversial road to follow. Screening out those dimensions of a situation attributable to luck may leave little left to praise or blame. So, however one looks at it, accepting the role of luck presents a major challenge to judgments of moral praise and blame – but perhaps something essential, too.

See also

1.2 Agency, 1.6 Character, 5.3 Bad faith and self-deception, 5.7 Free will and determinism

Reading

Thomas Nagel, "Moral luck" in *Mortal Questions* (Cambridge: Cambridge University Press, 1979)

Bernard Williams, "Moral luck" in *Moral Luck: Philosophical Papers 1973–1980* (Cambridge: Cambridge University Press, 1981)

*Daniel Statman, ed., *Moral Luck* (Albany: State University Press of New York, 1993)

5.9 Nihilism

In the Coen Brothers' 1998 film *The Big Lebowski*, nihilism is compared to one of the vilest creeds in human history – and found wanting. On discovering that the people menacing his friend "the Dude" are nihilists, and not Nazis as he had thought, the character Walter says, "Nihilists! Jesus! Say what you like about the tenets of National Socialism, Dude, at least it's an ethos."

"Nihilism" is often used as a term of criticism and even abuse. It's most often hurled by those who wish to defend "absolute" or divinely grounded morals against those they believe subvert them or the institutions built around them. But the term has also sometimes been used by the subversives themselves.

Deriving from the Latin *nihil*, meaning "nothing," modern usage of the term "nihilism" seems to have developed in the wake of its use in Ivan Turgenev's 1862 novel, *Fathers and Sons*. It came to characterize Russian social critics and revolutionaries of the nineteenth century like Alexander Herzen (1812–70), Mikhail Bakhunin (1814–76), and Nikolai Chernyshevsky (1828–89), who were associated with anarchism and socialism as well as with modern, secular, western materialism generally.

Anarchism, socialism, secularism, and materialism are not, of course, nothing. They comprise very specific truth-claims and moral values. But achieving their realization and acceptance requires the destruction or *annihilation* of the old order – of traditional morals and values and social systems said to be grounded in something divine or transcendent. After all, these thinkers aimed at the creation of a new, better world, a truly good world. But creating that world demanded first violently erasing the old world.

The threat of nihilism

But there's more to the charge of nihilism than the subversion of things based upon tradition and religion. Concepts and theories described as nihilistic are commonly taken to imply negative claims like these: (a) that there is no truth; (b) that there is no right or wrong, good or evil; (c) that life has no meaning; and even (d) that it's not possible to communicate meaningfully with one another. In short, any theory not ultimately grounded or finally justifiable may be subject to the charge of nihilism, whether its proponents realize it or not.

Most recently, intellectual movements collected under the moniker, "post-modernism" – like post-structuralism and deconstruction – have been called nihilistic. But nearly all things modern have also been subject to the charge – modern science, evolutionary theory, the Protestant Reformation, existentialism, pragmatism, modern relativism, rationalism, Kantianism, etc.

There's often a logical criticism wrapped up in all of this, a critique of *consistency* or *coherence*. The claim that "there is no truth" is itself a truth-claim. The claim that "language cannot communicate meanings" itself depends upon the ability of language to communicate. But does the claim that there are no values (no right and wrong) involve holding a value?

Thinkers like Friedrich Nietzsche (1844–1900) and Martin Heidegger (1889–1976) have held that in a perverse way it does. As they see it, it's a short hop from asserting that "nothing has value" to positively affirming the value of nothing. That is to say, nihilistic ideas and social movements, say the critics, inevitably lead to grotesque outpourings of violence and destruction.

Since nihilism cannot provide any foundation, ground, or reason for morality, ultimately "everything is permitted." Since everything is permitted, nothing is prohibited. That nothing's prohibited ought somehow to be exhibited and made manifest; therefore every act (even the most extreme acts) ought to happen. Some blame nihilism, therefore, for everything from the French Revolution's Terror, the Holocaust, and the Soviet gulags to pornography, drug abuse, abortion, divorce, petty crime, and rock and roll.

Overcoming nihilism

Traditionalists blame the modern abandonment of God for these mala-
dies and prescribe a return to tradition, absolutes, and a religiously based
society. One of the most influential analyses of the nihilistic characteristics
of the modern world, however, inverts this diagnosis and places responsibility for nihilism squarely upon the western philosophical and religious
traditions themselves.

Nihilism, says Nietzsche, actually results from the Christian-Platonic
tradition, from its attempts to acquire truth that is singular, universal, and
unchanging, together with its promoting the morals developed by a weak
and conquered people. One might call these pathologies the "God's Eye"
conception of truth and "slave" morality. After centuries of careful philosophical scrutiny philosophers have learned that truth of that sort is
unavailable to humans. The frustration and exhaustion of this disappointing
realization (the realization that "God is dead") together with the soporific
effects of slave morality have finally resulted in *thanatos* or the desire for
nothingness and death, even the desire to wreak revenge upon the world for
this disappointment.

For Nietzsche, our task is not to return to the pathological traditions
and philosophies that produced nihilism but, rather, to *overcome* nihilism.
Overcoming nihilism requires first recognizing and taking responsibility
for the fact that we are the source and creators of value. Next, overcoming nihilism demands that we find within ourselves the strength to make
new affirmative values, healthy values that honor our human finitude, our
embodiedness, and our desires, that love the human fate (*amor fati*) and
don't lead to nihilism. Existentialism has in many ways followed Nietzsche
in trying to achieve this project.

See also

2.14 Relativism, 5.2 Amoralism, 5.14 Skepticism

Readings

Friedrich Nietzsche, *The Will to Power* [1901], edited by Walter Kaufmann
  (New York: Vintage Books, 1968)
Karl Löwith, *Martin Heidegger and European Nihilism* [1953], edited by
  Richard Wolin (New York: Columbia University Press, 1995)
Stanley Rosen, *Nihilism: A Philosophical Essay* [1969], 2nd edition (South
  Bend, IN: St Augustine's Press, 2000)

5.10 Pluralism

Jean-Paul Sartre (1905–80) told a story of a young man who was caught in dilemma between his duties to his country and to his mother. Should he join the Free French Forces to fight Nazism or look after his sick, aged parent? Many moral theories would maintain that there must be some way of determining which of these duties carries more weight. Sartre disagreed because he thought it was finally up to each individual to choose his or her values, and no person or system could do it on anyone else's behalf. But there's another explanation for why the dilemma could be irresolvable: perhaps there are many values worth holding and no objective way of determining which should take priority over others – and sometimes these values simply conflict. This is the position known as pluralism, a doctrine most closely associated with Isaiah Berlin (1909–97).

Pluralism and relativism

Many critics claim that pluralism amounts to no more than relativism, so it is worth addressing this accusation directly in order to clarify what pluralism entails.

Relativism holds that there are no absolute moral values and that what's right or wrong is always relative to a particular person, place, time, species, culture, and so on. This position, however, differs from pluralism in a number of important respects. For one thing, the pluralist may well believe that moral values are not relative. For example, she might claim that the young man in Sartre's example really, objectively, has responsibilities to both his mother and his country. Nevertheless, the nature of morality is such that these duties cannot be weighed up against each other with any kind of mathematical precision to determine which has priority over the other. They both have a claim on him, yet he cannot adhere to both.

But conflicts among moral claims may not simply be a matter of imprecision. For the pluralist, there are many different values worth holding and many moral claims that may be made upon us. As W. D. Ross (1877–1971) and others have argued, goods, duties, values, claims, and principles may be irreducibly plural and complex. In certain cases, the constituents of this plurality may stand in conflict, and that conflict is simply *incommensurable* – that is, there may simply be no way to reconcile them.

Even if the pluralist does not hold that moral values are objective, the reason she has for claiming that moral values are plural and in conflict may not collapse into crude relativism. While there may be many ways in which human life has value, there isn't an unlimited variety. Some moral options –

for example, genocide – are not permissible. In addition, living in accordance with one option may in fact close off others. Take the example of the values of communal and individual life. There's value in living the kind of life in which one is very closely wedded to one's community, and there's a different kind of value in living as an autonomous, unencumbered individual. But if one lives to reap the benefits of one of these ways, the benefits of the other must be sacrificed. So, the values of community and individuality may be both equally important yet incommensurable.

This approach isn't a form of relativism because it's consistent with the idea that both ways of life have absolute value. Nor, again, is just any way of living valuable: there are limits to the plurality of value. While both community and individuality have value, racial purity does not.

The consequences of pluralism

The key claim of pluralism is simply that at least some values defy being pinned down in a hierarchy, whereas many other systems of morality contend that it will always be possible to determine which of our values are more fundamental than others and should thus take priority when there's a clash.

In practice, this means one has to accept that not all moral disputes can be resolved to everyone's satisfaction, and this isn't just because some people are mistaken in what they see as most important. If pluralists are right, then there are serious limits on the extent to which moral disagreements can be settled. Sometimes, the best we can do is to negotiate and reach accommodations with others, not actually agree on what value is superior to others.

This is particularly important for multicultural societies, where the plurality of values is more evident. A common ground can't always be found, but people must still live with each other. The pluralist warns that insisting that all moral disagreements are in principle resolvable forces people to conclude that those who disagree with them are fundamentally wrong, irrational, and immoral. That in turn generates tension and conflict, often violence. Pluralism offers the promise of a more peaceable alternative.

See also

2.14 Relativism, 3.1 Absolute/relative, 3.12 Individual/collective, 4.18 Universalizability

Reading

W. D. Ross *The Right and the Good* [1930], ed. Philip Stratton-Lake (Oxford: Oxford University Press, 2002)

Thomas Nagel, "The Fragmentation of Value" in *Mortal Questions* (Cambridge: Cambridge University Press, 1979)

*Isaiah Berlin, "The Idea of Pluralism" [1988], in *The Fontana Post-modernism Reader*, edited by Walter Truett Anderson (London: Fontana Press, 1996)

5.11 Power

The discourses orbiting around the recent war in Iraq include many arguments that the war is unjust, unnecessary, poorly executed, or illegal. Dealing with these arguments directly is one of the main ways in which the morality of the war has been debated. But there has been another way of criticizing these arguments, one that refuses to take any of the arguments at face value. This starts with the question *cui bono* – who benefits? Ask this question, many people say, and you will find the real reasons for war – or opposition to it. What people actually say is beside the point.

This approach reflects a strand in philosophy that analyzes events and discourses in terms of power relations. Look at the disagreeing parties in the debate and you'll find that each has some sort of interest in the stance it takes. The stance, then, whatever it appears to be, is fundamentally a device for protecting, securing, or enhancing its own power. The discourses about promoting democracy, advancing human rights, ensuring national security, upholding the requirements of international law, are therefore often – or even always – deployed to advance other agendas. Those opposed to the war have claimed these agendas might include securing access to oil, undermining Saudi power in the region, protecting Israel, stemming the advance of Russian and European power, weakening international institutions, galvanizing domestic support for the current government, creating a distraction and financial crisis to justify the dismantling of American social programs, transferring wealth to the shareholders of specific corporations, or weakening Islam. Those in favor of the war can also claim the anti-war movement is motivated by the desire to increase the power of Europe, the left, Ba'athists, or Islam.

Taken to its extreme view, this kind of analysis claims that, instead of making us excellent, or piling up treasures in heaven, or making more people happier, morality is largely, even completely, about power. Moral principles and moral terms are actually clever instruments of manipulation.

Marx, Foucault, and hierarchy

There are many ways to think about the way power works. One way is in a top-down fashion, where those above (the powerful) exert their power over those below (the powerless or less powerful). The classical Marxian model seems to follow this rule: owner/slave, lord/serf, capitalist/proletarian; that is, those who control the means of production (on top)/those who work the means of production (below). One of the things power of this sort can do is dictate the terms of moral and immoral, right and wrong, just and unjust.

So, slave owners, aristocrats, and capitalists invent systems of morality and politics that explain, justify, and secure their dominant position. Some people are born slaves and are intrinsically well suited to it, the aristocrat Aristotle (384–322 BCE) claimed. Slavery is actually good for slaves, American slavers argued. God has established the hierarchy where lords rule, said the lords. Their blood is superior. They create, cultivate, and sustain the refinements of civilization in ways the lower classes cannot. Capitalists have worked harder and smarter. They've been frugal, thrifty, diligent, disciplined, and have invested wisely.

It's no wonder, then, that Karl Marx and Friedrich Engels asserted that "The ruling ideas of society are in every epoch the ideas of the ruling class" (*The German Ideology*, I. B, 1845–6).

But, of course, power isn't simply exerted in a top-down way. Those underneath often struggle against those above, sometimes successfully. Those who occupy lower rungs in the hierarchy often marshal clever and effective forms of resistance and opposition.

There are, however, other models of power besides the top-down and bottom-up channels of hierarchy. Sometimes power struggles exist among those on the same rung. Sometimes players in power struggles change sides or play both sides against each other. Sometimes different power games go on at the same time, some along the lines of sex, other times through ideas about race, mental illness, criminality, economic status, political affiliation, family role, species, and personal history. Often these lines of power and struggle conflict with one another. Sometimes an individual may even be torn in different directions by different moral discourses, different lines of struggle.

For thinkers like Michel Foucault (1926–84), there is no grand *system* governing society – no single capitalist system, patriarchy, imperialist or racist order, etc. Rather there are instead countless power relationships constantly changing, realigning, breaking apart, and reconfiguring. Power is more like a kaleidoscope or a plate of spaghetti than a pyramid or a chain. On this view, to see something like the Iraq war as purely being about one group exerting its power over another is far too simplistic.

See also

5.2 Amoralism, 5.6 False consciousness, 5.9 Nihilism, 5.15 Standpoint

Reading

Michel Foucault, *Power/Knowledge: Selected Interviews and Other Writings, 1972–1977*, edited by Colin Gordon (New York: Pantheon Books, 1980)

Barry Barnes, *The Nature of Power* (Urbana: University of Illinois Press, 1988)

*Peter Ackerman and Jack DuVall, *A Force More Powerful: A Century of Non-Violent Conflict* (New York: Palgrave, 2001)

5.12 Radical particularity

In the debate preceding the invasion of Iraq in 2003, both supporters and advocates appealed to past precedents to strengthen their cases. Critics pointed to other attempts by western nations to interfere with the internal affairs of other states, while supporters compared leaving Saddam Hussein in power to the appeasement of Hitler.

Almost all moral debate requires some comparison. Similar cases require similar treatments, and what is right in one instance is also right in another, relevantly similar one. But then, as Jacques Derrida (1930–2004) puts it in *The Gift of Death* (1992): "*tout autre est tout autre*" ("every other is completely other"). No two individuals are the same, let alone identical. No two situations are utterly alike. Words don't mean precisely the same thing to me as they do to you, not the same thing in this context as in another, not the same thing on this reading as another, not the same thing this time as another. One might say that the very concept of *sameness* is itself problematic. There are a number of ethical implications to this.

The law, justice, and violence

Laws, rules, and principles are by definition general. None of them indicates precisely which rules apply to which cases in which manner. None of them can say whether a particular circumstance presents an exception. It's not possible for them to do so. So, when people appeal to a law, principle, or rule in some particular case, they can in fact only do so by making an utterly singular and unique decision, and that decision cannot be strictly determined by anything general.

The impossibility of avoiding undeterminable, foundationless choices about what to do, how to live, and what to believe was something Søren Kierkegaard (1813–55) emphasized as characteristic of the human existential condition. It's something that for him is most radically faced in a "leap of faith." It's a leap that, like all ethical choices, no reason, no principle, no theory could ever fully justify. When made "authentically," decisions like this particularize the self in a radical way (*Fear and Trembling*, 1843).

Laws, rules, and principles by their very nature attempt to produce order, regularity, consistency, and sameness in human practices. The *same* rewards are to be distributed for the *same* work; the *same* punishments are to be administered for the *same* crime. Laws, etc., like moral theories, would pretend to create an utterly closed system – a system that deals in a regular fashion with the same sort of cases in the same way without any arbitrary judgment. But if the presumption of sameness is baseless, then isn't it the case that this effort to make things the same necessarily involves a kind of *violence* against particularity? Mustn't the effort to expel the arbitrary, to close or complete that which cannot be closed or completed, necessarily lead to violence against whatever resists, what must resist? In short, aren't ethical rules, as rules, themselves unethical?

To the inevitably unethical nature of ethics, Derridian justice responds with what might be called permanent critique (echoing Leon Trotsky's call for "permanent revolution"). Permanent critique prevents – or at least limits – the way laws, rules, and principles must be used violently by subverting the fantasy of sameness and non-arbitrariness that captivates those who wield them.

It's a stirring call to arms. But what positive ideals of justice and morality does this make possible? What vision of a good or at least better society can such a view of justice and ethics yield us? The worry is that in its refusal to be pinned down and to accept any appeal to the general or the universal, such a permanent critique becomes hollow.

See also

1.5 Care, 4.2 Authenticity, 4.9 Justice and lawfulness, 5.3 Bad faith and self-deception

Reading

Søren Kierkegaard, *Concluding Unscientific Postscript to* Philosophical Fragments [1846], edited by Howard V. Hong and Edna H. Hong (Princeton, NJ: Princeton University Press, 1992)

Jacques Derrida, "Before the Law," in *Acts of Literature*, edited by Derrick Attridge (New York: Routledge, 1992)

Jacques Derrida, "Force of Law: The 'Mystical Foundation of Authority'" in *Deconstruction and the Possibility of Justice*, edited by Drucilla Cornell, Michael Rosenfeld, and David Gray Carlson (New York: Routledge, 1992)

5.13 The separateness of persons

Jane is an easy-going, hard-working person who does not let misfortune bother her. She has a moderately well paid job and has recently bought a small car, which gives her some pleasure, even though she doesn't use it very much. Mary, in contrast, is lazy and hard to please. But one thing she would really like is a car, which she can't currently afford, partly because she doesn't work very hard. If she had one, she'd be much more content. Mary and Jane both think that people should do whatever would increase the sum total of happiness. So Mary tries to persuade Jane that she has a moral duty to give her the car. After all, it will make Mary much happier, whereas Jane will soon get over the loss – she always does. What reason has Jane to say no?

Most people would think that Mary's suggestion is outrageous. Jane has worked to get her car, while Mary has been relatively idle. Yet, Mary is saying she should have Jane's car, not because that would be a kind and generous thing for Jane to do, but because it's the morally right thing. Ridiculous, no?

The trouble is that if one takes act utilitarianism seriously, Mary has a strong argument. Utilitarianism insists that everyone's interests should be considered equally, and that the right action is the one that increases the general happiness. This opens up the possibility that some people should be made worse off, even though they have done nothing to deserve any deprivation, simply because that would result in an increase in the general happiness.

What this seems to violate is a principle known as the "separateness of persons." Individuals are not simply carriers of welfare, happiness or utility that can be topped up, plundered, or combined like cups of water in order to achieve a fairer distribution of these goods. Harm to one individual cannot be compensated by benefits to another. If a person chooses to sacrifice some of his or her own welfare for the sake of another, that's an act of generosity, not the fulfillment of a moral obligation. Any moral system that ignores this – as utilitarianism allegedly does – is therefore flawed.

Against the separateness of persons

It's possible, however, to argue that the separateness of persons has no real moral significance, and that its apparent obviousness is illusory. For instance, in the case of Mary and Jane, other forms of utilitarianism, for example rule utilitarianism, just wouldn't demand that Jane give Mary her car. If one considers the whole picture, it's clear that a society operating upon rules that reward the lazy or don't allow individuals to keep the fruits of their labors will be dysfunctional, resent-ridden, and unproductive. So, contrary to appearances, utilitarianism doesn't necessarily require that the separateness of Jane's person be denied on moral grounds in order to deal with Mary's request.

Still, it's not clear at all either that people are fully separate (see 3.12 Individual/collective) or that, even if they are, it follows logically that redistributions of goods are unjust. Redistributions may be desirable for non-utilitarian reasons, say for reasons of duty or virtue. In addition, once one accepts that transfers of welfare may be *limited* by other considerations (e.g. the desire for security and stability of property and for effort and creativity to be rewarded), the idea that such transfers are unjust becomes less plausible. European welfare states, for example, routinely redistribute wealth from the rich to the poor through the taxation system, and most Europeans think this is a requirement of justice, not an affront to it.

Furthermore, the principle of the separateness of persons may lead to repellent consequences of its own. For example, suppose that the lives of many millions could be significantly improved by reducing the quality of life of a few of the best off in a very small way, a way that left them still much better off than the rest. Unyielding insistence on honoring the separateness of persons would, however, prohibit anyone from doing so. Is that prohibition something we should be morally willing to accept?

See also

2.1 Consequentialism, 4.7 Impartiality and objectivity, 5.12 Radical particularity

Reading

Derek Parfit, *Reasons and Persons* (Oxford: Oxford University Press, 1984)
John Rawls, *A Theory of Justice,* revised edition (Oxford: Oxford University Press, 1999)
Brad Hooker, *Ideal Code, Real World: A Rule-Consequentialist Theory of Morality* (Oxford: Oxford: University Press, 2000)

5.14 Skepticism

In June 2002, a local council of elders in the Pakistani village of Meerwala allegedly sentenced 29-year-old Mukhtar Mai to be gang raped by the male members of another local family in retribution for an allegedly improper relationship that Mukhtar's teenage brother had developed with one of the female members of the other family. International criticism of the sentence, as well as criticism from many quarters within Pakistan, was fierce.

But who's to say, and on what basis, that this punishment is unjust or just? Is it even possible to justify any moral claim, principle, or conclusion in anything but a provisional way? Are there really any moral "facts" or "truths" about her sentence, at least any that can actually be known? Even if there are, is there any reason to act morally or to care about morality's commands? The constellation comprising these and other questions has come to be called "moral skepticism."

Moral skeptics commonly hold that moral beliefs have purely subjective or internal bases, usually in feeling, and that no objective or external dimensions of the world can either explain or define moral practice and language. So, on this score, egoists, hedonists, and even moral sentiment thinkers would qualify as skeptics.

This recent usage, however, deviates from earlier usages, and overlaps quite a bit with moral nihilism. Ancient Hellenistic skeptics, like Pyrrho of Elis and Sextus Empiricus, seem to have held more cautious attitudes toward the possibility of moral truth. Rather than concluding negatively or positively about whether some doctrine is true, these skeptics withheld judgment, neither affirming nor denying. This, in turn, led them to a tranquil, undisturbed state (*ataraxia*), freeing skeptics from the conflict and disturbance of dogmatic belief. In particular, Hellenistic skeptics refused the Stoics' claim that people can apprehend the natural law and moral cataleptic impressions, which supposedly provide an indubitable and secure ground for moral argument and judgment. Although caricatures like those presented by Diogenes Laertius (probably third century CE) depict skeptics as paralyzed and unable to act (unable to move out of the way of runaway carts, for example), Hellenistic skeptics did act and reflect about action. Instead of pretending to absolute, divine, indubitable or universal moral truths, skeptics recommend deferring to custom, to what seems natural, and to the imperatives of feeling.

Early modern thinkers like Michel de Montaigne (1533–92) followed the ancients in this understanding of skepticism, criticizing dogmatists and rationalists for trying to become angels but instead becoming monstrous ("Of Experience," in *Essays*). For Montaigne, it's better to accept that one is no more than a finite, history and culture-bound human being.

Answering skepticism

Many of the claims that motivate moral skepticism are accepted by those who nonetheless believe meaningful morality is still possible. Non-cognitivists, for example, accept that there are no moral facts as such, but they still believe that moral discourse is meaningful and fruitful. What tips people over to skepticism is the nagging concern that morality may only be possible if there are absolute moral facts that we can know, but that there are no such facts. As such, and as with other forms of skepticism, critics claim that it only gets off the ground because it sets an impossibly high standard for what can qualify as genuine ethics, and then complains that nothing can meet the test.

On this view, the serious claims of skepticism simply undermine arrogant moralists who purport to base their claims on the apprehension of universal natural rights, divine moral principles, natural law, or the commands of reason. In any case, skepticism recommends that if effective moral criticism is to be made, it must be done in ways that makes sense in terms of the feelings, customs, traditions, and natural psychological features of those involved.

See also

1.13 Intuition, 2.9 Naturalism, 2.14 Relativism, 3.6 Cognitivism/non-cognitivism, 3.9 Facts/values, 3.15 Internalism/externalism, 5.10 Pluralism

Reading

Panayot Butchvarov, *Skepticism in Ethics* (Bloomington: Indiana University Press, 1989)

Clement Dore, *Moral Scepticism* (New York: Palgrave Macmillan, 1991)
*Walter Sinnott-Armstrong, *Moral Skepticisms* (Oxford: Oxford University Press, 2006)

5.15 Standpoint

G. W. F. Hegel's 1807 classic, *Phenomenology of Spirit*, tells an interesting story about the relationship between a master and a slave. While at the outset, the master in every way appears to hold a superior position to the slave, by the end of Hegel's exposition, we find that things are decidedly more complex and that the slave has achieved certain capacities denied the master – including the capacity to apprehend various truths the master cannot know. Karl Marx (1818–83) adopted this "master–slave dialectic," substituting the exploited working class for the slave and the exploiting ruling class for the master. Jean-Paul Sartre (1905–80), too, found influence in the idea, using it to devastating effect when he defended violent rebellion against colonialism in his Preface to Frantz Fanon's *Wretched of the Earth* (1963). The insight common to all three thinkers is that things look very different from different points of view. This insight underwrites a branch of philosophy that's come to be called "standpoint theory."

The claims of standpoint theory

In its most basic form, standpoint theory argues two propositions: First, what appears to be true or good or right to people is intrinsically related to the social, economic, and gendered position from which they see it. Second, moral reasoning is neither uniform nor universal. For a very long time, philosophers have held that reasoning is the same for any rational being at any place and any time – like $2 + 2 = 4$. But if moral reasoning is tied to one's standpoint, then those in different standpoints will reason about ethics differently. Contrary, to simple relativism, however, not all standpoints are morally or epistemologically equivalent.

While for example the wealthy may believe they understand the world better than the poor, the situation is actually just the reverse. The wealthy, because of their snobbery and their fear of the poor, isolate themselves in protected enclaves – seeing the world only from the top of the skyscraper, as it were. The poor, by contrast know both life at the bottom (where they live) and life at the top (where they work). Similarly, minorities know their own communities as well as the larger majority society because they must circulate in both. Those belonging only to majority races and religions, however, tend to know only themselves.

It has been feminist theorists, however, that have most fully developed the concept of "standpoint." Women, say these theorists, hold distinctive standpoints both as subordinates in the patriarchy and in their roles as mothers, caregivers, and the organizers of various social networks. Theorists like Sara Ruddick, in her book *Maternal Thinking* (1989), have accordingly argued that maternal practices render women more ethically competent to understand and resolve moral and political conflicts.

Attractions

One advantage often attributed to standpoint theory is that it allows theorists to attribute specific abilities to a class of people without claiming that the members of that class possess them in an essential way or by nature. If blacks or women, for example, possess superior capacities of some sort, they do so not because of some inherent essence that defines them but rather simply through their contingently occupying certain standpoints in the social order. So, in fact, males can adopt at least some of what are at present female standpoints when they start thinking and acting from that standpoint, when they take up "maternal practices."

If standpoint theory is correct, then significant, perhaps decisive weight must be given to voices from standpoints that have long been ignored or silenced, from the accounts, judgments, and narratives articulated by the oppressed. For example, with regard to issues of the sexual harassment of women, women's voices must be placed in the foreground. Moral assessments concerning the poor, the working classes, prisoners, and racial minorities must be attentive to the way things look from their standpoints.

Critique

Sometimes it's easy to tell whose standpoint has been neglected. For example, it was clear that the voices of blacks under South African apartheid should have been given a greater hearing. But perhaps some cases aren't so clear. In the case of the Israel–Palestine conflict, each adversary claims the standpoint of the oppressed, besieged, and victimized: Israeli Jews claim a privileged standpoint as victims of present and historical anti-Semitism surrounded by avowed enemies; Palestinian Arabs claim the standpoint of the dispossessed and of those living under illegal, brutal, racist occupation. How does one rank or adjudicate the competing claims of different standpoints?

Moreover, doesn't their superior education, access to information, and opportunity for travel tip the balance back in favor of the standpoints of privilege? Isn't it true that oppression brings deprivation rather than elevation, ignorance rather than understanding? If standpoint theory is right, then, doesn't it lead to the rather incredible conclusion that since the oppressed understand things better and possess better moral capacities, oppression, and deprivation aren't quite so bad after all? Or at least doesn't it lead to this strange trade-off: privileged ignorance on the one side or oppressed wisdom on the other? Which would you choose?

There's also the danger of presenting the viewpoint of a particular social group as being more homogenous than it really is. Can we really speak of a single, uniform standpoint that, say, all women, all workers, all members of a minority class, or even all slaves share? Or would that mask the individuality of people who happen to belong to a certain group?

See also

3.1 Absolute/relative, 4.15 Sex and gender, 5.11 Power

Reading

Georg Lukács, *History and Class Consciousness* (Cambridge, MA: MIT Press, 1971)
Linda Alcoff and Elizabeth Potter, eds., *Feminist Epistemologies* (New York: Routledge,1993)
*Sandra Harding, ed., *The Feminist Standpoint Theory Reader* (New York: Routledge, 2003)

5.16 Supererogation

Siblings Sly, Freddie, and Rose always entered the national lottery together, and one day they won $3 million − $1 million each. Sly spent some and invested some, but gave nothing away. Freddie gave away 20 percent to charity. Rose, however, bought herself a bottle of cheap champagne and gave away the remaining $999,975 to provide clean water for thousands of people in Tanzania.

When we think about what morality demands of us, many think that it requires a certain lack of selfishness. Sly may not be the most evil person alive, but a good person would have shared their good fortune at least a little, perhaps as much as Freddie. But Rose's generosity seems to go over and above what could reasonably be expected of her. Giving all her winnings away is said to be a *supererogatory* act. People praise such acts as good, but they don't criticize those who do not perform them. This because it's generally recognized that acts like Rose's involve doing more than one is morally obliged to do.

The exceptional nature of supererogatory acts means that they're thought to merit special praise. For example, the Congressional Medal of Honor is presented to a soldier who "distinguishes himself conspicuously by gallantry and intrepidity at the risk of his life *above and beyond* the call of duty." A soldier's simply performing his or her duty is respectable and honorable, but merely dutiful conduct doesn't merit an award like this. There are, it therefore seems, morally praiseworthy forms of conduct in addition to those that morality requires. There is, one might say, "heroic virtue" in addition to "ordinary virtue." Tzvetan Todorov raises this issue with particular poignancy in his reflections on moral life in concentration camps, *Facing the Extreme* (1996).

A special category?

Some moral theories, however, accommodate the supererogatory more easily than others. Deontological or duty-based ethics tend to specify a limited range of acts that people are duty-bound to perform – therefore leaving plenty of space to do more, if one so wishes. But act consequentialist theories can seem actually to require things that one would ordinarily think of as supererogatory.

For example, let's imagine Rose has a comfortable home and lifestyle before she wins the lottery. The extra pleasure she will get out of life from the winnings (the increase in *marginal utility*, as economists like to say) is therefore fairly minimal, considering that most research seems to suggest that once a comfortable material standard of living has been achieved, happiness does not increase much more with increased wealth. If, however, she spends the money on clean water provision for Tanzanians, thousands of people see their welfare and happiness increase significantly. Since this is the course of action that yields the best consequences by far, it would seem wrong for her not to do it. So, what seems like a heroic action turns out to be one everyone in her position should be expected to perform. Act consequentialists, therefore, would seem to be committed to the view that supererogatory acts are very rare.

Exceptional but not supererogatory

This needn't mean, however, that for consequentialists the intuition that some moral actions are more heroic than others is simply mistaken. It could be accepted, for example, that although people are equally bound by all moral duties, human nature and social circumstances make some duties much harder to perform than others. Rose isn't to be praised, therefore, because what she did was beyond her duties, but because the vast majority of human beings would find fulfilling this duty very difficult.

Another way to save the intuition that some acts are exceptionally praise-worthy without recourse to the supererogatory is to claim that some duties have a stronger claim on us than others. For example, the duty not to kill others makes so strong a claim that we legislate against it. The duty to be honest with our spouse seems to make a slightly weaker claim. Hence, lying to one's spouse about a serious matter isn't something people consider a sufficiently serious breach of duty to pass laws against it; but it is considered serious enough to warrant various kinds of reprimand and social sanction. The duty to give away wealth seems to make an even weaker claim. Not giving away a portion of one's wealth, therefore, although thought by many to be a violation of duty, doesn't make a sufficiently strong claim upon us to warrant much disapproval at all.

One problem with this solution, however, is that while it explains why sometimes people aren't punished for failing in their duties, it doesn't explain why they're praised in extraordinary ways for fulfilling them. It's not just that people *don't blame* those who fail to give away a portion of their wealth; they vigorously *praise* people who do.

It remains a serious possibility, therefore, that we should all act like Rose in the same circumstances and that our surprise that she was so generous does not show that she acted above the call of duty, but that we so often fail to fulfill the duties that fall upon us.

See also

1.20 Sympathy, 2.1 Consequentialism, 2.4 Deontological ethics, 4.7 Impartiality and objectivity

Reading

J. O. Urmson, "Saints and Heroes," in *Essays in Moral Philosophy*, edited by A. I. Melden (Seattle: University of Washington Press, 1958)

David Heyd, *Supererogation: Its Status in Ethical Theory* (Cambridge: Cambridge University Press, 1982)
*Andrew Michael Flescher, *Heroes, Saints, and Ordinary Morality* (Washington, DC: Georgetown University Press, 2003)

5.17 Tragedy

An airplane has been hijacked and is heading for a major city, where the hijackers say it will be deliberately crashed, bringing devastation and death to thousands. The air force commander doesn't believe it's right to kill civilians, especially those on one's own side of a conflict. But the only way he can stop the suicide mission is to order the plane shot down above an unpopulated area, killing approximately 200 innocent passengers – as well as, of course, the hijackers.

Most people would say that the commander is right to order the plane shot down. Yet, no matter how one looks at it, the decision involves killing 200 innocent people. It's true that it seems likely that they're going to die anyway. But isn't there a moral difference between killing and letting die? If someone's going to die soon, does that mean it's okay to kill that person? Isn't killing the innocent, even to save other innocents, morally wrong?

No good can come from it

One might say that this is an example of a moral tragedy. In the dramatic sense, a tragedy is when a bad outcome is the inevitable consequence, usually of the protagonist's fatal flaw. By contrast, a moral tragedy occurs when, no matter what one does, something morally bad must result, and the best one can hope for is to do the least bad thing. In morally tragic situations the choice is not between the good and the bad, but the more and less bad. Indeed, according to Martha Nussbaum (b. 1947), trying to lead a morally good life exposes one to moral tragedy. Goodness, in her rendering, is a fragile thing. Others, following Stanley Cavell (b. 1926), have argued that the pathological qualities of certain philosophical conundrums, especially those related to skepticism, lead to tragic results, at least in the dramatic sense.

Although the thought that some choices leave us with no truly good option seems perfectly understandable, there is nonetheless something odd about saying that someone did wrong if what he or she did was the best thing they could do under the circumstances. For this reason it might be thought that, contrary to appearances, moral tragedy is impossible: there's always some best thing that one can do; and if that is indeed what one does, one does no wrong. But there are several ways of explaining the seeming paradox of rightly choosing the wrong thing while retaining the idea of moral tragedy.

Good and bad; right and wrong

The key is to distinguish between the good and the bad, and two senses of right and wrong. If one thinks of "good" and "bad" as pertaining to outcomes or consequences, and "right" and "wrong" as pertaining to actions, then it clearly is possible for right actions to have bad outcomes (and wrong actions good ones). In this schema, it's quite easy to explain moral tragedy in terms of people doing the right thing, even though what results is a foreseeable bad. Moral tragedy, on this view, is about the inevitability of bad consequences, not of performing a wrong act.

This solution, however, isn't available to consequentialists, for whom an action must be wrong if its consequences are bad. They do, however, have another way of making moral tragedy sound more plausible. Right or wrong also bear the sense of "correct" and "incorrect." When someone chooses the lesser of two evils, therefore, it's true to say that they do wrong. But in another, important sense, one can say they did the right thing in the sense that they chose correctly between the options available to them. It doesn't make what they did morally right, but it absolves them of any blame for the bad consequences.

Whether moral tragedy is or isn't avoidable, to say that someone has behaved in a morally wrong but nevertheless correct way such that he or she is not morally culpable looks like a rather uncomfortable conceptual contortion. But perhaps it's a necessary one. It is usual to think that if someone knowingly acts wrongly and wasn't forced to do so, then that person is to blame for the act. But perhaps it should also be recognized that when there are no good options available, a person is, in a sense, forced to do wrong. In such cases, therefore, although the wrong is done knowingly, because the wrong was forced it's not blameworthy. This seems particularly pertinent in the case of political leaders, who often do find that their options are limited by circumstances. It's not only when there's only one choice that free will is compromised.

See also

2.1 Consequentialism, 3.14 Intentions/consequences, 5.8 Moral luck

Reading

Stanley Cavell, *The Claim of Reason: Skepticism, Morality, and Tragedy*, new
    edition (Oxford: The Clarendon Press, 1999)
*Martha Nussbaum, *The Fragility of Goodness: Luck and Ethics in Greek
    Tragedy and Philosophy*, 2nd edition (Cambridge: Cambridge University
    Press, 2001)
*Mervyn Frost, "Tragedy, Ethics, and International Relations," *Inter-
    national Relations* 17(4) (2003): 477–95

Appendix

Ethics Resources

I Online resources

Bioethics.net: http://bioethics.net
Bioethics Web: www.bioethicsweb.ac.uk
Episteme Links: www.epistemelinks.com
Erratic Impact: www.erraticimpact.com
Ethics Updates: http://ethics.sandiego.edu
Internet Encyclopedia of Philosophy (IEP): www.iep.utm.edu
Routledge Encyclopedia of Philosophy: www.rep.routledge.com
Stanford Encyclopedia of Philosophy: http://plato.stanford.edu

II Societies, institutes, and other organizations

American Medical Association (AMA) Institute for Ethics: www.ama-assn.org/ama/pub/category/2558.html
American Society for Bioethics and Humanities (ASBH): www.asbh.org/
Association for Feminist Ethics and Social Theory (FEAST): www.afeast.org
Association for Practical and Professional Ethics: www.indiana.edu/~appe/
British Society for Ethical Theory (BSET): www.bset.org.uk
Center for Medical Ethics Bochum (Ruhr Universität Bochum): www.ruhr-uni-bochum.de/zme/zme-e.html
The Hastings Center: www.thehastingscenter.org
The International Society for Environmental Philosophy (ISEP): www.environmentalphilosophy.org

Karolinska Institutet: www.mic.ki.se/Diseases/K01.316.html
Kennedy Institute of Ethics (Georgetown University): http://kennedyinstitute.
    georgetown.edu/index.htm
National Institutes of Health (NIH): http://bioethics.od.nih.gov/
National Reference Center for Bioethics Literature (NRCBL): www.george
    town.edu/research/nrcbl
Societas Ethica: www.societasethica.info/
The Society for Ethics: www-rohan.sdsu.edu/faculty/corlett/se.html

III Journals and periodicals

The American Journal of Bioethics
Bioethics
Business Ethics Quarterly
Cambridge Quarterly of Healthcare Ethics
Environmental Ethics: An Interdisciplinary Journal Dedicated to the Philosophi-
    cal Aspects of Environmental Problems
Ethical Theory and Moral Practice
Ethics: An International Journal of Social, Legal, and Political Philosophy
Ethics and Medicine: An International Journal of Bioethics
The Hastings Center Report
Jahrbuch für Recht und Ethik
Journal of Applied Philosophy
Journal of Ethics: An International Philosophical Review
Journal of Medical Ethics: Journal of the Institute of Medical Ethics
Journal of Moral Philosophy
Journal of Value Inquiry
Politics and Ethics Review

Index

Main entries in **bold**